T0402971

The California Gold Rush

In January of 1848, James Marshall discovered gold at Sutter's Mill in the foothills of the Sierra Nevada. For a year afterward, news of this discovery spread outward from California and started a mass migration to the gold fields. Thousands of people from the East Coast aspiring to start new lives in California financed their journey West on the assumption that they would be able to find wealth. Some were successful, many were not, but they all permanently changed the face of the American West.

In this text, Mark Eifler examines the experiences of the miners, demonstrates how the gold rush affected the United States, and traces the development of California and the American West in the second half of the nineteenth century. This migration dramatically shifted transportation systems in the US, led to a more powerful federal role in the West, and brought about mining regulation that lasted well into the twentieth century. Primary sources from the era and web materials help readers comprehend what it was like for these nineteenth-century Americans who gambled everything on the pursuit of gold.

Mark A. Eifler is Associate Professor of History at the University of Portland.

Critical Moments in American History

Edited by William Thomas Allison, Georgia Southern University

The California Gold Rush

The Stampede that Changed the World

Mark A. Eifler

Routledge
Taylor & Francis Group

NEW YORK AND LONDON

First published 2017
by Routledge
711 Third Avenue, New York, NY 10017

and by Routledge
2 Park Square, Milton Park, Abingdon, Oxon, OX14 4RN

Routledge is an imprint of the Taylor & Francis Group, an informa business

© 2017 Taylor & Francis

The right of Mark A. Eifler to be identified as author of this work has
been asserted by him in accordance with sections 77 and 78 of the
Copyright, Designs and Patents Act 1988.

Library of Congress Cataloging in Publication Data
Names: Eifler, Mark A., 1956– author.
Title: The California gold rush: the stampede that changed the world/
Mark Eifler.
Description: New York, NY: Routledge, 2016. | Series: Critical
moments in American history
Identifiers: LCCN 2016002861| ISBN 9780415731836 (hardback) |
ISBN 9780415731843 (pbk.) | ISBN 9781315849553 (ebook)
Subjects: LCSH: California—Gold discoveries. | California—History—
1846–1850. | Gold miners—California—History—19th century.
Classification: LCC F865.E37 2016 | DDC 979.4/04—dc23
LC record available at http://lccn.loc.gov/2016002861

ISBN: 978-0-415-73183-6 (hbk)
ISBN: 978-0-415-73184-3 (pbk)
ISBN: 978-1-3158495-5-3 (ebk)

Typeset in Bembo and Helvetica Neue
by Florence Production Ltd, Stoodleigh, Devon

For my son, Conor, who provided excellent feedback, editing, and ideas for the entire manuscript; and my wife Karen, who like the gold rush widows of 1849 carried too much of the load while I was off prospecting.

Contents

Series Introduction

Welcome to the Routledge *Critical Moments in American History* series. The purpose of this new series is to give students a window into the historian's craft through concise, readable books by leading scholars, who bring together the best scholarship and engaging primary sources to explore a critical moment in the American past. In discovering the principal points of the story in these books, gaining a sense of historiography, following a fresh trail of primary documents, and exploring suggested readings, students can then set out on their own journey, to debate the ideas presented, interpret primary sources, and reach their own conclusions—just like the historian.

A critical moment in history can be a range of things—a pivotal year, the pinnacle of a movement or trend, or an important event such as the passage of a piece of legislation, an election, a court decision, a battle. It can be social, cultural, political, or economic. It can be heroic or tragic. Whatever they are, such moments are by definition "game changers," momentous changes in the pattern of the American fabric, paradigm shifts in the American experience. Many of the critical moments explored in this series are familiar; some less so.

There is no ultimate list of critical moments in American history—any group of students, historians, or other scholars may come up with a different catalog of topics. These differences of view, however, are what make history itself and the study of history so important and so fascinating. Therein can be found the utility of historical inquiry—to explore, to challenge, to understand, and to realize the legacy of the past through its influence of the present. It is the hope of this series to help students realize this intrinsic value of our past and of studying our past.

William Thomas Allison
Georgia Southern University

Figures

Acknowledgments

Writing a short historical account of something as massive and far-reaching as the California gold rush requires the skills of a tight-rope walker. You must remain centered and balanced, not go too far or suddenly in any direction, and stay on the straight and narrow path, or you will fail. The reader will have to determine if I have succeeded. But if I managed to stay centered and balanced, it was due to the indispensable support of many people, including some who may be surprised to be included here.

My thinking on the gold rush is strongly indebted to Gunther Barth, whose classes and seminars introduced me to the academic history of the gold rush, and whose advice has guided my thinking for years. He is missed. Peter Blodgett and the H.E. Huntington Library staff supported my work professionally, helping me mine the archives for shining nuggets still to be discovered in the streams of gold rush memories.

As I was beginning to put this book together, Allie Judy asked: Do we really need another book on the gold rush? It is a great question that any author should keep foremost in mind throughout a project. I hope this book answers that question. After working on the book for about a year, I taught a gold rush seminar at the University of Portland. My students' responses dramatically changed many of my ideas on the structure and design of the book, and it is better because of that. Thus special thanks to: Alejandra Acosta, Benjamin Constantino, Scott Deal, David Dies, Jacob Fejeran, Jonah Grahek, Aily Girmaldi, Benjamin Heebner, Eva Klos, Monica Portugal, Rachel Saxby, Joseph Shorma, and Felicia Teba. I also need to thank my colleagues, Brian Els, Elise Moentmann, Christin Hancock, Brad Franco, Blair Woodard, and Fr. Art Wheeler for their support as I hid away to write. Genevieve Aoki and Dan Finaldi at Routledge have been wonderful, especially for their patience as deadlines for drafts slipped further and further down the road. And of course,

I acknowledge the time I spent with my P.C. (i.e., *Pippin*, a Dachshund-Jack Russell Terrier mix puppy, and *Coffee*), without which this book would probably be unreadable!

And finally, very special thanks to Bill Allison, who invited me to go on this rush; Helen Paris, who kept me sane on the journey; John Findlay, Peter Blodgett, Debbie MacKinnon and Virginia Livingston, who read drafts of various chapters and provided feedback; my son Conor, who provided excellent feedback, editing, and ideas for the entire manuscript; and my wife Karen, who, like the gold rush widows of 1849, carried too much of the load while I was off prospecting.

Timeline

1542	California coast explored by Juan Rodriguez Cabrillo.
1769	First Spanish mission settlements in California.
1821	Spanish rule in California ends with Mexican Independence.
1833	California missions secularized by Mexican government, Indian neophytes become domestic servants and laborers on *Californio* ranches, farms.
1839	John Sutter arrives in California, begins construction of outpost near mouth of American River.
1841	John Bidwell finds gold in California mountain stream, but is unable to relocate site again later.
1841	Gold discovered in Placerita Canyon, west of Los Angeles; sets off a short, local rush.
1845–1852	The Great Famine in Ireland.
Spring, 1846	Mormons begin organizing trek to Salt Lake.
April, 1846	Mexican War begins.
1848–1849	Revolutions sweep European nations.
January 24, 1848	Traditional date given for James Marshall's discovery of gold at Sutter's Mill.
February 2, 1848	Treaty of Guadalupe Hidalgo ends Mexican War, California and Southwest acquired by United States. Mexican citizens who stay in the region are promised full citizenship and property rights by the treaty.
February 13, 1848	Henry Bigler finds gold downstream from Sutter's Mill site.
March, 1848	Mormons finish work on Sutter's Mill, begin mining at "Mormon Island" on the American River below Sutter's Mill.
May 12, 1848	Samuel Brannan announces gold discoveries in San Francisco, kicking off local rush in California and eventually around the Pacific Rim.
August 19, 1848	New York Herald becomes the first major newspaper on East coast to report the discovery of gold in California.
Late Fall, 1848	Mining in California stops for winter, many miners return home, planning to come back next year. Estimates suggest that about 5,000 people have gone to the foothills, and gathered roughly 12,000 troy ounces of gold during the year.

December 5, 1848	President James Polk announces gold discovery in State of the Union. Samples of gold sent by Col. Richard Mason are placed on display.
Winter 1848/49	The Great California Gold Rush begins in eastern United States and Europe.
Spring 1849	First wave of sea-borne rush migrants begin arriving in San Francisco.
August 1849	First wave of overland trail rush migrants begin arriving in California.
September, 1849	Californians meet in Monterey, California to draft a state constitution, to set up a provisional state government, in the absence of congressional action to organize California as a territory. Ratified by local vote in November. Provisional state government set up to act, ten months before authorized by the US Congress.
November, 1849	Relief parties sent out from Sacramento to rescue migrants still trying to cross the Great Basin and the Sierras.
End of 1849	Estimated that over 90,000 people have arrived in California during this year. Of these roughly two-thirds were from the United States. Estimated that perhaps 20% died within the first six months of arriving. Estimated that over 490,000 troy ounces of gold gathered this year.
1850–1864	Taiping Rebellion in southern China, leads to rise in immigrants from Asia to India, Southeast Asia, Hawaii, and California.
Early 1850	Foreign Miners Tax Law passed by provisional California state government, requiring non-native miners—especially Mexican and Chinese—to pay the state a monthly fee of $25 in order to mine.
April 22, 1850	Indian protection act passed by provisional state government, which allows California settlers to enslave California native peoples.
August, 1850	Sacramento Squatter's Riot.
September 9, 1850	California becomes the 31st state. Compromise of 1850 allows California to enter the union as a "free state," due to "popular sovereignty."
End of 1850	Estimated that nearly 2,000,000 troy ounces of gold gathered this year.
March, 1851	California Land Act established the Land Commission, which requires holders of Spanish or Mexican land grants in California to prove they own the lands in a lengthy legal process. Most land will eventually be taken from original owners.
May, 1851	Australian gold rushes begin, after Edward Hargreaves, noting the similarity in the landscape between California and Australia, discovers gold in Victoria.
June, 1851	San Francisco businessmen, including Samuel Brannan, form Committee of Vigilance to prosecute crimes that they felt the city government was ignoring.
September, 1851	Treaty of Fort Laramie secures travel rights on plains between eastern States and California, but sets up-coming conflicts with plains Indians.
End of 1851	Estimated 3.6 million troy ounces of gold gathered this year.
1853	Filibustering William Walker establishes short-lived republics with the backing of his private army, in Sonora and Baja California, in attempts to extend US expansion. Three years later, he attempts a similar move in Nicaragua and Central America.
1854	The Kansas-Nebraska Act attempts to set up territories on plains in order to begin organizing transcontinental railroad to California; its provisions for popular sovereignty set off civil war in "Bleeding" Kansas.
1854	US Government opens San Francisco Mint, to turn California gold into standardized gold dollars.

1854	Stocks in mining companies, many purchased by British investors, collapse. "Honest Harry" Meigs accused of manipulating stock and land warrants, flees city. Though gold is still being mined, individual prospecting is all but over, and even raising capital for mining equipment becomes much more difficult. 1848–1854: over 16.7 million troy ounces of gold has been gathered, valued at the time at over $345 million.
January, 1855	Panama Railroad completed.
End of 1855	Estimated that over 300,000 people have moved to California since the beginning of the gold rush.
1856	British Columbia gold rush.
May, 1856	Second Committee of Vigilance in San Francisco formed, this time to conduct trials as well as to fight what it viewed as political corruption.
July, 1858	Pikes Peak/Denver gold rush begins.
1859	Comstock silver rush begins in Virginia City, Nevada. Between 1848 and 1859, over 28.7 million troy ounces of gold gathered in California.
1860	Lincoln elected President; Civil War breaks out the following spring.
1862	Pacific Railroad Act authorizes construction of transcontinental railroad to California.
1865	Samuel Clemens, under the pen name Mark Twain, publishes "The Celebrated Jumping Frog of Calaveras County," bringing him international attention.
1868	Burlingame Treaty between US and China allows Chinese subjects in the US rights of transit and religious belief.
1868	Bret Harte starts *The Overland Monthly*; his "The Luck of Roaring Camp" in the second issue raises him to national prominence and characterizes the gold rush as a comic romp.
1869	Transcontinental Railroad is completed, linking California to the eastern states.
1870	California Indian population, estimated at 150,000 before the rush, now estimated at less than 30,000.
1872	US General Mining Act codifies California mining practices for whole nation.
1872	*Roughing It*, Mark Twain's stories of his western travels, are published.
1873	*The Gilded Age* is published by Mark Twain and Charles Dudley Warner, portraying a comic yet dark image of western expansion and speculation.
1874	Black Hills gold rush.
1882	Chinese Exclusion Act, US federal law signed by President Arthur, based on earlier California practices, despite Burlingame Treaty of 1868
1884	In *Edwards Woodruff v. North Bloomfield Mining and Gravel Company*, US district court Judge Lorenzo Sawyer bans hydraulic mining, ending one of the more devastating practices of the early gold rush.
1890	Society of California Pioneers of New England tours California by rail.
1893	Frederick Jackson Turner presents his thesis on "The Significance of the Frontier in American History" in Chicago, painting a progressive view of western development, including the gold rushes.
1896–1899	Klondike gold rush.
1899–1909	Nome, Alaska gold rush.
1920s	Southern California scene of rushes similar to 1849 in the real estate, oil, and entertainment industries.

1925   Charlie Chaplin's *The Gold Rush* paints a comic picture of the Alaska gold rush, much in
            the tradition of Bret Harte.

1939   John Steinbeck's *The Grapes of Wrath* published, and produced as a movie the following
            year, suggests a new rush to California, but with a darker tone of realism.

1951   *Paint Your Wagon* opens on Broadway portrays California gold rush in comic musical
            production.

1990s   Several new historical studies, including works by Malcolm Rohrbough, Susan Johnson,
            and Richard Orsi, published around the time of the 150th anniversary of the gold rush,
            paint the rush in more complex and grittier terms. At the same time, Silicon Valley in
            California is touted as the "new California gold rush."

Introduction

In January, 1848, workers began gathering flakes of gold near a sawmill they were building for John Sutter on the American River in the foothills of California's Sierra Nevada Mountains. Though news of these finds leaked out slowly at first, by May the story was spreading rapidly throughout California, along the Pacific Coast, and throughout the Pacific Rim. By the end of the year the news had reached the Atlantic states of New York, Massachusetts, and South Carolina, as well as the European nations of Great Britain, France, and Germany. By the spring of 1849, the great California gold rush was in full swing. For much of the next decade, the lure of gold brought thousands of would-be miners from around the world to California.

This series examines critical moments in American history, moments when something happened that caused a major shift in American development. The California gold rush certainly caused a dramatic change in American development, but it was not a momentary event. It was not the initial discovery that was transformative, nor was it even the gold that would be mined in the coming years (though the amount of gold was substantial). It was the *rush* itself: the hundreds of thousands of individual acts of decision-making to pack up and get to California, the mass movement of people from around the world to one of the most isolated and remote places on earth at that time, and its almost overnight integration into not only the United States, but also into transportation and commercial networks that spanned the globe. It was a migration that seriously shifted political power not only in the United States, but throughout the Pacific Rim. And it set in motion a dream that, despite brutal realities, would become a powerful motivator in the American mind down to the present day.

The California gold rush was a mass movement, one organized from the ground up, not the top down. Its participants at times seemed to take

on the character of an army moving through foreign regions, setting out
to do battle with any obstacle in their way, be it the physical landscape
or human communities. Yet it was an army without officers to direct them,
without quartermasters to supply them, and at times without even a clear
sense of how to define victories or defeats. Little in American experience
seemed to provide a precedent for what was going on, and those who
have tried to understand the rush then and in the years since have seemed
unsure how to characterize and access the experience.

For many the gold rush has seemed to represent the American frontier
in all its contradictions. From a positive and colorful perspective, the rush
seemed to be a mad, greedy scramble of young men, out to strike it rich
in the sunny mountains of California. It has been portrayed as primarily
a male adventure, full of macho, drinking, and gambling. In this male
society, women were few, and their moral virtue slight. The character of
the event from this view is captured best in the humorous writings of Bret
Harte, quaint tourist towns along Highway 49, and the colorful and
boisterous comedy of the musical play and movie *Paint Your Wagon*.

Yet much as the positive character of the frontier has been called into
question, the gold rush has also been scrutinized for its negative and
destructive elements. Though the gold rush attracted people from all over
the world, the conditions they encountered in California were hardly
harmonious. Racial attitudes towards Hispanic and Chinese migrants were
harsh and cast into restrictive legislation that would have lasting
consequences. The rush unleashed genocide on the native peoples of
California, especially those tribes in the Sierra Nevada Mountains. Add to
this the violence of vigilante committees throughout the region, the
desperate condition of the many miners who did not strike it rich, and
the brutal environmental effects of unregulated mining, and the gold rush
hardly seems to be a progressive, celebratory event.

A third way of looking at the California gold rush suggests yet another,
perhaps more pragmatic interpretation. As an event in the development
of the West—and of California in particular—it is foundational. The gold
rush brought hundreds of thousands to the American West, laying the
social, economic, and political basis of California. The rise of San Francisco
was seen by contemporaries as perhaps even more impressive and important an effect of the rush as the gold itself. The California Dream, and
California's reputation as being "the Great Exception," was established
during the gold rush. The rush also stimulated a series of mining rushes
throughout the West and the Pacific Rim—in Colorado, the Dakotas,
Alaska, Australia, and British Columbia—that would replay the California
rush story over and over again, setting the tone for other extractive industries in the American West, as well as national policies and attitudes towards

these activities, for decades to come. In the history of the American West and California, the gold rush was the great event, a pivot of the nineteenth century.

And yet, looked at still another way, the California gold rush seems not to be foundational, or of any real significance at all. The rush took place during the decade of collapse of compromise in the United States over slavery, a series of crises that would lead to the greatest crisis in American History: the Civil War. In the growing division between the cultures and economies of the North and South, and the great issue of slavery versus personal freedom that characterized the 1850s, the California gold rush seems to be an insignificant side show, hardly more than a distraction from the weighty and critical issues of moral significance erupting back East. The gold rush, it seems, had little or no role to play in this great mainstream American drama.

Thus there seem to be four gold rushes—one of adventurous comedy, one of violence and racism, one of great regional importance, and one of national insignificance. Indeed, depending upon the approach one takes, it is hard to believe that these four interpretations all stem from the same event. Can these versions of history be resolved?

Assessing the gold rush requires that we look in the right direction. It is like a magic trick that uses misdirection to produce a wondrous result. The gold rush, it seems, was a mad stampede to gain "easy" wealth, and so the easiest way to assess it might be to ask: Did the miners make their hoped-for fortunes? And if not, did the gold mined during the rush quicken the nation's economy? These are valid questions, but they miss the historic legacy of the *rush*. The question is not what was the legacy of the gold, but of the *rush* for the gold? The legacy was the result of the massive movement of peoples world-wide to an isolated and, to most of the rest of the world, a remote place. Focusing on the movement, the *rush*, instead of the gold, we might ask: How did it affect world-wide transportation systems? How did it affect the isolated place that was California in 1848? And further: How did it affect the miners and their families, whether they found a fortune in gold or not? If we can ask how it affected the nation's economy, might we also ask how it affected national politics and society? Since it was an international rush, how did it affect other countries? Since it suddenly changed the demographic and economic foundations of the Pacific rim, how did it affect geopolitics? And what was its lasting influence on American culture and character?

This book attempts to examine the gold rush from a broader per-spective than western or California history alone. It examines the attitudes of rushing miners—both their naive quest for riches and their ingrained cultural racism—as elements of national traits in the late 1840s. It looks not only at the men who went to California, but also at the many thousands who stayed behind, yet who fully participated in the rush in other ways. To do this is to see the rush not as a male-only event, but as one that far more men and women participated in than we have usually thought. And rather than looking at how the rush created cultural, social, economic, and political structures in California and the West alone, this book attempts to draw connections back from this experience to the nation as a whole. The gold rush in many ways overwhelmed the previous socio-economic and political structures of California and the West, wiping away older traditions in many parts (but not all) of the West. The rush certainly was not as overpowering in the Atlantic-facing states as it was in the Pacific region, but the gold rush still had a major influence on the nation as a whole, not just the western half of the continent.

As a product of its times, the California gold rush reveals much about the world of the late 1840s in the United States. Attitudes towards wealth, work, men and women's roles, the nature of business, society, community, and government, and the possibilities of new formulations of these institutions are all revealed by and shaped by the California gold rush. Examined in this light the gold rush can indeed be viewed as a critical "moment" in the development of the United States in the mid-nineteenth century, one with lasting consequences for the American character on both sides of the continent.

This study is organized thematically as well as chronologically. Chapter 1 examines the isolated condition of California in 1848, and how news of the discovery of gold spread throughout the Pacific rim, and to the United States and Europe. This was not the first gold discovery in California, but the 1848 discovery occurred in a remarkable conjunction of conditions and events that would make this an international event. Chapter 2 examines the calculations, negotiations, and preparations made by the gold miners and their families. It was one thing to want to gather a quick fortune, but it had to be balanced against the dangers of travel in the Far West. Chapter 3 describes the rush itself—the routes to the gold fields, the impact of the migration both on the travelers and also on those whose lands they transited. It was a dramatic, brutal journey, one that reinforced the need to extend reliable transportation and communication systems to remote California. Chapter 4 looks at the ways the gold rush transformed California during the hey-day of the mining frenzy, roughly 1849–1854. The rise of California's infrastructure, especially the city of San Francisco, awed the miners as much or more than the amounts of gold they were finding. But it was by necessity a rushed accomplishment, sown with the seeds of future problems. Chapter 5 examines the balance sheet of the gold rush: what was gained, what was lost, by the miners and their families, from the perspective of the rushers as well as those who stood in the path of the rush. As we will see, the definition of success was never easy to determine. Chapter 6 looks past California to the wider political and social repurcussions in the United States, the Pacific Rim, and wider world in the aftermath of the rush. And Chapter 7 examines the cultural legacies of the gold rush dream in American history and culture from 1849 to the present day.

Years later, memories of the gold rush would be shaped by the great calamity of the Civil War, the crass materialism of the Gilded Age, and a "frontier thesis" of American history that tended to separate western development from the mainstream of American culture. The story of the gold rush became a distant tale of comic or brutal adventurism, far removed from present-day realities. Yet to examine the California gold rush today is to return to many of the roots of our current attitudes towards work and business, and the nature of a society obsessed with individual advance and material acquisition. If our interpretations of the gold rush are ambivalent, it may be in large part because the rush deals with issues that we still find unsettling and unsettled in our own age. At its heart are not only a "California Dream," but the hopes, dreams, and nightmares of American society itself.

CHAPTER 1

"Gold on the American River!"

On January 1, 1848, California was a Mexican province under American military control, with small settlements stretched along the coast from San Diego to San Francisco. Precariously perched on the western edge of the North American continent and surrounded by a native population of roughly 150,000, easily ten times larger than the non-native population scattered settlements near the coast,[1] California was isolated from the rest of the continent by mountains, deserts, and plains, and from the rest of the world by a huge ocean whose winds and currents made it difficult to reach by sea. In 1848, California was difficult to get to and little known or understood by the rest of the world.

The transformation of California within the next three years would be one of the most dramatic and dynamic events of the first half of the nineteenth century.[2] If the Mexican War (1846–1848) was an expression of America's sense of Manifest Destiny, the California gold rush was in effect destiny's reward. The resulting gold rush would almost over-night transform California from an isolated backcountry to a major center of American power in the Pacific and beyond. Between 1848 and 1854, over 250,000 people migrated to California, and mined roughly $345 million worth of gold.[3] The rush would reshape the transportation and communication systems of the world, and dramatically change the national economy. It would bring people from many different nations around the world together, while at the same time pushing the United States ever closer to a cataclysmic civil war. The experience would create a new version of the American dream, based on both reckless exploitation and almost unbelievable optimism.

James Marshall's discovery of gold at Sutter's saw mill has often been seen as the trigger of the California gold rush. Once Marshall discovered the gold, goes the thinking, the gold rush was a natural, even unstoppable, consequence. After all, who would not go to California as quickly as possible and simply scoop up the abundance of gold waiting to be found?

However, the story of the gold rush's origins is more complicated. The discovery of gold was not so much the story of a single discovery, but of a series of discoveries. Nor was discovery alone enough. Before a rush could begin, news of these discoveries had to be gathered, verified, and carried to a larger community. That community in turn would need to provide support for a mining community to function: food, security, and transportation and communication facilities.

In January 1848, during the last weeks of the Mexican War, California had very little organization by which it could investigate, report, regulate or support anything like a mining boom. The local Mexican authorities were clearly no longer in power, but American authority was stymied by California's distance and isolation, as well as by divisions within Congress between northern and southern interests regarding California's future. When the war officially ended in February, even the military authorities in California no longer had any official power to organize the territory.

It is easy to overlook the weaknesses of the communications, transportation, and political systems of California in 1848, and to imagine that the news spread swiftly and "naturally," and that Americans simply brought with them or created more formalized organization in 1849—to do this is to miss much of the real significance of the gold rush itself, both then and later. To understand the nature of that transformation, we need to look at how California in 1848 reacted to the discoveries of gold, and how the news actually spread to the rest of the world.

ON THE EDGE: CALIFORNIA IN 1848

Early in January, 1848, a winter storm barreling in from over the Pacific Ocean unleashed torrential rain on the mountains and valleys of northern California.[4] For the great majority of the people living in the area—the Native peoples who had called California home for thousands of years, and the Hispanic communities which had begun settling the region less than a hundred years before—the storm was simply part of the normal cycle of seasons in California. There was no reason to believe this storm would bring anything new to the region, but winter storms could be destructive, causing flooding and landslides, and in that sense the storm may have seemed a portent of things to come. For California was currently facing the aftermath of another storm: the Mexican War.

The war had begun in 1846, over a dispute between Mexico and the United States over the southern boundary of Texas. Mexico claimed that the boundary was the Nueces River, while the United States claimed it was the Rio Grande. The dispute, however, was merely the pretext for seizing the Southwest and California from Mexico. California had been the real prize. Though distant from American settlements in the Missouri River Valley, California was of vital concern to the United States for its location facing the Pacific Ocean. Since the 1780s, Americans had ventured into the Pacific, dispatching merchants to China, hunting sea otters along the northwest coast of America, sending missionaries to Hawaii, and building a whaling industry that in the 1840s was booming and still growing. The acquisition of California would not only give the United States a vital land base on the Pacific, but would allow the young nation to continue building trail connections between the eastern States and the Pacific. Andrew Jackson had tried to purchase San Francisco Bay for $5 million in 1835, only to be rebuffed by the Mexican government. An American naval officer, Thomas ap Catesby Jones, had prematurely "conquered" California in 1842, only to retreat ignominiously when he discovered that the US and Mexico were not actually at war. When the war came in 1846, two land expeditions, under John Charles Fremont and Stephen Watts Kearney, and the Pacific Squadron under Robert Stockton all descended on California to quickly secure the main prize of the war. In January 1847, the last battles in California were over, but the war with Mexico continued for another year. By January 1848, the war's ending was being negotiated and California was beginning to anticipate a new life within the United States.[5] Thus, as the January storm swept ashore in 1848, California was beginning to brace for a new storm of American settlers who would surely be arriving in the coming years.

Or perhaps not. Life in California did not develop quickly. Though initially "discovered" by the Spanish in 1542, 300 years later European intrusion into California had been relatively slight. California remained one of the most isolated places in the world in 1848, largely due to geography. Spanish explorers setting off north from the coast of New Spain found the currents and winds prevailing along the California coast pushing against them, making sailing to California difficult. Captains soon discovered that they had to sail hundreds of miles west and north before catching favorable conditions, an exercise that could take many

THE GOLDEN GATE

The name of the entrance to San Francisco Bay, the "Golden Gate," was given by John C. Fremont in 1846, two years *before* the gold rush. He named it this because of its potential as a gateway to the commercial riches of Asian trade. In other words, Fremont expected gold to come into California through the bay, not go out into the world from it!

weeks. Once they managed to get to the California coast, they found it to be a formidable shore. Most of the California coastline is rocky, with mountains dropping straight into the sea. There were few natural harbors. San Francisco Bay was the most famous, of course, but the entrance to it was often shrouded by fog, and was easy to miss. Monterey Bay had a barely usable port at that time, open to the sea and Pacific storms. San Diego would initially be the major port for Spanish California, but it was located too far south to be of much service to the settlements hundreds of miles to the north. The overland route north into California was long, and obstructed with deserts, mountains, and powerful native tribes. Traveling north into California was dangerous and difficult, and, in many years, Native uprisings closed the trail, making overland travel to California all but impossible.

Because of these conditions, Spain had waited over 200 years to begin even attempting to establish a colony in California. When it did so, in the 1760s, it was settled as a kind of buffer zone, intended more to keep American, British, and Russian explorers, merchants, and settlers in the Pacific out of northern Mexico rather than developing the area intensely as an important part of New Spain. California was initially colonized by Spanish missionaries, who established a series of missions, approximately a day's ride from each other, in a chain leading from San Diego to San Francisco Bay. This left the Spanish settlements strung out along the coast, dependent on each other and the ports of San Diego, Monterey, and San Francisco, and to a more limited extent a few other places along the coast such as near Los Angeles, where there was a break in the mountainous coastline. Since the region attracted few settlers, the Spanish officials and missionaries attempted to coerce the Native peoples of the coastal regions to live in the missions, and convert to Catholicism and Spanish customs and lifestyles. This policy had long been used on the Spanish frontier, essentially creating Spanish laborers from the local native population, and eventually mixing Spanish and Native peoples into a population that was loyal to Spain.

This practice had a somewhat limited success in California, however. First, because of the introduction of infectious disease, coastal Native peoples died in huge numbers, making it difficult to sustain the local population. Second, because the Spanish were limited to the strip of settlements along the coast, Native peoples who resisted the Spanish could escape into the interior regions, beyond Spanish control. As news of the Spanish spread throughout the region, the tribes of the Central Valley and Sierra Nevada foothills and mountains organized effective resistance to the spread of white settlement inland.

Mexico's independence from Spain led to the closing of the missions in 1833, and the Hispanic population of California converted many of the mission communities into ranchos, again using local natives as essentially enslaved laborers. The new Mexican nation, however, was torn by debate and turmoil, and California—an undeveloped buffer region far to the north and difficult to reach—was generally left to its own devices. Over the next two decades, the Hispanic population of California, bereft of support from Mexico, developed a strongly independent culture. Referring to themselves as *Californios* instead of Mexicans, they built their ranches and opened trade with passing ships from Britain, the United States, and elsewhere. Rich in beef, tallow, and hides, California became a common stop for American ships in the Pacific, especially as the hides sold for a profit in New England. To American visitors such as Richard Henry Dana, California seemed to be an underdeveloped backwater, just waiting for Yankee industry to transform it.[6]

Yet California's isolation still could not be easily overcome. The sea route remained long and difficult, and the overland route remained dangerous and exposed. In the 1820s, American fur trappers such as Jedidiah Smith began entering California from a new direction—from the east—crossing deserts and sometimes the mountains in search for animal pelts, and additional horses to carry them back to merchants at the Rocky Mountain rendezvous. Warned to stay out of the Hispanic settlements of the coast, these traders explored the interior valleys and mountains for hunting grounds and suitable passes to enter and leave California from a new direction. They found the trip rewarding: California's interior Native peoples were soon stealing horses from the Hispanic settlements of the coast and trading them to the American fur trappers, sometimes for guns in order to resist further expansion of the coastal settlements. However, the trappers found few easy ways into or out of California from the east. The Sierra Nevada Mountains were a formidable obstacle along most of its 400 mile range, and the deserts to the south, such as Death Valley, made it difficult to bypass the mountains. A few passes were found, and in the 1840s a few hardy souls had attempted to branch off from the Oregon Trail and tried to breach the Sierra wall. A few hundred had succeeded by 1848. Only two years before the Donner party had been trapped in the mountains in winter, where nearly half the party had died. News of the tragedy illustrated the dangerous nature of the trail to California.

Thus, as the January 1848 storm sweeping in from the Pacific lashed California, and its residents waited to see if there would be floods and landslides, they waited to see too if the coming American takeover would result in a flood of new immigrants or merely a trickle. Could the American conquest overcome the obstacles of geography?

SUTTER'S AND MARSHALL'S MILL

The storm that blew in from the Pacific in January 1848 may have appeared a symbol of the changes that were coming to California. To John Sutter, who lived far inland from the Hispanic settlements that generally hugged the coast of California, the storm was potentially a very real disaster. Sutter had moved to California nearly ten years earlier, and had set up an isolated trading post that he hoped would be the seed for a personal empire in the center of the great Central Valley of inland California, beyond the reach of the Mexican authorities settled along the coast. The war between the United States and Mexico, still officially unresolved at the beginning of 1848, had brought the American conquest of California, but had nearly destroyed Sutter's fragile empire. In an effort to restart his operation, Sutter had employed James Marshall to oversee the construction of a grist mill near his outpost, and a lumber mill in the remote foothills of the Sierra Nevada Mountains. Overseeing a crew of American workers—a small band of Mormons who had participated in the Mexican War and had been discharged in California—Marshall and Sutter selected a site for the sawmill about forty-five miles up the American River from Sutter's Fort. Work on the mill was slow going, however, and the Mormon workmen had promised to leave in the spring, to rejoin the Mormon community at Salt Lake. During the January storm, Sutter and Marshall worried that the sudden rise in river water had washed away the half-finished mill. After gathering more supplies and equipment for the mill, Marshall set out on January 14 to return to the mill site and see what could be salvaged.

Arriving at the site, Marshall was relieved to discover that the partially completed dam meant to channel the water to the mill had withstood the high waters, although the flooding had been powerful enough to cut deeply into the channel the men had been digging to the mill site. Seeing this gave Marshall an idea. The upper channel leading to the mill was now dug; it was only the lower reaches, the tailrace, which remained unfinished. Why not let the rushing water carve out its own path once it passed the mill? Marshall decided to close the gate at the head of the channel each morning, so that the men could work during the day. Then each night he opened the gate, letting the water tear through the lower channel, hoping it would dig out most of the gravel of the tailrace on its own. With luck, the river itself would do most of the heavy digging for the workmen at the construction site.

After only a few days of this experiment (January 24 is the usual date given, but the diaries of the men leave some question as to the exact date), Marshall was inspecting the tailrace in the morning to ensure that his scheme was working, or to see where, with a little directed digging, the men could help the river to follow a new course more efficiently. While examining the lower channel he discovered a small yellow pebble. Marshall showed it to the workers, saying he had discovered gold. The workers were skeptical, though a few simple tests on the rock—dropping it in lye, hammering it to test its malleability—all seemed to confirm that it was indeed gold.

The discovery was a surprise to the men, but it hardly seemed to be a major find. The crew had been digging and washing dirt through the riverbanks for weeks already, but no other gold had been found. A few workers began looking more closely at the gravel in the following days, and a few more flakes were found and gathered, but it certainly did not represent a major discovery. At Marshall's insistence, work on the mill continued.

On Thursday, January 28, Marshall rode back down to Sutter's Fort and showed his partner Sutter the gold. Sutter consulted an encyclopedia

Marshall Discovers Gold

Marshall had been in the habit of going down every afternoon to see how his Indians were progressing for they had struck the bed rock mostly of rotten granite yet the work was slow but this time when he went down towards the lower end of the race his eye caught the glitter of something laying in a crevice on the bare rock a few inches under water. . . . Before we went to bed Marshall came in and began to talk and said he believed he had found a gold mine near the lower end of the tail race and if I remember right he said he had been trying to melt some of the particles and could not and before leaving for his own quarters he directed Brown and me to "shut down the headgate in the morning, throw in some sawdust and rotten leaves and make it tight and we will see what there is." The next morning we did as he directed and while doing so we see him pass through the mill yard and on down the race. We went in for breakfast and had scarcely commenced our day's work in the mill yard—when Marshall came carrying in his arms his old white hat with a wide grin and said, "Boys, I believe I have found a gold mine," at the same time setting his hat on the work bench that stood in the mill yard. In an instant all hands gathered around and sure enough on the top of his hat crown, the crown knocked in a little, lay the pure stuff how much I know not perhaps the most part of an ounce for the size of very small particles up to the size of a grain of wheat.

Henry W. Bigler, *Autobiography*, quoted in Rodman Paul,
*The California Gold Discovery: Sources, Documents, Accounts,
and Memoirs Relating to the Discovery of Gold at Sutter's Mill*
(Georgetown, CA: Talisman Press, 1966), pp. 163–164.

4. JAMES MARSHALL, DISCOVERER OF GOLD, AT SUTTER'S MILL

Figure 1.1 Sutter's Mill. Daguerreotype of Sutter's Mill and James Marshall.

and tested the nugget with nitric acid and by weight and density, and came to the conclusion that the gold was real, and of a good quality, at least 23 carats. Marshall wanted to take Sutter back to the site immediately, but Sutter hesitated. The gold discovery was only of a few flakes. Though there was likely more, the amount that might yet be found could only be guessed at. Better to finish the mill than to go prospecting for gold.

Sutter was not necessarily being foolish or short-sighted. This was not the first time gold had been discovered in northern California. While leading the first emigrant party to California in 1841, John Bidwell had seen what he thought were gold nuggets in a mountain stream. He had not had the time to investigate, but over the next few years, several more of Sutter's workers had found flakes and reported it to Bidwell. Each time, the workers had been unable to find more, and Sutter had assumed the men were merely making excuses to escape work. Marshall's discovery thus seemed to fit the old pattern, and even after Sutter confirmed that it was gold of a high quality, he suspected the discovery would be used as an excuse for not finishing work on the mill.[7]

EARLIER GOLD DISCOVERIES

Gold was discovered in small amounts in California as early as 1775. In March, 1842, gold was discovered in Placerita Canyon, forty miles northwest of Los Angeles. For four years, roughly 6,000 people mined the region, removing roughly 5,000 ounces of gold.

Mary Hill, *Gold: The California Story* (Berkeley: University of California Press, 1999), pp. 16–18.

Furthermore, the land where the sawmill and the discovered gold were located was not part of Sutter's original Mexican land grant. Sutter and Marshall decided to keep the workers focused on building the mill while they tried to secure title to the land, negotiating a treaty with the local tribes and having that treaty recognized by US authorities in California— in this case, Colonel Richard Mason, head of the US Army occupation force in Monterey.

Meanwhile, Sutter and Marshall agreed to keep the news of the discovery a secret until they could get their claim in order. Their construction workers were asked to keep the discovery secret as well, but were allowed to look for gold on Sundays or on days when the weather had already halted work on the mill; otherwise, they were to be kept busy on the mill. Marshall also told the men that any gold they found had to be shared with Sutter, as the presumed owner of the land.

John Sutter and James Marshall

John Sutter and James Marshall were an unlikely pair to be immortalized by the gold rush. Yet the rush tied them together in history, in their attempts to gain recognition for the discovery, and ultimately for contributing to the failure of both men.

John Sutter was born in Germany in 1803, served briefly as a low ranking officer in the Swiss army, forced into an early marriage, failed in his dry goods business, fled debtor's prison, left his wife and children behind, and set out for America in 1834. Over the next five years, he engaged in the native fur trade, and visited fur trade centers in Santa Fe and the Oregon territory, where he likely developed the idea of setting up his own fur trade outpost/empire in the backcountry of Mexican California in 1839. Through boldness, bravery, coercion, and luck, Sutter generally succeeded in establishing his "New Helvetia" outpost, usually referred to as Sutter's Fort. By employing native workers through a combination of trade and force, Sutter soon established a working post at the center of a growing community of natives and settlers. He designed his own currency, had special uniforms made for his native "army," and purchased on credit equipment and cannons from the Russians. His business sense was never first rate, and he was suspected by the Mexican officials of the area, especially Mariano Vallejo, of using the natives and newly arrived settlers to set up a separate power base for himself in northern California.

James Marshall was born in New Jersey in 1810, and as a young man had drifted to new homes always westward—in Indiana, Illinois, and Missouri. After suffering from an unhappy romantic relationship, as well as failure as a farmer, Marshall set out for California, where he settled near Sutter's Fort in 1845 with a ranch provided by Sutter.

The Mexican War ruined both men's California operations. Sutter's allegiance was unclear in the beginning and his fort was briefly seized by John Fremont. Eventually both Sutter and Marshall supported the American cause, but both Sutter's post and Marshall's new ranch were essentially deserted by their workers during the war. It was in the aftermath of the war that they agreed to a partnership to build the sawmill where gold was discovered in 1848.

The discovery did not ultimately help either man. The land where the gold was discovered was not actually owned by Sutter and neither he nor Marshall thus had any preemptory right to the gold itself. The rush itself precluded either man from being able to find workers to help them on their other enterprises—both were eventually bankrupted by the rush.

For years, Sutter and Marshall pursued claims for compensation from the US government, based on their service as the initial discoverers and the damage that the discovery had done them but that had aided the nation so powerfully. The California state legislature did grant Sutter a $250 a month pension, but he died in poverty in 1880. Marshall also received a small pension from the state, but spent his last years doing menial jobs near the site of the original discovery, where he died in 1885.

For the next few months, work proceeded on the saw mill, as well as the flour mill further downstream. The famous moment of discovery passed almost unnoticed by most of the world, even by most of the population of California.

DISCOVERY AND COMMUNITY

Had Sutter used Indian laborers on the mill as originally planned, Marshall's discovery might have been forgotten. Even among the Mormon work crew, the excitement of the initial discovery quickly faded. The men had been digging in the area for months and had not noticed any gold before. Nor did they find more than a few flakes over the next few weeks. Yet the Mormon participation in the discovery would prove to be crucial.

The arrival of the Mormons in California was an offshoot of the greater Mormon migration westward. After being hounded and persecuted for their beliefs, the Mormon Church (Church of Jesus Christ of the Latter-day Saints) had moved out of upstate New York, where it had first organized, to Ohio, Missouri, and Illinois. After its founder, Joseph Smith, was murdered in 1844, church elders began looking for a refuge somewhere in the far West, away from American settlements. Brigham Young's famous exodus to Utah brought the main party of Mormons to the shore of Salt Lake in Utah. However, there were two other Mormon migrations, both of which ended up in California, and both of which would play a critical role in the gold rush.

One of these parties was under the leadership of Samuel Brannan, and had set out by ship from New York for California at about the same time that Brigham Young had set out overland for Utah. When Brannan's party arrived in California, it had already been taken over by the United States, which bitterly disappointed him and his followers. However, the American population of California was still only several hundred, and Brannan believed the Mormons could soon easily become the majority of California's white population.

Given the potential development opportunities in California as well, Brannan called on Young to bring the rest of the Mormons to join his group and settle in California, not in the isolation of Utah. Throughout 1847, Brannan and Young quarreled over where the future of the Mormon community should be located. Young remained adamant, arguing that Salt Lake would be safer, as Americans would never want to settle there as they clearly would in California. Brannan set up a Mormon colony in California, but it was short-lived and, by the fall of 1847, Brannan's followers were growing restless to join the rest of the church at Salt Lake.

Meanwhile, a second band of Mormons had marched their way across the Southwest and into Southern California wearing uniforms of the US Army. This "Mormon Battalion" had been recruited by the US in Council Bluffs, from the great Mormon encampment then preparing to set out for Utah. It might seem strange that Mormons would join the army of the nation that had so bitterly harassed them for years, yet Brigham Young had encouraged the men to sign up. The coming migration west, he knew, would be difficult. By sending some of his party off to fight for the US Army, Young hoped to improve relations with the United States, but he would also have fewer mouths to feed on the church's western journey, and the soldiers' pay could be used to help support and establish their new settlement.

The Mormon Battalion had accomplished much in the recent war, had marched to Los Angeles, and then in 1847 had been discharged. Now they were seeking to join the rest of the church at Salt Lake. Their first move was to move north to join Brannan's colony near San Francisco. Once again, Young warned the California Mormons to delay coming to the struggling early settlement. The Salt Lake outpost was too weak to support a sudden influx of new settlers. Better to stay in California for the

THE MORMON BATTALION

The Mormon Battalion was composed of over 500 volunteers, who served from July 1846 to July 1847. The volunteers marched nearly 2,000 miles from Council Bluffs through the Southwest to San Diego, and constructed a wagon road into southern California.

remainder of 1847, supporting themselves there and looking for jobs that might pay money, and then rejoin the church in 1848.

Thus in the fall of 1847, Sutter's attempt to establish a settlement in the California backcountry and the economic needs created by the recent war temporarily combined with the migration of Mormons on their way to a new home at Salt Lake. Sutter and Marshall soon put the veterans to work building a sawmill on the American River, at a site the local Indians called Coloma.

Henry Bigler was one of the Mormon Battalion veterans working at the mill in Coloma. Bigler was fascinated by the possibility of discovering more gold, and although it was deep winter, Bigler kept looking in his spare time. He was nearly the only worker who was willing to go out in the icy water and dig through the gravel and rock looking for more evidence of gold in the area. Each weekend, Bigler searched near the mill site. Using a knife, he had discovered a few more flakes, lodged in the crevices of rocks along the riverbanks. It had not amounted to much, but it was enough to capture his imagination. Bigler was inexperienced at prospecting, but two factors drove him to explore farther away from Sutter's mill. First, he had seen that the water was washing the gold flakes downstream, so he imagined he would be more successful heading down river. Second, he wanted to get away from the mill site, where he hoped any gold he found would not have to be shared with Sutter.

In March, on the pretext of going goose hunting, Bigler set out down the river, and was rewarded by finding more gold flakes. A few weeks later, about twenty miles downstream, Bigler found a concentration of gold that matched his imagination. Within days he had harvested about $30 dollars' worth of gold—at a time when Sutter was paying the men $25 per month to build the mill.

As a member of California's Mormon community, Bigler soon contacted the rest of the Mormons under Samuel Brannan's direction down near San Francisco Bay. It was unthinkable that Bigler would keep the news of his good fortune to himself. He alerted other Mormons, both at Coloma and working on the flourmill, of his discovery. Within days, Mormons from both sites and from down around San Francisco were coming to the stretch of the river, where the south and middle forks of the American River converged. The Mormons found gold readily, and were soon making over a hundred dollars a day. The site became known as Mormon Island. By the end of April there were several hundred people working the site. Sutter was having trouble keeping his workers focused on their contracted duties. The Mormons retorted that Sutter was in arrears in paying their wages. Soon another site was found nearby, quickly known as Negro Bar, where more gold turned up.[8]

The presence of the Mormon community was critical to the discovery of California's gold in 1848. Not only had a Mormon, Henry Bigler, managed to figure out where to prospect for gold, but the Mormon community had established the first substantial mining camp in the Sierras—at Mormon Island, not at Sutter's Mill in Coloma. Even more importantly, the Mormons formed a large enough community that the gold discovery did not remain an isolated find. Together they fanned out across the region, looking for (and finding!) more places to mine gold. As the Mormons told each other about the news and organized work parties to gather the initial gold, they proved that the golden flakes found at the mill were not an isolated discovery. Their efforts suggested not only that the gold existed, but solid detail and fact about what had been found, and trustworthy information as to where to begin looking for it elsewhere. It was from this activity in April and May of 1848 that the real extent of the California gold rush began to become known.

Most of the Mormon miners did not give up their religious mission to hunt for gold, at least not those who had been part of the Mormon Battalion. They mined at Mormon Island until mid-summer, 1848 then made their way over the Sierras and the Great Basin to the Mormon settlement at Salt Lake. During that trek, they also built a road from the mines over the mountains to Salt Lake, to make it easy to return to California in the future. It would in coming years be one of the most heavily traveled paths into California.

BRANNAN'S OPPORTUNITY

Yet not all of the Mormons would return to the church in Utah.

In the fall of 1847, Brannan had traveled to Salt Lake to plead with Young to come to California. Young had steadfastly refused, and ordered that the California Mormons come to Salt Lake in 1848. Brannan returned to California in the fall of 1847 believing Young was making a big mistake.

Brannan, of course, heard about the gold being collected at Mormon Island and Negro Bar, and in April and May decided to ride out to investigate the truth of the stories for himself. He did not stay long in the region, but later stated that he had been convinced that the gold being mined there was a major discovery, likely to last for at least five years.

Instead of taking up a pick and a shovel, Brannan—the leader, entrepreneur, planner—looked at the bigger picture instead. It was a natural position for him. For over two years he had been responsible for seeing to the needs and supplies not just of himself but of his followers in California. He had been thinking of establishing the main church settlement in California, before Young had refused to take his advice. Seeing several hundred miners busy at work, Brannan noted the lack of tools and supplies needed to do the early mining. To do the job properly, they would need shovels, picks, pans, blankets, food, and a variety of supplies. While the miners at Mormon Island saw the gold, Brannan saw the whole community, and it was that perspective, plus his recent argument with Young, that led him to take a different path. Leaving the mining camp, he went first to Sutter's Fort, where he arranged to have a warehouse and store built, and stocked with goods the miners were likely to need in the coming months. Then, once this was well underway, Brannan journeyed to San Francisco, and, in a publicity stunt that would echo through history, walked up and down the streets, holding aloft a glass bottle filled with gold dust, and waving his hat, while shouting "Gold! Gold! Gold on the American River!"

The small town had already heard rumors of the gold discoveries, but Brannan's bottle, and his place as leader of the Mormon colonists, proved those rumors were true. Within hours, his announcements had excited the imaginations of the settlers by the bay. Within a few days, San Francisco was virtually deserted as townspeople journeyed up to Mormon Island to see for themselves the gold fields, and to try their own luck at prospecting. Of course, when they needed supplies and equipment to sustain them, Brannan's store was nearby, ready to meet their demand—

BRANNAN AND YOUNG

Relations between Brannan and Young over leadership of the Mormon community in the West grew increasingly strained. Brannan continued taking tithes from California Mormons but did not forward them to the Salt Lake community. Supposedly, when Young demanded the money, Brannan replied that he would only do so if he got a receipt signed by God. Though this may be only a legend, Mormons in California complained to US authorities over Brannan's collection of church tithes.

Early Newspaper Accounts

Edward Kemble, the editor of the California Star reported on the rumors of the gold discoveries, at just the moment that Bigler and the Mormons were beginning to find significant deposits. He could not help ridiculing their excitement, however:

From the San Francisco *California Star*
March 18, 1848

THE MINERAL MANIA—*all not Coal that glitters*—The Philosopher's Stone never called into the field, and away from honest labor such a host of diligent bodies, as have the recent discoveries in the mineral kingdom, in California. Gold—the veritable gold itself has been dragged forth, and now that it has been turned from the earring without sowing, we wouldn't be willing to risk a prediction where the excitement caused will cease.

   Some silver-seeking 'uns, in the course of their researches, not many miles off, happened upon a shining substance, and *coal* at this particular juncture being preferable to suspense, or valueless black rock, coal it must be. Yes, coal has been brought to light! Coal enough to provide the proposed line of Panama steamers with fuel! Perhaps, though, it would be well to bring it to the light and heat of the furnace. Ah! there did exist a slight difference between this and the bona fide, lucklessly for the people. It did certainly look like coal and the scientific say it felt like coal! The only difference between this and the coal then, was, coal would burn and this would not!

> Quoted in Rodman Paul, *The California Gold Discovery:*
> *Sources, Documents, Accounts, and Memoirs Relating to*
> *the Discovery of Gold at Sutter's Mill* (Georgetown,
> CA: Talisman Press, 1966), p. 77.

at a healthy profit. Indeed, Brannan was able to sell all the goods they wanted, at ten times the price they had been going for only a few days before! Brannan thus became the first to see the gold rush as an opportunity not just for mining but also for mining the miners themselves!

CALIFORNIA'S GOLDEN SUMMER

The reaction to Brannan's announcement is sometimes seen as the beginning of the rush, but it is important to keep what happened next in perspective. After Brannan's announcement, San Francisco was basically deserted as its residents set out to see for themselves what was in the foothill streams. Ranches and farms in the area were abandoned in the early summer of 1848. It must be remembered that the total population of San Francisco at that time was only a few hundred—it was barely a hamlet, let alone a town. There were only a handful of ranches and farms in the area in the first place and the California economy in 1848 was still suffering from the long isolation of California, compounded by the effects of the Mexican war. If people went off to the foothills, it was not as if there was a buzzing business keeping them at home. Most probably set out with the intention of only seeing if it was true and maybe spending a few days digging around. It was an easy trek, and many went with their whole families, almost as if on a vacation—which in a way many were. Nearly everyone returned home after a few weeks or months in the foothills, even when they were successful.

If residents in central California found it easy to go to the foothills, residents from both northern Mexico, especially Sonora, and settlers from Oregon also found it easy to wander to California to try their luck. Oregonians, for the most part, were recent arrivals, and like Californians, the pace of business in Oregon was slow and flexible. Travel by ship down the coast of California from Oregon was easier, as winds and currents usually favored a quick voyage.

The Sonorans who came from Mexico were a special case. Many were miners, in fact they were generally the only ones in California in 1848 with any real mining experience. Since California had been part of Mexico only a few months before, this trek into the gold region hardly felt like a distant adventure. By the summer of 1848, there were around 5,000 people in the mining camps.[9]

Throughout 1848, mining in California seems to have been almost a holiday. Families had gone to the mining region, lived together there for a while gathering gold, and by the end of the year most returned home— though most also planned to return the following summer. Gold turned out to be abundant and widespread, contributing to the holiday atmosphere, and reducing tensions in the mines considerably. If no gold was found in one place, searchers often discovered it nearby. The surface gold disappeared quickly, and the seekers found they needed to dig the gravels and pick through the dirt to find the gold. The earliest mining usually required only rooting around along the river's gravel banks. Most early miners used a pan to scoop up gravel, then swirled water through the pan, causing the lighter materials to slosh out, leaving the heavier gold behind. The Sonoran miners introduced the cradle and rocker, which were larger wooden boxes with cleats nailed to their bottom. Gravel was shuffled into the box, and water poured or diverted in as one or more miner shook the entire box, shaking

1848 GOLD

Gold is measured in *troy ounces*, which are 2.75 grams heavier than a "normal" ounce. It is estimated that 11,866 troy ounces of gold were gathered during the summer of 1848, worth about $245,301 at that time. The same amount of gold today would be worth over $12,000,000.

Mary Hill, *Gold: The California Story* (Berkeley: University of California Press, 1999), p. 263.

out the lighter materials. Rockers and cradles usually required several miners working together as a team, but more gravel could be washed in a single day, thus increasing the chances of gathering more gold. By the end of the year, the first gold rockers and cradles were already showing up in the foothill camps to wash the gravel. It was back breaking work, but it tended to pay off. If it was not a sure thing, persistence generally rewarded the diligent worker and the average daily take was good. In many places, workers could make as much money in a few days as it would take months to make back east.

By the late summer of 1848, a regional California gold rush had begun. Yet its reach remained largely local. Nearly all the miners had needed to make only a few weeks' journey, at most. Many went home again after a short visit in the area, but two factors were already giving the early mining increased momentum. First, the amount of gold was not diminishing significantly, fueling rumors that the gold deposits were substantial. Second, and perhaps more important, the sheer number of discoveries was amazing. The gold was not limited to a single canyon or river valley, but was being discovered nearly throughout the entire western range of the Sierra foothills. It was this aspect of the discovery—not the single discovery by Marshall or even the more significant discoveries by Bigler and the Mormons—that was beginning to draw widespread attention to California. Even this discovery could not set off an international rush. Before that could happen, news of the discoveries had to reach the outside world and, given the weak state of communications between California and the world in 1848, the spread of that news was bound to be indirect and unsubstantiated. The ways that the news reached the outside world illustrates the great isolation of California, as well as one of the great challenges the rush would have to overcome.

REACHING AROUND THE PACIFIC

Samuel Brannan's dramatic announcement of the Mormon gold discoveries did more than set the local and regional population moving towards the foothills. It also indirectly began spreading the news of California's gold discoveries to the rest of the world.

As small as San Francisco might then have been, it was still a potentially important Pacific port—one that, now in American hands, attracted the attention of merchants all over the Pacific Rim. In particular, the merchants of Valparaiso, Chile, were keeping a close watch on developments in San Francisco. Valparaiso had been built by the Chilean government after its independence from Spain in the 1820s, specifically to be a major headquarters of trade in the Pacific. Chile hoped through its open port to engage in trade with any nation, and thus capitalize on the growing commercial activity of the Pacific and Valparaiso was uniquely suited to do this. The Pacific coastlines of North, Central, and South America were mostly rocky, with few natural ports. By establishing a modern port in the Americas, Valparaiso was poised to dominate trade in the Pacific. Ships coming from the Atlantic and rounding Cape Horn found Valparaiso to be a secure shelter, repair, and re-provisioning station. Its merchants kept tabs on the prices and commodities available throughout the Pacific. By 1848, Valparaiso was rapidly becoming one of the most prominent ports in the Pacific—a major crossroads of European, American, and Asian trade.

California under Spain and Mexico had not developed the potential of the port of San Francisco. America, it was understood by all, would not be so backward. Already American merchants were beginning to calculate the potential value of Asian trade that might flow into America through California's Golden Gate. In 1848, however, San Francisco was a minor hamlet of only a few hundred people, and hardly yet counted as a major port of call. To the merchants of Valparaiso, however, it bore watching.

Brannan's announcement of gold drew the close attention of Chilean merchants already looking to establish trade in San Francisco. One in particular promised to buy all the gold brought to him at a high price—higher than it was going for in California. It was not a bad deal, as he knew he could trade it in Valparaiso for an even higher price. When his ship, the *JRS*, arrived in Valparaiso with gold from California, the captain brought both news and proof of the gold discoveries with him to the merchant community at the crossroads of the Pacific.

It was as merchants that they responded. News traveled from San Francisco and Valparaiso to the edges of the Pacific. The news reached Hawaii in May, only a few weeks after Brannan's announcement. It had spread to China and Australia a few months later. As each of these reports reached a new port, it was the merchants who had the news first, and who had to decide whether or not to believe the stories coming out of California. Most, it seems, did believe that gold had been found—though

AUSTRALIAN MIGRATION

British officials in Australia actually discouraged migration to California during the gold rush. They feared that if the colony's workers went to America, the cost of hiring those laborers who remained would rise so high that it might undermine Australia's economic viability.

the exact extent of the find was still unknown. They reacted to the news in a sensible, business-like manner. Most gathered materials that they believed would be demanded by miners in California—shovels, blankets, clothes, mining equipment, etc.—and sent that to California.

Few initially seem to have set out to try their hand at mining themselves. This was a logical response by men who had spent years involved in Pacific trade. Already hoping to make money by supplying the needs of California's early settlers, the gold discoveries promised to make the California trade even more profitable. The idea of actually going to mine upon hearing the initial reports seems to have been dismissed. In response to the initial news, some young men from around the Pacific Rim did set out for California almost immediately, but their numbers depended upon how close they were to California: the closer and easier it was to get to California, the more likely a young man might make a trip to see for himself if the gold rush was real. As the news of the gold rush grew and became more certain during the summer of 1848, however, more young men around the Pacific Rim began to make plans to go to California, not merely send goods to sell there.

MASON'S WARNING

The first news of the gold discoveries had spread between Marshall, the work crew, and Sutter. The second discovery was reported among the Mormons in California. Brannan announced the news both to the local California community and indirectly to the merchant community of the Pacific. In each case, the news was reported in terms of its importance to the local members of the community. Sutter had interpreted the news to be something of a work dodge, but something out of which he could later potentially make money. Bigler and the Mormons had seen it as something that could enrich their community, both in California and Salt Lake. Brannan had seen business opportunities, as had the merchants around the Pacific Rim who responded by organizing shipments of goods to sell in California. Each response was slightly different, depending upon the motives of the person reporting the news.

Of all the reports beginning to come out of California, the most distinctive and perhaps ultimately the most influential was that made by Col. Richard B. Mason in the summer of 1848. Mason viewed the gold discoveries not as a potential miner or calculating merchant, but from the perspective of a military officer who was nominally in charge of California in the closing months of the war. As he waited to see how the US Congress would deal with establishing a government for California, he viewed the discoveries from the perspective of an administrator. As such, what he saw and reported was in many ways very different from the reports initiated by Brannan.

Mason's first inkling that something was up in the Sierra foothills seems to have come when Sutter approached him to approve his treaty with the Indians in the Coloma region. Mason informed Sutter that his own authority in California was coming to an end, and that in any case it was US policy not to allow individuals to make Indian treaties. Mason suspected—rightly—that Sutter was up to something in the region, though he did not initially know what. When Brannan set off the local rush to the foothills, local residents began to abandon their homes, and his own soldiers began deserting their posts to join the rush, he knew he needed to investigate.

In July of 1848, Mason and his aide, Lt William T. Sherman, set out on a tour of San Francisco, Sutter's fort, and the gold camp region. His concerns were not those of someone planning to jump into the rush, but to see if the rumors were accurate or exaggerated. Mason was a careful observer. His report of the mining regions detailed the locations of the camps, numbers of men hunting for gold, and the amount of gold being found. He collected specimens of gold from each site, labeling each specimen as to its purity and appearance. It was the first carefully researched, written, and documented examination of the gold fields. Mason concluded that the gold resources in the foothills were extensive and likely to remain productive for years to come.

His report, however, was hardly an enthusiastic endorsement of the local rush. He noted that while the rush was going on, other local industries were abandoned, which would ultimately hurt the region and make it difficult to feed and house the many newcomers that were starting to show up in the gold fields. There was no regulation in the gold camps, he pointed out, which could produce chaos. The government should find a way to regulate and tax the miners; the gold was legally US property, and thus the revenue should be shared with the government. Yet he also warned that the scale of the mining returns would make that nearly impossible to enforce. Regulators would have to be paid a very high salary in order to keep them actually at their jobs. Further, he advised, the salaries

William T. Sherman's Account

I remember one day, in the spring of 1848, that two men, Americans, came into the office and inquired for the Governor. I asked their business, and one answered that they had just come down from Captain Sutter on special business, and they wanted to see Governor Mason in person. I took them in to the colonel, and left them together. After some time the colonel came to his door and called to me. I went in, and my attention was directed to a series of papers unfolded on his table, in which lay about half an ounce of placer-gold. Mason said to me, "What is that?" I touched it and examined one or two of the larger pieces, and asked, "Is it gold?" Mason asked me if I had ever seen native gold. I answered that, in 1844, I was in Upper Georgia, and there saw some native gold, but it was much finer than this, and it was in phials, or in transparent quills; but I said that, if this were gold, it could be easily tested, first, by its malleability, and next by acids. I took a piece in my teeth, and the metallic luster was perfect. I then called to the clerk, Baden, to bring an axe and hatchet from the backyard. When these were brought, I took the largest piece and beat it out flat, and beyond doubt it was metal, and a pure metal. Still, we attached little importance to the fact, for gold was known to exist at San Fernando, at the south, and yet was not considered of much value.

Colonel Mason then handed me a letter from Captain Sutter, addressed to him, stating that he (Sutter) was engaged in erecting a saw-mill at Coloma, about forty miles up the American Fork, above his fort at New Helvetia, for the general benefit of the settlers in that vicinity; that he had incurred considerable expense, and wanted a "preemption" to the quarter-section of land on which the mill was located, embracing the tail-race in which this particular gold had been found. Mason instructed me to prepare a letter, in answer, for his signature. I wrote off a letter, reciting that California was yet a Mexican province, simply held by us as a conquest; that no laws of the United States yet applied to it, much less the land laws or preemption laws, which could only apply after a public survey. Therefore, it was impossible for the Governor to promise him (Sutter) a title to the land; yet, as there were no settlements within forty miles, he was not likely to be disturbed by trespassers. Colonel Mason signed the letter, handed it to one of the gentlemen who had brought the sample of gold, and they departed.

That gold was the first discovered in the Sierra Nevada, which soon revolutionized the whole country, and actually moved the whole civilized world.

William T. Sherman, *Memoirs of General William T. Sherman, by Himself* (2 vols., New York, 1875), Vol. I, pp. 40–42.

of soldiers and other public officials charged with keeping law and order would also have to be quite high, or the rewards of mining would simply tempt them to abandon their jobs, leaving California in a lawless condition. Mason admitted that the salaries he had in mind would seem much too high for Congress to approve, but, he noted, the scale of money here was not so far above what Congress would consider "normal" that nothing less would do. He despaired in his report that Congress would likely not be up to the job.

Mason's report was a danger signal of one of the most significant aspects of the coming gold rush. It would be self-organized, self-managed, self-regulated—which meant that it was likely to be a massive, chaotic event that any government (local, state, or national) would have a very difficult time managing or organizing. Unlike Brannan's ebullient announcement, Mason's report was a red flag, a pointing not just to the promise, but also to the massive problems likely to be unleashed by the gold discoveries.

Getting that report to his superiors, however, was a difficult task. In 1848, there were no direct communications between California and Washington DC. Mason sent Lt. Lucien Loesser on August 30 with his report and a sample of the gold to Washington DC. He set out by sea, crossed Panama, and arrived in Washington on November 23. To insure delivery, Mason also sent out a second messenger two weeks later with a copy of the same report who crossed Mexico instead, and actually arrived the day before Loesser.[10]

Mason's report arrived in Washington at about the same time that the news was beginning to create a buzz in the merchant community of the Atlantic world. As merchants and businessmen were wondering if the rumors coming out of California could be true, Mason's report seemed to provide absolute proof. Bigler had seen the gold discovery as a personal opportunity and Brannan as a commercial opportunity, but if Mason saw it as a potential administrative nightmare, President James K. Polk turned Mason's report upside down. In his State of the Union address he proclaimed that the gold discoveries were authentic, that the mining regions were going to be productive for years to come, and that it was a just reward for the expenditure of money and lives in taking California in the recent war. "The accounts of the abundance of gold in that territory," Polk proclaimed, "are of such an extraordinary character as would scarcely command belief were they not corroborated by the authentic reports of officers in the public service."[11] In other words, far from a political nightmare, he saw the gold as a political blessing, as assurance that his recent war had been divinely sanctioned. Polk's political enemies in the Whig party grumbled that Polk's announcement was a sham, designed to make the costs of the war more acceptable to the American public.

Foreign observers suggested that Polk was trying to build a rush of Americans to California in order to get enough citizens there quickly to hold the territory securely for the United States.

Polk, who was about to leave office, seems to have been concerned with his legacy. He released Mason's report to several newspapers, and put the gold on public display in Washington. Hundreds lined up to see it. American and European newspapers quickly touted the news, echoing in most ways the astounding and providential nature of the gold strikes. Mason's warning was drowned out by a sea of media enthusiasm.

★   ★   ★

The great 1849 gold rush was about to begin.

NOTES

1   Albert Hurtado, "Clouded Legacy: California Indians and the Gold Rush," in Kenneth N. Owens, ed., *Riches for All: The California Gold Rush and the World*, (Lincoln: University of Nebraska Press, 2002), p. 95.

2   Malcolm J. Rohrbough, *Days of Gold: The California Gold Rush and the American Nation* (Berkeley: University of California Press, 1997), p. 2.

3   Owens, *Riches for All*, pp. 16–20.

4   Both Sutter and the men working at his mill noted the storm and its effect on raising the water of the Americans River to high levels. See for example the Sutter's Fort Diary, and Azariah Smith's Diary, both reprinted in Rodman Paul, *The California Gold Discovery* (Georgetown, CA: Talisman Press, 1966), pp. 59, 66.

5   Walter A. McDougall, *Let the Sea Make a Noise: Four Hundred Years of Cataclysm, Conquest, War and Folly in the North Pacific*, (New York: Avon Books, 1993), pp. 194–238. See also Neal Harlow, *California Conquered: The Annexation of a Mexican Province, 1846–1850* (Berkeley: University of California Press, 1982).

6   Richard Henry Dana, *Two Years before the Mast* (New York: Harper & Brothers, 1840), pp. 215–216.

7   Mary Hill, *Gold: The California Story* (Berkeley: University of California Press, 1999), pp. 12–14.

8   Kenneth N. Owens, "Gold-Rich Saints: Mormon Beginnings of the California Gold Rush," in Owens, *Riches for All*, pp. 37–39.

9   Rohrbough, *Days of Gold*, pp. 8–15.

10   Hill, *Gold*, p. 29.

11   James K. Polk, message to Congress, December 5, 1848, quoted in Rohrbough, *Days of Gold*, p. 24.

CHAPTER 2

Deciding to Go

The gold rush of 1848 was local. Most miners came from California, Oregon, and northern Mexico. By the end of 1848, roughly 5,000 people had visited the mining region. As the year ended and the winter rainy season returned, most of these miners had gone home again. The number of prospectors at this point was roughly on par with the mining rushes in North Carolina and Georgia in earlier years, and even California's earlier Placerita Canyon rush of 1842.

Over the winter of 1848–1849, something new happened. The California gold rush "went viral." It exploded from its local setting and became an international stampede. Hundreds of thousands of people, with no mining experience, gambled their lives and fortunes on a long and dangerous journey to the new "El Dorado." A new illness seemed to sweep the nation: "gold fever." Sufferers appeared obsessed with rumors and news from California, studied maps and guidebooks on ways to get there, and began planning how to leave for the West as soon as possible.

Traditionally, the abundance and ease of mining gold in California accounts for this sudden rush, and these causes certainly cannot be ignored. President Polk and eastern US newspapers all seemed to confirm the availability and ease of mining at the end of 1848. Yet, ultimately, these explanations cannot explain the rush fully. At the beginning of 1849, the exact extent of mining could only have been guessed at; going to California was still a gamble. The rush continued strong for nearly a decade, long after it was clear that California's gold could not be easily gathered from the surface, and even as the amount of gold being mined seemed to be diminishing. Nor could the real dangers of the trip be ignored, either in 1849 or for the following decade. Yet the "fever" continued. Perhaps half a million people or more had come to California by 1860, including those who came, participated in the rush, and then left.[1]

Something other than the dream of golden riches drew these men and women to California. Four factors can be traced beyond the lure of California's rumored riches that ignited the gold fever of the 1850s: political instability, economic transformation, societal change, and improved transportation and communications systems all helped to create the golf rush. By examining these features, we can understand the rush not merely as a crazy dream of fortune hunters, but an attempt to deal with the remarkable changes sweeping the world in the middle of the nineteenth century. It turns the caricatures of crazed argonauts into real people, and it points to one of the most important hidden aspects of the rush: that there were far more people involved directly and indirectly in the rush than we usually realize.

POLITICAL INSTABILITY

Reports of fortunes already gathered in California played a large role in the thinking of feverish argonauts in 1849, but more was required to make hundreds of thousands of people journey to a distant land. Generally speaking, people do not leave if their homes are comfortable, secure, and stable. The high participation in the gold rush suggests the miners were leaving an uneasy, insecure, and unstable world. Perhaps surprisingly, many gold seekers wrote of being reluctant sojourners, pushed to trek to California by difficult circumstances at home.[2] As we consider why so many men went to California, we should consider why so many men were willing to leave their homes in the first place.

Much of the world in 1848 was in a state of political, economic, and social upheaval. Europe, Asia, and North America were all undergoing significant turmoil that would soon play an important role in both the creation and character of the gold rush experience. Large parts of both Europe and Asia seemed poised on the threshold of starvation and revolution. In North America, the US-Mexican War had ripped half of Mexico from its parent state and was now in the process of setting the United States at war with itself over what to do with its new conquests. Even before the gold rush, major movements of people were beginning around the world. The discovery of gold in California not only created a mass movement, but also channeled mass movements of people worldwide that had already begun gathering force.

EUROPE

Europe in the 1840s was on the verge of a political collapse that would reach into nearly every nation on the continent by 1848. In the aftermath of the Napoleonic wars, European nations had turned conservative and authoritarian, re-instating a strict class system and limiting the social and economic mobility of the lower classes.

This restrictive political climate coincided with a series of agricultural failures in the 1840s. The best known of these today is the Irish potato famine, but similar wheat failures also occurred throughout Europe in the late 1840s. These harvest failures, beginning in 1845 and lasting throughout the decade, led to widespread destitution and desperation. Irish refugees left home by the millions. The British government made it easy for shipping companies to offer Irish immigrants cheap passage to America. Conditions for the Irish in America were not ideal, but they were an improvement over earlier conditions at home, and Irish immigrants wrote home of their success, further directing more attention to the idea of migrating to America.

ALEXIS DE TOCQUEVILLE ON UNREST IN FRANCE, FEBRUARY 1848

I am told that there is no danger because there are no riots; I am told that, because there is no visible disorder on the surface of society, there is no revolution at hand.

Gentlemen, permit me to say that I believe you are deceived. True, there is no actual disorder; but it has entered deeply into men's minds. See what is passing in the breasts of the working classes, who, I grant, are at present quiet. No doubt they are not disturbed by political passion, properly so-called, to the same extent that they have been; but can you not see that their passions, instead of political, have become social? Do you not see that there are gradually forming in their breasts opinions and ideas which are destined not only to upset this or that law, ministry, or even form of government, but society itself, until it totters upon the foundations on which it rests to-day? Do you not listen to what they say to themselves each day? Do you not hear them repeating unceasingly that all that is above them is incapable and unworthy of governing them; that the present distribution of goods throughout the world is unjust; that property rests on a foundation which is not an equitable foundation? And do you not realize that when such opinions take root, when they spread in an almost universal manner, when they sink deeply into the masses, they are bound to bring with them sooner or later, I know not when nor how, a most formidable revolution?

This, gentlemen, is my profound conviction: I believe that we are at this moment sleeping on a volcano. I am profoundly convinced of it.

Alexis de Tocqueville, *The Recollections of Alexis de Tocqueville* (New York: Macmillan, 1896), p. 14.

"NO IRISH NEED APPLY"

The Irish Famine lasted from 1845 to 1852. Approximately one million people died and a million more migrated from Ireland. As a result, Ireland's population fell by nearly 25%. Many came to America, though the refugees often faced discrimination in housing and employment on the east coast. Still, America offered opportunities not found elsewhere.

The "hungry forties," as these years would be called, were leading to the continent-wide dramatic political upheavals of 1848.[3] Nearly every country in Europe experienced a revolution. In their aftermath, thousands of defeated revolutionaries desperately sought asylum in another country. Political refugees believed that America offered a sympathetic haven, a place to find both shelter and to raise new funds and support for continuing the revolution. And, once the news of the gold discoveries reached Europe, not only was there an extra reason for migrating to America, but for many governments, there was the opportunity of dumping radicals in America to rid Europe of potential troublemakers. The French government, for example, sponsored a special raffle of tickets to the California gold fields. Close observers noted that they were one-way tickets.

Thus, in the end, the gold rush from Europe needs to be placed in the context of these events: a long history of migration to America, generally positive reports from American immigrants, and government policies encouraging the deportation of its own citizens to America. The gold rush occurred, in other words, at a time when the population of Europe was already growing mobile, sending people looking for new opportunities. The rush, in effect, focused this general mobility for a few years on California.

CHINA

What was true for Europe was also true for parts of Asia, especially China. Japan in the 1840s was still a closed society, under the Sengoku policy of the government. China was a different story. China had traditionally been one of the most advanced and organized nations on Earth, but it had become a victim of its own success. A booming population had out run its ability to grow food, and the bureaucratic structure of the government had made it difficult for the nation to respond easily to crises. The humiliating loss to the British in 1842 in the First Opium War, combined with increased population and a massive rise in inflation, contributed to a collapse of internal order and a rise in banditry. In 1847 a secret society in Guangxi province, led by the visionary leader Hong Xiuquan, initially formed to bring order to southern China would soon clash with government forces, which would culminate in the Taiping Rebellion in 1851. The conflict would last over a decade and be the bloodiest struggle of the nineteenth century.[4]

> **THE TAIPING REBELLION: 1850–1864**
>
> The Taiping Rebellion was one of the bloodiest wars in world history. Estimates place the casualties as ranging between 20 and 70 million killed, and many more millions displaced.

As in Europe, many people were leaving home to seek economic security elsewhere. For several decades, young Chinese men had become sojourners, manual laborers working abroad for a number of years to raise money to send home to their families. These workers, known as "coolie" workers (from "ku li," meaning "bitter strength"), had migrated away from home to Southeast Asia as a growing labor force. Many of them were hired by the British in India and throughout the Malaysian peninsula, and the movement of workers was expanding both in numbers and in distances. Again, as in Europe, this was a large mobile mass of young men looking abroad for relief from conditions at home. New transportation technologies and the potential of new Pacific marketplaces already drew attention to California before the rush began. The gold rush in California did not create this movement, but did provide a focus for it for a number of years.[5]

THE UNITED STATES

By far the largest number of California gold miners, roughly two-thirds of the total, came from the United States.[6] Though many Americans may have believed they had an edge because the nation had recently acquired California in the Mexican war, that advantage counted for little in the effort and cost required to reach the gold fields. Like most miners worldwide, the majority of Americans set out to reach California by sea. The difficulties in getting to California were roughly the same whether setting out from New York or London, Boston or Hong Kong, New Orleans or Sydney. While many Americans had the option of reaching California by land, the overland route was long, costly, difficult, and dangerous. Nor would being an American provide any protection from the dangers of the journey—cholera, accidents, isolation, or just bad luck.

In 1848, the American westward movement was already nearly a century old. Colonial migration into Kentucky had begun in the 1770s, and the nation rapidly swept over the eastern half of the continent to the

Mississippi River valley. American farming families were thus traditionally "rootless" and expansive, and looked to the West for new opportunities and lands. This migration would be radically different: over 90% of the migrants were men, the majority between twenty and thirty-five years of age. These fortune hunters never intended to stay in the West. Most believed they would be in California for only a year or two before returning home. Most intended to use the gold they would find to build new farms and businesses in the East, not to resettle on the frontier. Unlike previous American Western migration, the California gold rush would not be centered on families seeking new lives in the West, but on young men seeking to improve their lives in the East.[7]

At the heart of the gold rush was a quest for wealth. The quest for gold was universal; hopeful miners came from every state in the union, but the conditions at home that pushed them to leave varied. Census figures show that the majority of the American migrants came from the northern states, especially the New England states and those bordering the Ohio and Missouri rivers. In part, this is to be expected since the northern states had a larger population in 1850. However, even after accounting for this difference, the gold rush clearly had a special appeal to young men in the North. As Asia and Europe were undergoing political upheavals, the United States was itself experiencing a social and economic transformation that had a powerful role in determining who would participate in the coming rush.

By the 1830s, the agrarian migration to the west had begun to ebb. The Great Plains were unsuited for farming, at least as it was practiced in the 1840s. American famers needed regular rainfall, navigable rivers, and plenty of wood to grow and transport crops, and to build and fuel their farms, all elements the plains lacked. Farther west, the Rocky Mountains and the Great Basin were even less hospitable. The Willamette Valley of Oregon was considered a farmer's paradise, as were parts of California, but both were distant and, before the Mexican War, not under exclusive US control. Farmers, which traditionally had large families, increasingly found themselves with little opportunity for their many growing children.

Unable to get new lands for farms of their own, many young men and women began traveling within the United States looking for work. Following roads, canals, river and steamboat lines, and the new railroads, many turned to cities, which began booming in the 1830–1840s. Looking for work as laborers, clerks, merchants, or any number of urban-based jobs, these booming urban populations began to give rise to a new society. It centered along cities and transportation lines of the North; the existence of slavery tended to limit the rise of both cities and middle class employment in the South.

The "Great American Desert"

In regard to this extensive section of the country [the Great Plains], we do not hesitate in giving the opinion, that it is almost wholly unfit for cultivation, and of course uninhabitable by a people depending upon agriculture for their subsistence. Although tracts of fertile land, considerably extensive, are occasionally to be met with, yet the scarcity of wood and water, almost uniformly prevalent, will prove an insuperable obstacle in the way of settling the country. . . . This region, however, viewed as a frontier, may prove of infinite importance to the United States, inasmuch as it is calculated to serve as a barrier to prevent too great an extension of our population westward.

Edwin James, *An account of an Expedition from Pittsburgh to the Rocky Mountains, performed in the years 1819, 1820* (London: Longman, Hurst, Rees, Orme, and Brown, 1823), Vol. 3, pp. 236–237.

Figure 2.1 1850 Farm Ideal. Though the majority of Americans remained farmers in the 1840s, this ideal of a bountiful farm depicted by Nathaniel Currier in 1853 was becoming harder to acquire by most Americans. Lack of available farm land, the difficulty of city and business life, and the growing stagnation of social mobility prompted many to seek their fortunes in California in 1849.

This shift away from an agriculturally-oriented community toward an urban society was not easy. Moving to a city to find work brought with it a whole series of associated changes that were difficult to either create or accept. For example, wealth in a farming region could be pegged to the amount of land one owned, its fertility, and its productivity. Money, profits from the annual crop, in many ways, was a by-product of land-ownership. In towns and cities, though, money not land, in the form of capital investment, was the basis of wealth. In a way, it was a reverse of the traditional equation of life. Land brought security, shelter, and money. In cities, money bought security, shelter, and (in the form of real estate investments) land.

This new centrality of capital created an unfamiliar basis for a moral life. For generations, preachers had cried out against the greedy ambition of merely making money the center of life's pursuits. Benjamin Franklin, who was seen as a model of rising respectability, also made money a

Ben Franklin's work ethic

Benjamin Franklin's Autobiography *was one of the most popular books of the early nineteenth century, promoting hard work, frugality, savings, and many other virtues that would help a young man rise in the modern world. For many in the years leading up to the gold rush, it was a kind of informal guide on how to get ahead in business. The pressure to follow Franklin's advice, however, was not universally admired. Mark Twain would later write of how Franklin's Autobiography made life miserable for young boys during his youth:*

His [Franklin's] simplest acts were contrived with a view to their being held up for the emulation of boys forever—boys who might otherwise have been happy. . . . With a malevolence which is without parallel in history, he would work all day, and then sit up nights, and let on to be studying algebra by the light of a smoldering fire, so that all other boys might have to do that also, or else have Benjamin Franklin thrown up to them. . . . And that boy is hounded to death and robbed of his natural rest, because Franklin, said once, in one of his inspired flights of malignity:

Early to bed and early to rise
Makes a man healthy and wealthy and wise.

As if it were any object to a boy to be healthy and wealthy and wise on such terms.
Mark Twain, "The Late Benjamin Franklin,"
in *The Galaxy*, July 1870, p. 138–140.

secondary, not a primary goal. Yet in cities money—capital for investment —now seemed the center for life. It was needed to buy or rent a home, to secure food, to invest in business—all things which land had done for farmers in the past. To this new generation, a focus on money was necessary but also deeply troubling.[8]

One way to understand this uneasiness was real estate speculation. In the booming cities of the early nineteenth century, with the growing scarcity of land in or near cities, it made sense (and cents) to buy land in or near a city, wait for its value to go up as the city grew, and to sell or lease the land at a much higher price. On the one hand, it was a rational way of making capital in an urban setting. It even had a kind of echo of farming, where value was placed in the land. Yet on the other hand, it was deeply disturbing. Unlike farming, the investor did not necessarily improve the land, growing crops or building structures on it. The sale of real estate made money, but money without the security of a sheltered home. Capital was fluid, it had to be reinvested continually in order to keep "working."

Those who engaged in speculation were viewed with suspicion. They seemed to be somewhat immoral, chasing fortunes for fortunes sake, untethered to the local community (as a farmer and his land), constantly on the lookout for a new investment opportunity, even one in a different region or city. What is remarkable about this is how people at the time described those who were engaged in this activity. They were said to be absorbed with speculation "fever," that they seemed obsessed with making money, with shifting their interests, with a kind of spiritual illness akin to greed and immorality, unusual by community standards.

Of course, what is remarkable about this is how precisely these descriptions match those afflicted with gold rush fever in 1849. The sense that this was somehow immoral, that it was based only on money, that it was not really tied to one's community. To a certain extent, while it was immoral, it was also a model for how the new world actually worked— and thus might actually be a smart move!

That it might be a smart move was based on yet another reality: that American society was beginning to calcify.[9] For generations, Americans had prided themselves on living in a society where men could better their condition. This was certainly true, especially in comparison with the societies of much of the rest of the world! The availability of land and resources to the west had essentially guaranteed that a person who was willing to take his family to a new location could with hard work better his condition was a touchstone of American faith.

However, by the 1840s, that faith was being shaken. As noted above, available lands were becoming scarcer. As people moved to towns and

Speculation Fever, *BEFORE* the Gold Rush

"Dress strictly respectable; hat well down on forehead; face thin, dry, close-shaven; mouth with a grip like a vice; eye sharp and quick; brows bent; forehead scowling; step jerky and bustling": thus did Walt Whitman describe (and instruct) youngsters seeking to make their way on Wall Street. The young poet's passion for New York City was almost erotic, yet he acknowledged that the merchants and money traders had "their brains full and throbbing with greedy hopes or bare fears about the almighty dollar, the only real god of their i-dollar-try." Highbrow New Englanders rued the spirit of speculation moving over the continent from New York. Preachers such as Henry Ward Beecher, Horace Bushnell, and William Ellery Channing described stock markets as a sinful temptation to "feverish, insatiable cupidity." Yankee intellectuals such as Henry David Thoreau and Ralph Waldo Emerson denounced both speculation in capital and the industrial market it fueled (albeit Emerson clipped 6 percent coupons on his own portfolio). Spokesmen for the southern plantation economy despised the ethic and monopoly power of northern financiers, whose "code of laws is that of the gambler, the sharper, the imposter, the cheat, and the swindler." Westerners deemed their dependence on moneyed men back East to be a species of servitude. Their leader was Andrew Jackson himself, who roared against "brokers and stock speculators," hoped they would all "break" (go broke), feared Americans "shall yet be punished for their idolatry," and in his farewell address endorsed "sober pursuits of honest industry." Charles Dickens's Martin Chuzzlewit spoke for foreign visitors when he described Americans' conversation as "barren of interest, to say the truth; and the greatest part of it may be summed up in one word: Dollars." All their cares, hopes, joys, affections, virtues, and associations, seemed to be melted down into dollars. Whatever the chance contributions that fell into the slow cauldron of their talk, they made the gruel thick and slab with dollars. Men were weighed by their dollars, measures gauged by their dollars; life was auctioneered, appraised, put up, and knocked down for its dollars.

Walter A. McDougall, *The Throes of Democracy: The American Civil War Era, 1829–1877* (New York: Harper Collins Publishers, 2008), p. 7–8.

cities and sought work in non-agricultural fields, money became more critical to success. At the same time, the availability of money was becoming restricted.

Part of the problem lay with the amount of actual money available for circulation. In the early 1830s, the renewal of the US Bank became a political crisis, and Andrew Jackson vetoed its renewal. He then transferred general moneys out of the bank, and issued the Specie Circular, which essentially ended the informal governmental regulation over US currency.

The result was a sudden collapse in faith in paper money, hurting the US economy generally and especially anyone basing their lives on capital investment. It also led to the rise of a large number of state licensed private banks that very often printed up far more paper money than it could possibly cover with their reserves. The reputation of paper money sank even lower, just as it was becoming more and more necessary in urban and business life.

This had a very restrictive influence on American business and trade, and on social mobility more generally. Unable to get the money to start businesses, or for investments generally, while also finding it harder to get good farmland easily, a new generation of Americans was finding that the American dream of self-betterment was not working. Unable to get a farm or investment capital, this generation saw itself not only failing to get ahead but also beginning to sink. Life in the cities, already unusual by traditional American standards, was also coming to be seen as akin to the society of European cities: sink holes of desperation, disease, and immorality. As conservative authoritarian social systems grew in Europe after Napoleon, Americans could look at their cities and wonder if the opportunities which democracy in America seemed to promise had perhaps been an illusion.

Both religious evangelicals and secular reformers sought to explain and fix American society in this new era. The Second Great Awakening gave Americans the sense that they were the captains of their own souls. Americans were swept up by the idea that they could make their society better through hard work and a moral lifestyle. While on the one hand this belief reinforced traditional ideas of the American dream, it also placed the burden of success on the individual. Reformers suggested you could succeed; those who did not had only themselves to blame.

The pressure to succeed—economically, socially, and morally—was thus intensified just as the arena in which such success was judged—the new industrial urban world of the North—presented what seemed like a diminishing world of choices.

The discovery of gold in California must have appeared to many to be a heaven-sent opportunity. Like many opportunities at that time and place, it was nontraditional. Its morality was questionable. It appealed to individuals rather than families. It required the investment of time and money, and its rewards were measured in cold hard currency. It seemed to promise a chance to reinvigorate the American dream of social mobility. For a young generation seeking to establish themselves in the new society of America in the 1840s and 1850s, the quest was not for farmland, but for real investment capital. California seemed to offer the golden answer.

If the actual journey to California was difficult and dangerous, that too could be considered an argument in favor of going. The shift from frontier farming to city life in the 1830s and 1840s was accompanied by a great reduction in the patriarchal power and authority—the "manliness" —of young men, and no clear way to reverse this sense of loss. Furthermore, this was a period when women's roles were elevated as moral guardians of the family, including their spouses. Men, it was understood, had to make moral compromises in the new urban environment. The home, the traditional "woman's place," was meant to be a refuge and an island of salvation for urban males. Again, men lost something in the power relationship between the genders. Manliness was diminished.[10]

The rush provided the chance to prove one's manliness against an urban background where human worth was often diminished. California acquired a reputation, not only as a place filled with gold, but also as an exotic and foreign land, filled with Hispanic women and Pacific trade connections. As portrayed in newspaper stories, advertisements, and guide-books for hopeful miners, California seemed to be a place worth seeing. The gold rush provided young men the opportunity to declare their independence from families and the old ways of life, to participate directly in a New World of capitalism, to prove their sense of manhood.

In this light, the often-expressed need for a macho gold rush adventure takes on a deeper meaning. This was not merely a lark, it was an attempt to regain a manliness that was seen as being diminished. What better way to do this than in a traditionally masculine activity such as going to war (i.e., volunteering of the Mexican War) or adventuring in the American far West—a land of mountains and deserts, fur trappers and Indians, and struggle in the service of national expansion?

Critically, the goal of the trek to California was radically new in American history, not a simple extension of the American frontier. Tied to the idea of getting gold as a stake to establish a life in the new urban-oriented world of the United States in the mid-nineteenth century, as well as the perceived availability of travel to the far West, the idea of heading to California began to take on features that would appeal to a vast number of men. To the hopeful miners setting out in 1849 from the United States, California represented not the dream of a new home in the West, but the golden key to a new, secure life in the East. They set out as sojourners, determined to make their fortune in distant, exotic California and to return as respected, manly adventurers with the money to make a foundation in the new American society of the East.

That goal, they would later discover, would significantly shape their experiences in California and beyond.

REACHING CALIFORNIA

Since newspapers reported the abundant, easy fortune to be gathered in California, the only major obstacle to that wealth seemed to be California's great distance from much of the rest of the world. Generally speaking, there were three routes to the California gold fields. Would-be miners could go by sea, by land, or by some combination of both. American migrants, who accounted for the bulk of the migration, generally divided almost evenly between the sea routes and the overland trails. Each possible route had advantages and disadvantages.

The trip by sea, usually out of Boston or New York, to Rio de Janeiro, around South America, up the coast of Chile to Valparaiso, then swinging out into the Pacific to pick up winds and currents to reach San Francisco was generally considered the quickest and safest route. Passengers could generally leave any time of the year, could carry personal goods more easily, and could be reasonably certain of reaching California within a few months. The downsides were the cost—it was the most expensive way to California; the passage of Cape Horn—one of the most feared places to navigate on earth; and the general problems associated with ocean travel—seasickness, a possibly tyrannical captain, poor food, disease, etc. For migrants coming from Hawaii, Australia or Asia, ship passage was the

The California Herald

James Gordon Bennett, publisher of the New York Herald, *created a special edition on news of the California gold rush, which he called the* California Herald. *The edition was meant to be a guide to California gold seekers, as he explained in the opening edition:*

The great discovery of gold, in dust, scales and lumps, of quicksilver, platina, cinnabar, &c. &c., on the shores of the Pacific, has thrown the American people into a state of the wildest excitement. The intelligence from California, that gold can be picked up in lumps, weighing six or seven ounces, and scooped up in tin pans at a rate of a pound of the purest dust a scoop . . . has set the inhabitants of this great republic almost crazy. "Ho! for California," is the cry everywhere. . . . All the intelligence from the gold region, and all the information relating thereto, is therefore sought for with the greatest avidity; and it is with the view of satisfying the public on this point, that we publish THE CALIFORNIA HERALD.

Quoted in Richard T. Stillson, *Spreading the Word: A History of Information in the California Gold Rush* (University of Nebraska Press, 2006), p. 21.

only option. For Europeans, ocean travel accounted for the first leg, and it was more common that migrants would simply travel the whole route by sea or take the Panama short cut.

Many believed that they could shorten the trip and the expense, and reduce the danger as well, by sailing to Panama, trekking across the isthmus, and then catching a second ship to California. On paper, such a trip seemed very attractive. In reality, this route held a number of hidden obstacles. The journey across Panama was through a tropical climate that few Americans were truly equipped to deal with. It included a passage up the Chagres River in a jungle, then a harsh, difficult and dangerous march over mountains. Nor were food or other supplies required by a sudden influx of thousands of travelers readily available along the route. Perhaps the worst surprise, however, was reaching the Pacific coast and discovering that they were stranded there! Many captains that stopped in San Francisco in 1848 and 1849 found their crews had abandoned them for the mines. In the words of historian H. W. Brands, San Francisco became a kind of nautical "black hole": ships that sailed in did not ship out again.[11] As a result, there were fewer ships in the Pacific available to pick up passengers, and many that were available were reluctant to sail through the Golden Gate for fear that their crews would abandon them. Thus would-be miners found themselves stuck in Panama for months at a time, in a location unsuited to a sudden boom in residents and unprepared to handle the crush, especially when disease started breaking out. To make matters worse, when ships did appear, ticket prices rose in response to supply and demand, eating away at the "cheaper" cost of taking this short cut through Central America. Again, though, this was a popular route for Americans and many Europeans.

The third route was overland along one of the western trails, generally setting out from towns along the lower Missouri River valley. This route was considered the cheapest, as there were no tickets to buy. Migrants could merely buy a wagon and team and set out along the trail. Even these costs could be reduced if miners shared expenses—as many did —by forming associations and companies in which all members paid into a pool to share the costs of the wagon, team, and supplies for the trek.

Yet if this route had the advantage of being cheap, it also took the longest time to reach California, and was the most difficult and dangerous of the routes. Crossing the continent by wagon involved a careful calculus. The wagon could not leave too early across the plains, before the grass had grown enough to provide fodder for the teams. This meant leaving around May. Leaving too late, however, risked being caught in the western mountains by winter snows. The Donner Party had been caught in just this way only three years before, and was very much on the minds of the travelers. The trip itself was long and arduous, and there was little support along the way for resupply or assistance.

Disease was also rampant along the trail. Cholera was an especially prominent scourge in 1849, breaking out in several US cities as the migration began. Overland migrants would soon discover the disease accompanied their travels as well, leading to an appalling death rate along the march.

The realities of the journey to California, however, were often ignored. The excited stories in the newspapers inspired men to dream and plan. Though the passages to California were difficult and dangerous, recent events suggested they were at least surmountable. The 1840s had seen the rise of steam ships, railroads, clipper ships, and new rapid forms of transportation. Newspapers proliferated, and the telegraph promised to spread information faster and farther than ever before. These innovations shrank the world, drawing even distant places closer together. As a result, even the backcountry of California seemed to be closer than it had ever been before.

The Mexican War also altered peoples' perceptions. The war had begun with a series of rapid moves by US forces into Santa Fe, Northern California, and Los Angeles. These forces had been set in motion before the war actually broke out, but the effect of US troops moving apparently effortlessly into these three regions so quickly suggested that travel in the West was not as difficult as had been previously supposed.

Global events also suggested that the world had become a smaller place. The US Pacific whaling industry was already reaching its zenith, and US missionaries had already settled in Hawaii. The Opium Wars of the early 1840s proved that Britain could project its power across the globe. Early British efforts in Hong Kong showed the new potential of Pacific trade, and San Francisco was expected to give the United States a similar Pacific outpost. Thus, by the late 1840s, the possibilities of trade and transportation throughout the Pacific had already sparked the imagination.

The problem with these expectations, however, was that they very likely misled the forty-niners far more than they painted an accurate picture of the difficulties of traveling in the West. They made the passage seem easier and more secure than it actually was. It would undoubtedly be a challenging and difficult passage, but one that they believed was ultimately surmountable. That idea may very well have increased the numbers of hopeful migrants to the gold fields, but it would also contribute to a rude awakening when the migrants actually faced the reality of the journeys.

Cholera

Cholera was virtually unknown in the United States before the middle of the nineteenth century. It was endemic in the Ganges Valley in India, and most Americans assumed it was a disease of the poor. Yet it appeared in the United States in 1832–1834, 1849–1854, and in 1866. Cholera was caused by *vibrio cholerae* organisms, which breed in polluted water. They can only be transmitted to human beings by swallowing contaminated food or water. Large numbers of people living crowded together and sharing contaminated water created the perfect breeding grounds for cholera epidemics.

The 1849 epidemic began in Europe the previous year, undoubtedly increased by the famine and revolutions of that year. Americans understood that it was likely to reach the United States in 1849, and early cases broke out in January. Attempts to quarantine patients proved ineffective, though a particularly cold winter slowed its progress. The disease also broke out in New Orleans, however, and with its milder winter it soon spread up the Mississippi and Missouri river valleys. By the summer of 1849, it was raging in New York.

Gold rush emigrants in 1849 originally worried more for the families they left behind in crowded urban environments than they did for themselves. They were shocked when they found cholera breaking out on crowded steamers, ships, and along the trail. Many believed that simply keeping fit and taking preventatives such as mint powders or "a diet of bacon covered in cayenne pepper and washed down in whiskey" would keep them safe None yet understood that the disease was transmitted by water, and few Americans gave much thought to drinking water straight from the same rivers and streams where they disposed garbage and human waste.

From 1849 to 1854, the zenith of the California gold rush, cholera broke out continually within the United States. Hardest hit were western towns and mining camps, where overcrowding and unsanitary conditions were at their worst. Transportation lines, especially those carrying large numbers of passengers, were also vulnerable.

In the 1860s, the English physician John Snow discovered the link between cholera and contaminated water, though he still did not understand the workings of the *vibrio cholerae*. It was enough, however, for doctors and public health officials to point to contaminated water as the cause of the disease. Cholera as an epidemic in the United States ended quickly after this discovery (see Charles Rosenberg, *The Cholera Years: The United States in 1832, 1849, and 1866*, 2nd edition (Chicago: University of Chicago Press, 1987); Edward Dolnick, *The Rush: America's Fevered Quest for Fortune, 1848–1853* (Boston: Little, Brown and Company, 2014), p. 126; and Steven Johnson, *The Ghost Map: The Story of London's Most Terrifying Epidemic—and How it Changed Science, Cities, and the Modern World.* (New York: Riverhead Books, 2006)).

THE DECISION

During the winter of 1848–1849, hundreds of thousands of young men worldwide struggled with the decision of whether or not to go to California. The weight of the various motivations for going to California varied greatly from individual to individual, of course. They weighed potential costs versus benefits, their physical fitness versus the dangers of the journey, and their own sense of karma. They asked themselves, "Do you feel lucky?" As news of the gold discoveries were trumpeted in the newspapers, and men discussed the advantages and possibilities of going, a bandwagon effect began to build. As each person declared his intention to go to California, the adventure seemed less a fool's errand and more a golden opportunity. As more and more young men prepared to head west, a new competitive edge entered into their deliberations. A growing awareness that so many others were going to California suggested that if they did not go now they would miss this wonderful opportunity.

Yet for the majority of young men, this decision was not theirs alone. In the mid-nineteenth century, family mattered. Fathers expected sons to contribute their labor to the running of a farm or business. Wives expected husbands to provide emotional and economic support, not to set out on a long Western adventure. Convincing family and friends that the trip was worthwhile, and getting their permission and support to go, was not easy. Of course, many simply decided to go, whether their family was supportive or not. Many, already cut off from family networks by the shift to urban settings, may not have had strong family ties, but, for the majority of young men, family permission and support were required, both physically and psychologically.[12]

The majority of Americans in the 1840s still lived in extended family groups, and usually sought to maintain these ties even in urban settings when possible. There were good practical reasons for this. The United States in the 1840s had very limited policing and medical facilities. Banking was, as we have seen, limited. There was no Medicare or Social Security, and life insurance was not widely accepted or participated in. All this is to say that the public support system for individuals was weak; families were units of protection and support in a much greater measure than we usually understand today.

This factor cut two ways: young men who set out for California took enormous risks, abandoning their support structure; and families who let their young men go—men in the prime of their ability to work and protect the family unit—risked weakening the ability of those who remained behind to cope with the daily struggles of life. The decision thus determined not only on the young man who sought to go to California, but also on the extended family left behind.

Getting permission to go to California was rarely easy. Parents, particularly mothers, usually argued strenuously against letting their sons head west. For the older generation, the idea of an easy path to riches seemed foolish and immoral, and directly opposed to their own experiences in life. The journey itself provoked nightmarish fears for parents, who feared their wandering sons might never be heard from again. Newspapers painted garish images of a war-torn American West filled with vengeful Mexicans, savage Indians, epidemic diseases, and brutal landscapes. The costs of getting to California also represented a substantial investment. Often those most desperate to go to California for economic reasons had the most difficulty in raising the funds needed to purchase passage aboard ship or a wagon loaded with supplies for the overland trek.

Overcoming these obstacles represented the first steps on the road to California. Many who wished to go were unable to overcome family objections in 1849. For many of these young men, though, each year in the coming decade offered new opportunities to renew their arguments, and many eventually won permission to go. Those who succeeded in convincing their families of the potential of the trip most often won these permissions only after intense negotiations. Young men needed to cover a variety of concerns. Brothers or cousins often needed to agree to step in for him and provide additional labor and support for families for as long as the miner was gone. Families demanded that the young man return according to a prearranged deadline, usually within two to three years, or once a given amount of gold was harvested. The costs of getting to California were often raised by seeking a loan from a family member or by pooling their resources available within the family. Successful miners were expected to repay these loans and to share their newly gained fortunes when they returned. Single young men with sweethearts sought arrangements to ensure a continuing relationship during their absence. Even when young men were anxious to go to California, these negotiations forcefully reminded them of the potential dangers they faced, as well as the increased vulnerability they created for the families they left behind. Even for those who expected the journey to be a glorious adventure, the hardships that they and their families would face in the coming years could not be ignored.

Fears for the young men's safety prompted another series of negotiations. In the 1840s, families were the first line of security against crime and disease. Young men heading west alone were seen as dangerously vulnerable. Most were expected to join formal or informal associations that would provide for their security. Men sought where possible to head west in the company of a brother, cousin, or neighbor. The vast majority of forty-niners, whether going by sea or land, joined formal associations or companies with written bylaws. Members promised to nurse other members who fell sick; some companies boasted the inclusion of doctors within their membership. Most associations also demanded that their members agree to behave in an upright and moral manner. Most miners promised to write home regularly with news not only of their own condition but also of friends and relatives participating in the trek to California.[13]

The traditional image of the gold rush is of hundreds of thousands of young men taking every kind of transportation available in a mad scramble to get to California. This image is not entirely wrong, but it is also very misleading. It suggests that the majority of miners were young, single, and unattached, and that their behavior was thus that of a boisterous fraternity, boasting of its excessive manliness and behaving badly. In many cases this was true, but a closer look shows that for the most part the gold seekers never completely left a tightly-knit community. They traveled with relatives—fathers, brothers, cousins—or with men from their home communities. They supported each other, and wrote about themselves and their companions to family back home. They needed family connections and expected to return home to a strengthened position in society due to their journey. They reported on their successes, both masculine and economic, and expected to have their resulting hard-won status affirmed by family members at home. Wives, sweethearts, and sisters were often the principal recipients of their letters, and thus the audience for their performance as well as the future partners of their imagined lives. Family ties, though stretched by great distances, were still maintained and valued by most miners.

This aspect of the gold rush is perhaps one of the most hidden, but also one of the most important. We imagine hundreds of thousands of young men participating in the rambunctious chaos of the gold rush as the only participants. Yet they stayed in as close connection with their distant families as possible. They included their home communities in their adventures, knowing that their successful return depended on it. Those stay-at-home family members—which far outnumbered the men who went to California—directly participated in the rush as well. They supplied advice, money, and emotional support. They covered for the absence of their young men, often at great cost to themselves. They maintained and supported gold rush "widows and orphans," trying to make do with an absent husband or father. If the gold seekers risked their lives on the journey, families at home equally risked becoming permanent widows and orphans, and a difficult future if the young men never returned. In the coming years, their participation in the rush would often be decisive as young men in California decided to come home rich or poor, stay a longer period than expected, or try to relocate their families to California permanently.

★   ★   ★

As the 1849 rush began, then, we need to consider not only those who hit the trails or boarded the ships, but also those supporting them and waiting for their return. They were also direct participants in the great California adventure.

NOTES

1   The 1860 US Census for California lists 379,994 residents. By this time, many of the miners of the early 1850s had gone back home, headed off to another rush such as Nevada, or had died of disease or starvation.

2   Malcolm J. Rohrbough, *Days of Gold: The California Gold Rush and the American Nation* (Berkeley: University of California Press, 1997), pp. 31–34.

3   Mike Rapport, *1848: Year of Revolution* (New York: Basic Books, 2010), p. 35.

4   Jack Gray, *Rebellions and Revolutions: China from the 1800s to 2000,* 2nd edition (New York: Oxford University Press, 2003), pp. 53–55.

5   Gunther Barth, *Bitter Strength: A History of the Chinese in the United States, 1850–1870* (Cambridge, MA: Harvard University Press, 1964), p. 3.

6   Rohrbough, *Days of Gold*, p. 33.

7   Rohrbough, *Days of Gold*, p. 33.

8   Ibid, 36–37; Brian Roberts, *American Alchemy: The California Gold Rush and Middle-Class Culture* (Chapel Hill: The University of North Carolina Press, 2000), pp. 49–53; Edward Dolnick, *The Rush: America's Fevered Quest for Fortune, 1848–1853* (Boston: Little, Brown and Company, 2014), p. 11.

9   Rohrbough, *Days of Gold*, pp. 2, 78–81; Dolnick, *The Rush*, pp.14–15.

10   Roberts, *American Alchemy*, pp. 69–92; Mark Eifler, *Gold Rush Capitalists: Greed and Growth in Sacramento* (Albuquerque: University of New Mexico Press, 2002), pp. 219–224.

11   H. W. Brands, *The Age of Gold: The California Gold Rush and the New American Dream* (New York: Anchor, 2003), p. 85.

12   Rohrbough, *Days of Gold*, pp. 33–45.

13   Rohrbough, *Days of Gold*, pp. 73–74.

CHAPTER 3

The Stampede of 1849

Throughout the winter and spring of 1849, hundreds of thousands of young men joined mining companies and associations, and left home for California. Franklin Buck, writing to his sister, tried to convey the scene. "Look out on the docks and you will see twenty to thirty ships loading with all kinds of merchandise and filling up with passengers," he wrote. All knew that the coming journey would be difficult and dangerous. As emigrants set out for California, tears were shed on both sides, as mothers and their sons, husbands and wives, wondered if they would ever see each other again, but most tried to rally themselves, to face the journey manfully, to experience the adventure of a historic journey into the unknown. Buck wrote to his sister,

> There is something about it—the excitement, the crossing the Isthmus, seeing new countries and the prospect of making a fortune in a few years—that takes hold of my imagination, that tells me "Now is your chance. Strike while the iron is hot!"[1]

Members of gold rush traveling associations and companies sought to cheer themselves and find new resolution in memories of western bravery. Stories of historic explorers filled their imaginations. Dr. J. C. Tucker, writing his memoirs years later, remembered

> No little courage and enterprise was required then to travel thousands of miles by land or sea to explore a wilderness said to be infested with fierce animals and Indians. California was then less known than is, by the researches of Livingstone and Stanley, the heart of Africa today.[2]

This sense of heroic adventurism gave satisfaction to the deep emotional need to appear manful, brave, and daring in the face of the unknown.

Later historians and writers often adopted that same attitude towards the gold seekers of 1849. On one level, this is very appropriate. This vision of themselves as explorers is how they wrote up their travels, in part because—to them—it seemed accurate. Very few of the emigrants had been on extended sea voyages or had made long wagon treks across the plains. To them, the experiences were new, exotic, and unusual. Writing letters home, they shared their reaction to these scenes with family, friends, and neighbors who they knew would also find these adventures remarkable. They certainly knew that, in telling such stories, they were making themselves the heroes of an adventurous story.

However, on another level, this aspect of the journey can be over drawn. In nearly every case, the gold rush emigrants traveled along established routes and known terrain. What was new was the overwhelming *scale* of the migration. It was the crowding, pressing multitudes of people trying to get to California—one of the most isolated places in the world in 1849—that would create the greatest difficulties and dangers of the journey. The transportation systems in place in the West in 1849 could have supported a few thousand emigrants; they were completely unprepared to handle the hundreds of thousands who would set out for California over the next decade.

From 1849 until at least the mid-1850s, the original routes for getting to California proved inadequate for the sudden press of numbers of people frantic to reach the gold fields. Ships had sailed from New England to California and the Pacific for decades before the gold rush, but never had ships transported so many passengers, who needed food and water and other services along the voyage. This also changed the demands made on the ports where these ships stopped to resupply. Much the same was true of the overland trails. Trail emigrants needed to secure food and water for themselves and their draft animals for months while traversing the continent. This was a relatively easy task when only a few hundred traveled the long, isolated trails, but when hundreds of *thousands* hit the trail at once, resources disappeared quickly. The scale of the rush—the very volume of humanity flooding down the trails—so stressed the trail itself that, what had once been a difficult undertaking, now became far more harsh and deadly. If the story of the rush is a story of struggle and hardship, it was a story made harder by the vast number of men themselves, traveling at once to a distant and isolated destination.

Our vision of the gold rush also needs to be enlarged. In traditional tales of the gold rush, the spotlight is on the young men anxious to get to California, but these were not the only people who were affected by the rush. The men and women who lived in the port towns that were rushed, or who lived along the trail sides of the American West, had their lives turned upside down by the rush. Travelers demanded resources without a care to the future because they were only transient visitors. Those who lived there, however, saw essentially a voracious army stripping an area of resources and then leaving nothing in their wake, like a plague of locusts. This tension was further aggravated by the fact that the Americans had just won the Mexican War, acquiring California and the Southwest, and thus had a more aggressive attitude towards the local communities they were passing through, as well as towards emigrants from other nations who were also heading to California on the same routes. American chauvinism was often brutally on display along the routes to California.

Nor was this attitude exclusively shown towards "outsiders." As the journey progressed, many emigrants began to fear that the ultimate obstacle in their way was their fellow travelers. Competition for food or water, for wagons and mules, or for trailside services frustrated the would-be miners. They worried about getting to California in time, and about securing their own share of the wealth. Men who formed companies to work together to support each other and share the wealth often started quarreling, broke up their associations, and struck out on their own for the mining camps, often immediately upon reaching the docks of San Francisco, or crossing the last of the mountains into California. The men who set out on the rush in a cooperative spirit of adventure and camaraderie began to see themselves as rivals in a great race.

Meanwhile, yet another group of gold rush participants discovered their own world was dramatically changing. The gold rush was, in many ways, similar to a wartime mobilization. Those who were left behind still needed to cover the jobs and responsibilities of their absent young men, and often were expected to follow and support their distant fathers, husbands, brothers and sweethearts—even as their own burdens at home increased. Worldwide, there were families trying to make do with the absence of a family member—absences that could last a year, two years, or forever. In many ways, they also found themselves exploring new worlds of responsibility, navigating difficult decisions and living quarters, and enduring hard work and toil in the quest of a better future.

When we look at the rush in this larger perspective—viewing not just the emigrants, but also the natives whose lands they rushed through, and the families they left behind—we see that the rush was not an event focused only on the hundreds of thousands of young men in California. It literally involved millions of people throughout the United States, the Americas, and Europe and Asia. The scale of the rush was larger and more far-reaching than the images of young men heading down a dusty trail can ever suggest.

Figure 3.1 Off to California. The mania to set out for California is captured in this satirical cartoon of a gold rush migrant. In fact, most gold rushers set out in groups, and pooled resources and equipment.

THE RUSH BY SEA

The majority of all gold seekers set out for California by sea, either rounding Cape Horn, or sailing into the Caribbean, crossing Central America, and embarking once more by ship to San Francisco. For European and Asian immigrants, of course, ocean passage was essential.

Transoceanic passenger travel was still in something of its infancy when the gold rush began. Most ships carried cargo, few if any passengers, and set sail on irregular schedules. The transportation of large numbers of people before the gold rush had not usually been concerned with comfort. Slave ships had been operating on the Atlantic for two hundred years before the gold rush, treating their passengers as chattel, packing them into cargo ships in horrific, inhuman conditions. Little to no thought had been given to health, much less comfort, aboard these ships. In 1849, slave ships still operated, though they were becoming rare, but the arrangements for large groups of passengers were hardly improved. The ships that brought large numbers of starving Irish men and women to America were known as "famine ships," or "coffin ships" due to their terrible conditions and high death rates. The ships that carried most of the Chinese "coolie" laborers out of Asia were also overcrowded and deadly.[3]

Few European or American passengers would willingly tolerate the conditions of a coffin ship or coolie ship but, in the press to get to California, most traveled on ships originally designed to haul bulk cargoes such as lumber, cotton, coal, whale oil, or manufactured goods, not passengers. Many ships simply raised temporary partitions in the hold, stacked berths in the compartments, and sold as many tickets as they could. When looking for a ship, most Americans sought fast ships, especially the "down-easters," built in Maine and with roomy hold but enough sleekness to move through the water swiftly.[4] Accommodation on these ships thus varied considerably.

Arranging regular scheduling was difficult in an age of sail, when fickle winds and strong currents could force any captain to adjust his plans. Passengers were simply told the ship would be sailing within a range of days, and to be available for departure on short

FREDERICK DOUGLASS ON THE COOLIE SHIPS

Abolitionist and former slave Frederick Douglass was particularly struck by the harsh conditions of ships carrying "coolie laborers" out of China, noting that they were as terrible as the slave ships. The mortality rates aboard these ships sometimes reached 50%.

Lincoln Paine, *The Sea and Civilization: A Maritime History of the World* (Knopf, 2013), p. 530.

notice. Delays in departure might take weeks. Regular, scheduled passenger services across the North Atlantic began fitfully in 1817, when New York investors tried to schedule one ship per month between New York and Liverpool. The operation was risky and hard to make profitable, as it required ships to sail by a timetable, whether full or not. Regular service, especially passenger service, to the Pacific however did not exist yet. Ships simply set out when their holds were filled, sailed to a profitable location in the Pacific, traded, and then moved on, often with several stops before returning, and usually with no certain stops in the Pacific. Rumors of likely profitable markets along the Pacific Rim directed ship routes more than a scheduled plan. Establishing direct and swift passages to San Francisco had not been a profitable enterprise before the gold rush.

Steamships offered one solution to regular, scheduled travel. Steaming under their own power, these new ships could essentially ignore winds and currents—as long as they had a supply of coal to burn. Steamers were already common on inland rivers and lakes and coastal waters by the time the gold rush began, but it was not until the late 1830s and 1840s that larger and more far-reaching steamships began to appear on the oceanic crossings between Europe and North America. Even then, the profitability of the steamer service was difficult to maintain, and steamer schedules were unreliable. Nor were any steamers available for direct passage from the Atlantic around Cape Horn to the Pacific.[5]

Competing against the new steamers, American shipbuilders had for some time been interested in making ships that were fast, even if it meant reducing the cargo capacity. Ship designs that added sail and reduced hull widths were usually referred to as "clippers," and had a growing reputation in regional, coastal waters. The age of the great clipper ships reached its peak at the same time as the gold rush. Initially built for service to Europe, the gold rush redirected their routes. Clipper ship construction boomed, becoming one of the first of many non-California businesses to profit from the gold rush. Clipper captains competed to see which ship could reach California in record time, both for personal glory and to advertise the advantages of clipper travel. Records were indeed set during the gold rush; the average clipper could reach from New York to San Francisco in 120 days, while the fastest could make it in less than 100 days.[6] In the spring of 1849, however, few clippers were yet available, and the $400 ticket price was expensive.[7]

One last consideration made booking passage to San Francisco difficult. Once the gold rush began, ship captains and owners also began to be leery of sending their ships to San Francisco. Arriving in port, crews abandoned their posts to try their luck in the gold fields, and could not be persuaded to return. While captains were willing to consider making a profit hauling

Robert Waterman, James Douglas, and the *Challenger*

The rush to California spurred excitement about clipper ships. Over 150 clippers were built in the five years after 1848, and clipper captains were the celebrities of the 1850s. Robert Waterman, who commanded the *Sea Witch*, was considered one of the greatest, having broken records on his runs to China. When Nathan and George Griswold commissioned the building of the *Challenge*, they challenged Waterman with a $10,000 bonus to reach California within ninety days of departure. Setting out in July, 1851, Waterman and his first mate James Douglas violently pushed their crew, and had to put down a mutiny in the South Atlantic. A storm off Cape Horn delayed the ship by eighteen days; the *Challenger* reached its destination after 108 days, missing the goal by exactly the duration of the storm. The San Francisco public, however, demanded that Waterman and Douglas be tried for their abuse of the crew. Though neither was ultimately sentenced, the trial began a series of investigations and trial of ship captains, ultimately resulting in the passage of the Seaman's Act of 1915, to protect sailors and seaman (Brands, H. W. *The Age of Gold: The California Gold Rush and the New American Dream* (New York: Anchor, 2003), pp. 106–121).

passengers to California, it would mean nothing if they could not return home again. By the spring of 1850, there were over 600 abandoned ships in Yerba Buena Cove.[8]

One popular solution was for the emigrants to purchase their own ship and then hire an experienced captain and crew to get them to California. Emigrants would form large companies or associations, pool their resources, and set out together as a mutual support and protection society. These associations would often sign up a doctor or two to travel with them, in order to insure the emigrants' health. They would purchase enough food to last the company for the whole voyage, and would sometimes purchase mining equipment as well to ship to California. Members of these associations bought shares on an equal basis, expected to draw on support from each other during the trip to the mines, work together as a team, and share the profits of their labors equally. Mark Hopkins, for example, helped organize the "New England Mining and Trading Company," an association made up of twenty-six men, each of whom put up $500 to secure goods and passage from New York to California. It was against this background that the purchase of a ship by a company also seemed to make sense. Having purchased the ship, the company usually expected to sell it again in California, and thus recoup their investment. Captains and crews thus would be free to join the rush as well, if they wished, or seek passage home again on their own.

By the end of 1849, 777 ships had set sail from the East coast head for Cape Horn and San Francisco, a trip over 13,000 miles—and often much longer due to having to navigate contrary winds and currents.[9] Whether as individual paying passengers or as a company of new ship owners, the voyage at sea was difficult for everyone involved. Seasickness plagued many of the men. Sheer boredom was another problem. Once at sea, the scenery was monotonous, and, in the crowded conditions of the ships, there seemed little to do to pass the time. Meals might mark the passage of the day—if they were not too sick to eat—but the quality and often the quantity of the food deteriorated as the days passed.

Sea-going passengers generally divided the trip into three roughly equal lengths. The first was from Europe or North America southward down the Atlantic to Rio de Janeiro, which covered roughly a third of the distance and in theory the time of the trip. During this leg passengers gained their sea legs (or not), and became accustomed to the monotony of the trip.

They also came to know the intimate personalities of their fellow passengers. Dr. Tucker remembered

> Most of these pioneers were sons of rich families, and many far above mediocre mental ability. The cost of reaching these shores then was not within the reach of every one, and many a slouched hat covered a cultivated mind, replete with classic lore.[10]

To some, the chance to study people so closely deepened their understanding of the strangers around them and their true natures. "Selfishness and mere pretense will show itself if it exists in an individual here," Mark Hopkins wrote in a letter to his brother. "'Tis impossible long to conceal immoral & infidel principles, they will peep out. . . . We become known pretty much as we really are."[11]

Crossing the equator was usually celebrated by the crew, often with a hazing of new crew members and sometimes participated in by the passengers. By the time the ship put in to port at Rio de Janeiro or another South American port, the passengers were ready for fresh food, a day or two perhaps of dry land, and the excitement of an exotic foreign city.

They might also be ready to mutiny against their captains. Few emigrants had any experience of life at sea, especially under the authority of the captain of a ship. They were internationally recognized as having the unquestioned power of life or death over anyone on board—crew or passengers. Such power was believed to be needed on ships sailing in

Mark Hopkins at Sea

We have a great variety of character on board, and the contact is productive of an endless variety of amusement. Sometimes I think their golden visions and high hopes of successful expedition to California does much to keep up their spirits and good humor. . . . We have many very intelligent and gentlemanly men among us. On the whole we are the most truly republican community I have ever seen. Mere class and formal politeness does not distinguish the gentlemen among us. We are thrown together in such close and continued contact that the spurious are certain to be detected—none but the genuine will pass comment. True gentility must be the offspring of intelligence and generous good will. Selfishness and mere pretense will show itself if it exists in an individual here. Tis impossible long to conceal immoral & infidel principles, they will peep out. Coarseness, rudeness, and sensuality of thought & feeling are here striped of their disguise of formality, fine cloth, and casual intercourse. We become known pretty much as we really are, valued according to real worth, and intimacies formed according to affinity of tastes and thought. This is true republicanism.

Mark Hopkins, *Letter to Brother, Moses,* March 3, 1849;
Huntington Library manuscript, HM 26036.

international waters, without the traditional support of law enforcement, and in a situation where all men needed to do their duties or all men could perish. Captains ordered, and expected instant obedience. The gold rush, however, challenged this order. For the middle class men seeking adventure, fortune, and independence, a captain's authority seemed patriarchal, arbitrary, and undemocratic. It was especially a problem when the emigrants had purchased the ship and thus felt entitled to order the captain about in his job. The new and harsh conditions of life at sea shocked many emigrants, and while some welcomed them as part of the manly adventure of the trip, others demanded that their needs and desires be attended to by the captain and crew. Likewise, many captains, unused to carrying passengers, were either unprepared or uninterested in the requirements of their complaining, landlubber, cargo.

Mark Hopkins reported that after his ship, the *Pacific*, reached Rio Janeiro, the passengers marched to the American Consul and demanded that their captain be removed from command. Hopkins noted that, though his legal authority to remove the captain was questionable, the Consul had pity on the passengers and relieved the captain. Hopkins' association then found another captain to take them the rest of the way to California. Hopkins noted that the passengers had been ill-treated and poorly fed, but

TUCKER HORDES OF YANKEES HOWL

Dr. J. C. Tucker described the America immigrants in Rio Janeiro as "the hordes of irrepressible Yankees [that] made Rio howl with their wild orgies and eccentricities."

Tucker, J. C. *Diary of a Voyage Around Cape Horn in 1849 to California* (Kindle Edition), Kindle Locations 198–199.

while in Rio began to see other ships coming in on their way to California that had faced much worse conditions under much harsher captains.[12]

American attitudes towards the Spanish-speaking natives they met while in port were chauvinistic, especially given the recent war with Mexico. The frustrations and anxieties of the emigrants began showing itself in the ports of South and Central America. Charles W. Haskins, who set out for California in the spring of 1849 aboard the clipper ship *America* noted what he called "an incident" while the passengers were disembarked at St. Catherina, South America. When a passenger was killed by a native, "for what reason was not known, although supposed to be from jealousy," the Americans demanded the killer be arrested. When local officials seemed unwilling to act, the Americans took the law into their own hands. The Americans "threatened to capture the fortress upon the hill and to bombard the town." Haskins noted that local officials were led to believe that the Americans intended to

> capture the entire country and annex it to the United States. This idea arose from the fact, as we heard related, that the passengers from one ship did actually enter the fortress and unfolded to the breeze the stars and stripes from the flag-staff, and some one, for fun or accident, had with a piece of charcoal put in an additional star which, of course, represented Brazil. . . . The Governor had the culprit arrested, and after a fair trial he was shot in the presence of those who demanded his execution.[13]

Haskins was unrepentant and jingoistic in his attitude, one reflected by many emigrants in South and Central America.

> At this period in their history . . . this nation of people were not held in very high esteem by the various governments and peoples of the South American continent, for the reason that their ports were but very seldom visited by our ships of war . . . but they were dealing now with the passengers of three or four ships who were on their way to California—a crowd of Americans who were determined to have the culprit arrested and punished at all hazards.[14]

After re-provisioning in Rio Janeiro or some other South American port, the California bound ships then set out for the second leg of their voyage, the one that most passengers feared the most—rounding Cape Horn at the southern tip of South America, or passage through the equally difficult and dangerous Strait of Magellan. It was one of the most feared and dangerous stretches of ocean in the world. Winds and currents threw walls of sea against any ship trying to sail into the Pacific. Storms in these latitudes were frightening. Ships attempting to round the Horn faced the full brunt of these forces, and could be blown hundreds of miles back eastward for every dozen miles they progressed westward. The storms often made it impossible to get celestial readings, and captains often had to sail on for days through the crashing waves and furious winds, without even knowing from day to day if they were still in the Atlantic or had reached the Pacific. Ships that took the Strait had the advantage of knowing where they were, but risked being dashed onto rocky coastlines, with a loss of all hands.

Once the ships reached the Pacific and began sailing northwestward, everyone on board breathed a sigh of relief and began to look forward to the next port: Valparaiso, or perhaps Lima. Again, it was a chance to get fresh food and water, to walk on dry land, to see a fabled old Spanish city, to interact with Peruvian culture, and to begin to get excited about the prospects of California again. Here emigrants could also gather fresh news from California: Was gold still being found in abundance? (It was.) Were there other people going to California, too? (Yes, and in worrying numbers!) Had other ships that had left Rio at about the same time reached here ahead of them—or at all? (Sometimes yes, sometimes no.) By the time they set to sea again for the last leg of their journey, the emigrants were growing anxious to get to California quickly.

Yet it was this last passage that was in some ways the most frustrating for many of the emigrants. The distance was perhaps the shortest of the three legs, measured on a map, and contained no terrible, life-threatening passage. Yet ships sailing up the coast to California ran into prevailing winds and currents that ran directly against where they wanted to go. The only way to make headway was to tack against the wind, bit by bit, and to sail far out into the Pacific in order to find conditions that would allow the ships to make it to San Francisco. Most ships struggled day after day, making little or no headway, sometimes losing miles rather than gaining them. Here at the threshold of the gold fields, just as their anxiety levels were rising, nature was creating an unbearable delay. For many ships, it took several days of maneuvering just within sight of San Francisco in order to get safely into the Bay.

> ## FRUSTRATION NEAR SAN FRANCISCO BAY
>
> Dr. J. C. Tucker, after nearly six months at sea aboard the sailing ship *Tarolinta*, recalled that, for many of the emigrants, the final leg into San Francisco Bay became "so unbearable, that those passengers having boats were thinking to launch them to row into port."
>
> Tucker, J. C. *Diary of a Voyage Around Cape Horn in 1849 to California* (Kindle Edition), Kindle Locations 498–499.

By the time these ships finally reached San Francisco, most passengers were finished with the sea and also growing tired of their fellow passengers. Five to six months trapped aboard an overcrowded ship under difficult conditions likely did little to endear the men to each other, but the growing sense of anxiety and competitiveness among them also played a large part of their attitudes. Having arrived in San Francisco, most associations broke up. Despite the initial schemes for working together, most men quarreled over which direction the association should go, where they should mine, whether they should wait to sell the ship or just abandon it, or a host of other issues. Deserting crewmembers often left before the ships were unloaded, delaying and frustrating passengers even further. Most associations sold what they could, pooled and divided the profits, and members then headed out for the gold fields as individuals or in partnerships of two or three, often brothers, cousins, or neighbors from back home, but the larger companies and associations of fifty to 100 men virtually all dissolved on reaching San Francisco.

ACROSS PANAMA

There was an alternative to the long and difficult voyage around South America: sailing to Central America, crossing the Isthmus of Panama, and then taking ship passage the rest of the way to San Francisco. In theory, this was the fastest route to California, though it was also expensive. It was perhaps the most popular and well used of the various routes to California, and grew in popularity throughout the 1850s. Yet, especially in 1849, it held hidden dangers.

The Panama route was first used by British merchants and diplomats with their interests on the west coast of South America. Ships would carry passengers across the Atlantic into the Caribbean, passengers would then cross the Isthmus of Panama and be carried to their final destination by British ships operating on the Pacific coast. Once the United States conquered California, the Polk administration called for similar mail and light passenger services across Central America to California, which was authorized by the Mail Act of 1848. William Henry Aspinwall received the contract to establish a steamer service between Panama City and California and Oregon, and with three new steamers organized the Pacific Mail Steamship Company (PMSS). The first steamer to make up the service, the *California*, left New York for the west coast in October 1848, before the news of the gold discoveries in California had reached the United States. As the gold rush began, Aspinwall soon promised to connect California bound passengers from east coast steamers to his soon arriving fleet of Pacific steamers via a short overland journey across Panama. Ticket prices initially ranged from $200–$500 for those willing to brave the journey.[15]

The first leg of this trip was similar to the beginning of the South Atlantic run—hopeful emigrants gathered in increasingly crowded ports, seeking passage to Panama. Unlike the southern route, however, this shorter passage was easier to arrange. Shipping was more common, and new routes to Panama were eagerly added to profit from the rush. Likewise, captains did not fear losing crews or ships in Panama, so emigrants need not consider purchasing. Ships from New York or Boston might sail or steam to New Orleans or Havana, and emigrants would then travel on to Panama. Passengers unaccustomed to sea travel faced many of the same conditions on the voyage to Panama, and if they stopped in Havana they experienced the strangeness of a different culture, if only temporarily. However, the voyage was usually short, and most seemed to weather it well. Accommodations were usually better than on the South Atlantic runs, and conflicts between the passengers and the crews less likely. Yet, again, the biggest obstacle was the sheer numbers of people trying to get to California. Passengers could not all be easily accommodated; ticket prices rose, and wait times for the next available passage lengthened, but securing passage to Panama, even if delayed, usually still seemed faster and safer than the southern all-ocean route.

Arrival in Chagres, Panama, however, was an assault on the senses, as well as on the emigrants' understanding of what this route actually entailed. Chagres had previously been a rather small, disreputable, and un-policed backwater. The port was simply unprepared to house and feed the number of passengers suddenly unloaded on its docks. Finding food and shelter was a serious problem. Once again, the scale of the rush—which overwhelmed the town—also overwhelmed the emigrants, who not only had to compete with each other for basic services, but who now also realized that they would soon be competing with each other in the gold fields of California as well. The sense of adventure still prevailed, but a growing edge of rivalry began to appear in their letters home.

The trip across Panama was also more difficult than they had expected. It began by chartering a small boat to ascend fifty miles up the winding

CHAGRES FEVER

Yellow fever, called "Chagres fever" by the emigrants, was prevalent, as were malaria, typhoid, and cholera.

Chagres River. Emigrants were plunged into a tropical jungle, witnessing not only strange and exotic flowers and plants, but also seeing new and dangerous animals. The environment overwhelmed them—it was stifling, humid and oppressive, and strange, unusual in ways that were unfamiliar and challenging.

After three or four days going up river, emigrants disembarked at Gorgona, and prepared to hike the last twenty-five miles to Panama City. The trail over the mountains and down to the Pacific was rocky, and in the constant tropical rains, muddy and slippery. Emigrants found they needed to carry their own baggage, often weighing 250–300 pounds. Mules were available for carrying people and their goods over the trail, but never plentiful enough for this number of people. Most emigrants shared mules, taking turns riding and walking, or walking the whole way and letting the animals carry their belongings. For many, unable to secure mules or struggling to carry their belongings over the peaks, it was easier to just discard their belongings by the trailside. It was not long before the trail over the mountains was littered with abandoned goods, some valuable, but all too impractical to carry.

Stumbling down the trail to the Pacific coast town of Panama City, most emigrants now expected that they had indeed survived the worst of their trip, and would soon be gathering gold in California. Yet it was here that the emigrants were in for another surprise. As the thousands of travelers poured down the mountainsides, day after day into Panama City, they discovered they were trapped. They had expected Aspinwall's Pacific Mail Steamship Company steamers to be waiting to carry them the last leg to San Francisco, but they found few if any ships.

Aspinwall had sent out three steamships—the *California*, *Panama*, and *Oregon*—around the Horn to provide passenger and mail service along the Pacific coast. The *California* set out first, in October 1848, before the rush. She was designed to carry sixty passengers, but had only seven aboard. She reached Callao, Peru, in late December, and first got word of the rush, leaving port now with seventeen cabin passengers and another eighty in steerage. When she arrived at Panama City, there were over 1,500 people waiting to board. When she left this port late in January, she now had roughly 375 passengers aboard. Upon reaching San Francisco, the crew abandoned the *California*, leaving it unable for months to return to relieve the overcrowding in Panama City.[16] Similar stories were recreated on the *Panama* and *Oregon* in the coming months. Other attempts were made to transport passengers out of Panama City. The captain of the Pacific whaling ship *Niantic*, for example, set up berths where whale oil casks were usually stored, set sail for Panama City, took on 249 passengers at $150 to $250 apiece, and headed for San Francisco.[17] On arrival, it, too, was abandoned. Panama City took on the characteristics of a vast refugee camp. Months passed before regular passenger service to Panama City finally began to reduce the number of frustrated emigrants.

Once again, relations between the travelers and those around them suffered. American travelers grew anxious and frustrated, and it was easy to take out these frustrations on the Spanish-speaking residents of Panama City. The mixed-blood culture of the region struck many Americans as unsavory, given the existence of racial slavery in the States. Americans had

Hopkins on San Francisco arrival's death

Travel by sea or across Panama took a heavy human toll. Mark Hopkins reported the following to his brother Moses upon arrival in August 1849:

Captain Richardson of the ship Brooklyn is charged with treating his assenters badly, & provisioning them so badly that the scurvy broke out among them until it has caused the death of seven and many more were disabled for the season and perhaps for life if they live at all. Our Doct Stillman is attending upon several of them. Some have had their teeth drop out & others have in a measure lost the use of their limbs. One of the passengers, Mr. John Blovelt, died near out camp of scurvy soon after landing. I attended his funeral & followed his remains to the grave. The coffin was covered with our American flag & the procession was joined by almost every American who saw it. The funeral discourse was preached by the Revd Mr Wheeler from Jersey City, at the camp where he died. The text was Mark 8th chapter 16th verse. It was an impressive scene & is often called to mind as see the same flag floating in the breeze over our camp. He was a man highly esteemed by all his fellow passengers. He was a jeweler from New York, did business in John St, and resided on Thompson St & leaves a wife and seven children. All the tented inhabitants of the valley rendered him all the assistance in our power, but could not save him. Poor fellow, it was hard to pass away so—to reach California to die, so far away from his family—with no relative near to receive his dying message or feel sympathy that none so well as near friends can feel. I felt glad I was not a married man with wife and children to care for me if such a fate is to be mine.

Mark Hopkins, *Letter to Brother, Moses,* August 30, 1849; Huntington Library manuscript, HM 26039.

just finished a war against Mexico, fueled in part by jingoistic racism and a sense of divine destiny. It was easy to transfer many of these attitudes towards Panamanians. As resources grew scarce, and much more expensive, conflicts between "Americanos" and the people who lived along their path grew more frequent.

Nor was the stay in Panama City the end of the ordeal. For travelers who did finally escape from this increasingly squalid encampment, there were still the contrary winds and currents that so frustrated the other voyagers trying to reach California from the south. After a long wait in Panama, another long frustratingly slow passage to California added insult to injury. Arriving in San Francisco at last, many found themselves reaching the gold fields at about the same time as thousands of others who had taken the long journey around South America. And as they set out, at last, for the Sierra foothills, they would be arriving at about the same time as the third great migration route was delivering its army to California from across the plains and deserts of the far West.

OVERLAND

The journey overland was longer and more difficult and dangerous than the ocean passage, but it was also cheaper. The cost of outfitting could range from $100 to $200, especially when emigrants formed traveling associations or companies for mutual support. The majority of emigrants set out from jumping off places such as St. Joseph or Independence, Missouri, in the late spring, journeyed up the overland trails alongside the Platte River, crossed South Pass over the Rocky Mountains, crossed the Great Basin of current day Utah and Nevada, and then scaled the Sierra Nevada Mountains before the winter set in, arriving at last at the gold fields after roughly a five or six month trip. Some instead set out down the Santa Fe Trail, crossed the Southwest to Los Angeles, and hoped to catch a steamer to San Francisco. Some decided to cut across northern Mexico instead of the Isthmus, but the unsettled conditions of the southern trails, so recently the front lines of the Mexican War, persuaded most to take the central overland route. To many who planned to take a trail, the routes were demanding but fairly well established. Most of the trails had been used for a decade before the gold rush. Men on the trail before the gold rush sometimes viewed the long trek with at least some sense of relief, as a diversion from the usual chores of summer work on a farm, but, once again, it was the press of thousands on the trail that would be the emigrants' greatest obstacle. The reality of 1849 proved to be much more crowded and grueling than their expectations.

The overland journey did not actually begin on the lower Missouri, but usually much farther east. As gold seekers decided to go overland, the first leg of the journey was just getting to the jump off points in Missouri. William Swain, for example, left his home in Buffalo, New York, in mid-April, traveled by steamer through the Great Lakes and Mississippi and Missouri rivers, arriving in Independence, Missouri, in order to prepare to "jump off" for the overland trail. He had already traveled nearly 1,000 miles, on a journey that, officially, had not yet begun.[18] For many if not most, this first leg of the journey represented the farthest they had ever traveled and the greatest distance they had ever been from home. During this first journey, they experienced their first bouts of worry and homesickness, as well as the thrill of adventuring and traveling to distant places. They wrote home with a mix of homesickness and adventurousness.

At the same time, they began to get early letters from home, often filled with misgivings about the trip, worries, even panics. Wives, mothers, sweethearts wrote of the first shock of reality of having their loved ones far away. To some, these letters may have had the effect of changing minds. For those who continued on, there was another realization: that they were not alone. As more and more would be gold-seekers headed west towards the lower Missouri Valley, emigrants began to see more and more crowds heading to the same region. The realization added to their sense of being part of a great, historic event, but also began increasing the sense that they were in competition with each other.

What happened next was something akin to the scenes in port cities around the Atlantic in early 1849, as gold seekers gathered seeking passage on ships, but in this case, the gathering was more intense and concentrated. Travel across the plains needed to begin between the end of April and the beginning of May. Starting out too early could leave a wagon stranded on the plains where grass for the draft animals had not yet grown; leaving too late risked seeing the available grasses already depleted by the earlier wagon trains. Mistaking the timing could bring disaster. In port cities, ships departed throughout the year; in the lower Missouri jump off towns, roughly the same

TURNING BACK

Joseph Banks, traveling west with a company from Ohio, noted in his diary meeting one of the many who turned around early. "Says he can't go all the way. Has money enough; loves his wife more than gold."

Joseph Banks quoted in Edward Dolnick, *The Rush: America's Fevered Quest for Fortune, 1848*–1853 (Boston: Little, Brown and Company, 2014), pp. 93–94.

number of those who would go by sea over the year was concentrated into one close region, and all set out within a few weeks, rather than throughout the year.

The result was the concentration of tens of thousands of people in small towns that usually only numbered a few hundred. This massive crunch of people needed to be fed and sheltered until the conditions were right to set out on the trail. At the same time, the gathering emigrants needed to purchase food and draft animals for the journey, far in excess of what the local region could provide. St Louis had, for years, been something of the entrepôt of the far West, and could send goods up the Missouri River to the jump off towns, but the scale of this rush challenged even St Louis. Draft animals, for example, were gathered from throughout the Mississippi valley, and were still in short supply. This created not only difficulty in securing these animals, but insured that the prices for them would be high, even if their condition was poor. One emigrant noted that the price of oxen doubled as soon as the buyer made it clear he was heading to California.[19]

Waiting in these towns increased feelings of anxiety, of falling behind in the race. Gold seekers increasingly felt a need to move as more and more emigrants crowded into the area and prices for goods rose to unprecedented levels. Yet the reality of the trail meant that they had to wait. Many, if not perhaps most, of these emigrants not only needed to secure a wagon, food, equipment, and animals, but also needed to learn how to harness and handle teams of animals, something many had no experience in. William Swain noted that breaking oxen "was a mean job."[20]

Most were relieved to finally be setting out, and the first travelers began hitting the trail in late April. Some broke down and returned almost immediately, as they had set out before the conditions were good. Many began to throw out extra equipment, food, and supplies as being too heavy, slowing down their progress. Soon the trailside was littered with goods, many of which had been purchased at high prices only weeks before.

BREAKING MULES

Isaac Wistar set out overland for California in 1849. As he noted in his diary, his traveling company "had a high old time breaking the mules to harness. . . . They were lassoed, thrown, harassed, and dragged into place by sheer and simple force. . . . Each animal had a rope with a choking noose around his neck, at the other end of which was a mad and excited individual who walked, ran, jumped, fell, swore and was dragged."

Isaac Wistar, quoted in J. S. Holliday, *The World Rushed In: The California Gold Rush Experience* (New York: Touchstone, 1983), p. 105.

The trail itself underwent a startling change. Before 1849, the trail was not a road so much as a series of directions; guidebooks instructed emigrants to follow one river to another, to cross various passes, etc. The press of thousands in this confined area actually began to create a true trail, in the sense of being a visible road, worn down and marked by hoof prints, wheel ruts, and abandoned goods across most of its distance. The trail or road, however, grew wider and wider as the summer progressed. Trailside rivers became increasingly polluted and stripped of resources. Grasses, required by the grazing draft animals, were chewed away or trodden down to such an extent that travelers needed to wander farther and farther away from the main "trail" beside the river. Meanwhile, the emigrants themselves swept up as much brush and wood as they could for cooking fires. The gold rush "trails" created devastated corridors many miles wide across the central plains. As the gold seekers rushed through the plains, they left a wide resource desert in their wake.

They also left a series of graves. In some cases, it was the result of accidents. Emigrants unused to handling animals, to packing and unpacking wagons, tired from hours of monotonous walking in a hot sun—all these factors led to accidents. Without much medical care along the way, an accident on the trail could be fatal. Yet the greatest killer on the trail was not accidents, or Indian attacks (which the emigrants feared, but which very rarely occurred), but disease, especially cholera.

Cholera was a frightening killer in the early nineteenth century. Its causes were not understood, but its effects were savage. As historian Charles Rosenberg noted,

> The onset of cholera is marked by diarrhea, acute spasmodic vomiting, and painful cramps. Consequent dehydration, often accompanied by cyanosis, gives to the sufferer a characteristic and disquieting appearance: his face blue and pinched, his extremities cold and darkened, the skin of his hands and feet drawn and puckered. . . . Death may intervene within a day, sometimes within a few hours of the appearance of the first symptoms. And these first symptoms appear with little or no warning.[21]

Cholera was most concentrated in cities, and was caused by disease in drinking water. It could swiftly strike great numbers of people in days. It had broken out in several American and European cities before the gold rush. It broke out in New York City in 1849. For many gold seekers, news of the New York and other urban cholera epidemics in 1849 drastically increased their concern for families left behind. Mail services were uncertain at this time (see below), and gold seekers worried when they did not hear from relatives at home that cholera had claimed their lives in their absence.

It was not long before cholera began to show up on the trails heading to California. Today the reasons are clear: the disease was carried by the rushers, infected the water they used along the trail, and spread quickly through the trail population. Nor should we be surprised that what had essentially been an urban disease now hit the "rural" emigrants. With over 30,000 emigrants hitting the trail all within a couple of weeks of each other, the overland rush was the equivalent of a large US city picking up and moving along a single trail. One trail goer climbed a hill during the rush, and saw a series of campfires lining the Platte River as a single line from the eastern horizon to the western horizon. This concentration of people, in the jump off towns, along the trails, and at various bottlenecks of passes or outposts along the trail, was the perfect breeding ground for the disease. The death rate was enormous. It was said that travelers coming late in 1849 or 1850 on the trail were never out of sight of grave markers along the length of the trail. Many, if not most, were simply buried beside the trail without ceremony, a coffin, or a grave marker.

The emigrants carried the disease to California as well, and it spread among the mining camps and in the booming gold rush tent cities. Combined with malnutrition, exposure, and accidents, the death rate in gold country was catastrophic; it is often suggested that one in every five immigrants who rushed to California in 1849 died within the first six months of arriving.

The ramifications of these effects of the trail need to be seen on a larger stage. For every miner who died along the trail or in California, there were usually family members back home who now bore the loss not only of a loved one but of an important contributor to the family's survival. Many were young husbands or fathers who left behind widows and orphans. Perhaps worse still, many never learned of the deaths of their

> ## TRAILSIDE GRAVES
>
> Luzon Wilson, traveling to California in 1849, saw many trailside burials, noting that the emigrants simply dug shallow graves, covered the bodies with dirt, and then moved on, "leaving the lonely stranger asleep in the silent wilderness, with only the winds, the owls, and the coyotes to chant a dirge. . . . There was not time for anything but the ceaseless march for gold."
> Edward Dolnick, *The Rush: America's Fevered Quest for Fortune, 1848–1853* (Boston: Little, Brown and Company, 2014), p. 134.

absent young men. Though most miners sought to relay news to families where they could, often letters home went missing, or surviving partners were unable to send the news home again. For many of these families, young men who went off to California simply disappeared without a trace.

Likewise, the environmental and disease corridor created across the central plains significantly affected the Plains Indians. Before the gold rush, the Sioux had become a major power on the northern plains, defeating or creating alliances with other tribes in the region, and aggressively expanding their power towards the southern plains. The Platte River Valley was at this time essentially their southern frontier. The tribe most affected by the disease and resource devastation was the Pawnee, who lived and hunted primarily along the Platte and Republican River watersheds. The 1849 rush essentially weakened the Pawnee to the point that the Sioux advance was made easier. Yet, at the same time, it created a serious problem for the Sioux. During the summer, the Sioux and other Plains Indian tribes tended to hunt buffalo on the high plains, away from the Platte River and its trails. This is one of the reasons why interactions between the Plains tribes and the gold rushers were actually rather limited, but cholera struck the Sioux, who used the same water that the emigrants had contaminated.[22]

In the winter, the Plains tribes needed to seek refuge off the exposed plains, in the timbered river valleys such as the Platte which bisect the plains. Thus, when the Plains tribes returned to the Platte during the winter of 1849, the devastation wreaked by the gold rush emigrants was felt not primarily by the rushers, but by the natives who needed these resources to survive the winter. Over the next few years, the gold rush trail along the Platte would create increasing difficulties for the Plains Indians, and become an increasingly bitter point of debate between the tribes and American travelers and government officials.[23]

THE FAR WEST

Passing out of the plains, the California gold seekers next faced a series of decisions. Should they strike out directly for California, or take a side trip to Fort Hall or the new Mormon settlement at Salt Lake. The detour offered the possibility of refreshed supplies, repairs to equipment, and news of the trail ahead, but it also added to the length of the trip, and for every immigrant that passed on ahead of them, there would be less grazing and water available for those who followed. The decision was yet another difficult calculation needed to be made along a trail that was increasingly offering bad options.

For those who stopped at Salt Lake, it was a chance to see the religious sect that had been so maligned and persecuted, and that had secret religious rites and practices. To many Americans, the Mormons seemed as foreign as natives along the trail. Potential conflicts between the Mormons and gold rush emigrants always lurked close to the surface. Brigham Young, the Mormon leader, tried to keep the Mormon settlers from selling wheat and flour to the emigrants that, he noted, was desperately needed by the Mormon community itself.[24]

On balance, however, the church, benefitted from the rush in these early years. Mormon scavengers gathered discarded goods from along the trail, set up trading posts, and profited from reselling the goods, or using the iron from abandoned or broken-down wagons for other uses. Hundreds of emigrants poured into Salt Lake City daily between early June and the end of August, seeking provisions, repairs, and fresh draft animals. To some emigrants, the Mormons proved to be a needed lifeline in the desert; to others, they were profiteers squeezing them in a time of need. Like the residents of Independence and the Sioux and Pawnee, however, the Mormons were deeply affected by the fleeting contact with the massive movement of emigrants headed to California.[25]

The next leg of the trip involved crossing the Great Basin, a geographical feature unlike any the emigrants had ever experienced before. Indeed, it was unlike nearly any other place on earth.

Stretching between the Rocky Mountains and the Sierra-Cascade Mountains, the Great Basin covers nearly 185,000 square miles. There was no way to go around it; emigrants needed to cut across it, a journey of over 500 miles. It is rough terrain, largely composed of a series of north-south running mountains and hills, each an obstacle to the overland emigrants. Yet the real problem was the aridity of the region. The Humboldt River was the lifeline of the Great Basin. It was a narrow and shallow river, hardly worth the name, running through rough, desert terrain and long stretches of alkali flats. What was worse, the Humboldt simply disappeared about halfway across the region, dropping into a sink, leaving the emigrants in the middle of the Basin with over a hundred miles still to go. Overland emigrants needed to follow its somewhat meandering course through the central region of the Basin, but it was not a straight line, it ended before the Basin itself ended, and the river grew increasingly precarious and insubstantial as the emigrants followed it into the desert.

SALT LAKE'S VISITORS

At least 10,000 visited Salt Lake in 1849 alone. Selling goods to the miners quickly became a vital business for the struggling Mormon colony.

The Basin was an anvil that broke many of the emigrants and their animals, equipment, and psyches. Perhaps the best passage after leaving the Humboldt sink was to head for Donner Pass, but the reputation and rumors surrounding that route were so feared that most travelers sought another route. Some headed further south for Carson Pass. Others headed for "Lassen's Cut-Off," a supposed shortcut that headed north. Other guidebooks suggested short cuts or alternative routes that seemed safer or more direct—many of which were complete figments of the authors' imaginations, written primarily to make a quick buck off the gold rush migration.

Leaving Humboldt Sink, emigrants set out to cross dry, dusty ground without water. Many traveled at night, to reduce the heat and to try to push through the landscape as quickly as possible. The trail began bleak and strange, and the lack of sleep and water only heightened the difficulty. Emigrants wrote of a ghostly environment, of passing in the night covered in alkali dust like apparitions. Gaunt, stumbling, staring ahead for landmarks in the landscape that did not seem to exist, this leg of the trail was perhaps the worst of the whole trip.

Once again, the sheer number of travelers on the trail made the conditions worse. Those at the head of the rush generally passed safely through the Basin. Those coming later found a landscape already stripped of limited resources. All along the trail, emigrants had passed abandoned equipment and supplies. Here the trailside debris looked different. Wagons broke in the dry, rocky region. Others were abandoned to make it easier for the draft animals to carry supplies for a last dash to the Sierras. However, without water, the animals too began to falter. Soon carcasses of dead oxen lay strewn on the trailside. Those who came later in the herd of emigrants encountered a gruesome scene. Oliver Goldsmith came upon Rabbit Hole Wells in late September, expecting to find a freshwater spring.

> I had associated with the name 'wells' a vision of an oasis. . . .
> The whole environment as far as the eye could reach was simply
> an abomination of desolation. . . . Ash heaps of hills into which
> slowly percolated filthy-looking, brackish water. More than half
> the wells were unavailable as they were filled with the carcasses
> of cattle that had perished in trying to get water. To add to the
> natural horrors of the scene, about the wells were scattered the
> bodies of cattle, horses, and mules which had died here from
> overwork, hunger, and thirst; broken and abandoned wagons,
> boxes, bundles of clothing, guns, harness, or yokes, anything and
> everything that the emigrant had outfitted with.[26]

At this point, especially for those later in the rush, the alternative trails seemed more promising. Yet travelers soon discovered that the trails either were poorly marked, poorly thought out, inaccurately described, or sheer lies. Wandering desperately in the Basin now, short of water and supplies, unsure if they should keep following an uncertain trail or retrace their steps and try again, the traveler's plight became serious. By September it became clear to many in California that a large portion of the emigrants were still out in the Basin, struggling to reach the Sierras before the winter snows fell, possibly lost on their way. Many who had already reached California now organized relief and rescue parties to find and guide the stragglers home. The emaciated travelers they found seemed barely alive. Many would take months to recover from the ordeal.

By the end of 1849, over 100,000 people had reached California. They had begun arriving by sea early in the spring, and continued in a steady stream directed at San Francisco for most of the year. In the fall, the great overland trail emigrants had begun pouring in over the mountains. By November, that migration had all but ended, and with the winter rain and snow settling in over the mountains, most of the miners left the foothills for shelter in Sacramento or San Francisco.

The great rush itself was one of the largest voluntary mass migrations in human history. It was also one of the most cosmopolitan, bringing people from all over the world, and marching through a wide range of populated regions and nations. Organized from the bottom up rather than the top down, it was composed of hundreds of thousands of individuals, all acting essentially on their own, as they formed partnerships and associations to band together to face the difficult journeys. The death toll of the trip,

Enos Christman's "Manly Fortitude"

I have crossed the broad American continent from shore to shore. . . . And have seen human nature under a great variety of circumstances, and in every stage of development. . . . I have a more enlarged, a more comprehensive view of the works of nature, a more accurate conception, and a nicer appreciation of their beauty and grandeur. I am sensible that I have obtained a more thorough knowledge of mankind, of their character, their energies and capabilities, of the motives and springs that govern human actions. In short, I am thus far satisfied with my enterprise, though, in some respects it may not turn out as favorable as I could wish.

Enos Christman, *One Man's Gold* (New York: Whittlesey House, 1930), p. 135.

especially along the trail, is impossible to judge accurately, but must be estimated in the thousands.

What is perhaps more amazing is that this rush, despite the death toll, would be repeated, year after year, throughout the 1850s. Though we sometimes refer to the emigrants as the "49ers," in honor of the first year of the rush, they came out in huge numbers year after year—even as the dangers of the journey became well known. The goal, many believed, was worth the risk.

The coming months and years working in California would test that belief.

LEFT BEHIND

As thousands of young men journeyed over the seas, jungles, plains, and mountains to California, hundreds of thousands of other participants in the rush also began exploring new worlds and creating new lives. Whether in the United States, Europe, or Asia, the loss of a young man to a multi-year adventure created problems for those left behind. Parents and siblings missed their absent sons and brothers, worried about their safety, and feared that they might never see their loved ones again.

For women engaged or married to absent gold seekers, the gold rush dramatically turned their worlds on end. Early letters from wives and sweethearts speak of a sense of bewilderment, of dread and fear at letting their partners leave them. As would be miners drew ever closer to California, the women they left behind realized that their loved ones were moving farther and farther away from them. Panic at the realization of their abandonment caused many to write frantic letters, begging their loved ones to give up the quest, turn around, and return home at once. In many cases, this likely happened as young men also grew homesick, or got cold feet in the face of the challenging journey. Once aboard a ship, or embarked on the far western trails, however, few were able to return even if they wanted to, and, after the first month or so, many women realized that they had to move forward in their own new circumstances.

For young women engaged to a westering miner, it meant waiting, usually for a period of years, to be finally reunited with their fiancées. The strength of these long distance relationships was difficult to sustain, though both parties usually understood that it would be at least two years before the couples were actually married, but absent beaus could not compete with other prospective suitors who stayed behind in the East. Letters between lovers were essential, and both men and women eagerly waited for word from each other. The difficulties in establishing a regular and reliable mail service, especially in the early years of the rush, severely tested the bonds of affection. When neither men nor women heard from their loved ones for months at a time, fear and imagination often ran wild.

Perhaps the most difficult circumstances were those faced by young wives and mothers who watched their husbands head out alone to California. In some cases, the separation was too difficult and whole families headed out to California together, but most wives and children were left behind while their husband/father set out alone to reap a family fortune. These women faced all the same anxieties for their husbands and worries over delayed or missing letters, but they faced added responsibilities. Children, especially infants, needed care, and family businesses usually needed tending, even without the husband's participation, if the family was to survive. The struggle to maintain a farm or family business was a strain. In most cases, women were familiar enough with the work or business to oversee operations while their husbands were gone, but lack of his direct contributions made these businesses more difficult. If a woman had very young or infant children, finding the time to raise them and run a business was extremely wearing. In the cases where men had gone west to help a struggling family, the business the wife now ran might already be in difficult straits.

Often young wives and children found themselves at the mercy of extended families, very often needing to live with their in-laws—a situation often difficult enough already, without the added problem of a missing husband. A husband's brother might help out to keep the family afloat, but often they had their own farms or businesses to run as well. The unspoken tension underneath the miner's absence was that the whole family was pitching in to cover while he was gone, but there were limits to this charity. Wives not only wondered when (or if) their husbands would return, but faced the tacit questioning of those helping them as well. Relations among such families could grow strained.

SARAH'S PLEA

Sarah Nichols, writing in April 1849 to her husband Samuel and son George on the trail to California, could not keep from an emotional outburst. "I cannot live if you go any further. Oh return home, sell your things and return to me. Save Oh Save my life I cannot live if you go to California. There is war, famine, pestilence, murders and every evil there to await you have mercy on a poor mother. Oh come home. I'm sick and depressed. I know not what to do."

Sarah Nichols, *Letter to her Husband, Samuel and Son, George*, April 7, 1849; Huntington Library manuscript, HM 48291.

The letters of Sabrina Swain to her westering husband William suggest the difficulties of young wives awaiting the return of their husbands. Sabrina had given birth to a young girl only a few months before her husband had left. She was originally opposed to William's adventure, but she was overruled by her in-laws, especially her mother-in-law. While William was away, Sabrina was to move in with his family and be looked after by his brother, George. In her first letter, she makes the depth of her feeling of abandonment clear.

> I want very much to describe my feelings as near as I can, but in doing so I hope not to crucify yours. I feel as though I was alone in the world. The night you left home I did not, nor could not, close my eyes to sleep. . . . William, if I had known that I could not be more reconciled to your absence than I am, I never could have consented to your going.[27]

In following letters, she sought to appeal to his sense of guilt in going.

> Most of the people tell me that I am a fool for letting you go away and that no man that thought anything of his family would do so. They say that I need not indulge a hope of seeing you again.[28]

By the end of 1849, Sabrina was reporting to William that George was taking good care of her, that she was still struggling to reconcile herself to her fate. Of their daughter, Eliza, who was now toddling around and learning to speak, Sabrina reported, "she has long ago forgotten that she has or ever had a father. As she grows older, the more I feel the need of a father's care and assistance in lightening the responsibility of governing and training her right."[29]

★   ★   ★

As 1849 turned into 1850, eastern families adjusted, waited for letters or news, and looked forward to the day they would see their young men return. As news of the cholera epidemic along the trail, or the death rate in California filtered back to these families, their tensions could only increase. Some would never hear from their young men again. Some would hear only infrequently, or through rumors from other letter writers on the health of their gold seekers. Some would see their young men return, eventually, either wealthy or poor. Some would soon discover that their husbands wanted them to come to California to join them. In every case, however, the world of these young women and their families would be forever touched by the California gold rush.

NOTES

1   Katherine A. White, ed., *A Yankee Trader in the Gold Rush, the Letters of Franklin A. Buck* (Boston: Houghton Mifflin and Company, 1930), p. 27.
2   J. C. Tucker, *Diary of a Voyage Around Cape Horn in 1849 to California* (Kindle Edition), Kindle Locations 55–57.
3   Lincoln Paine, *The Sea and Civilization: A Maritime History of the World* (New York: Knopf, 2013), p. 530.
4   Paine, *The Sea and Civilization*, p. 521.
5   Paine, *The Sea and Civilization*, p. 513.
6   Paine, *The Sea and Civilization*, p. 521.
7   Alex Roland, *The Way of the Ship: America's Maritime History Re-envisioned, 1600–2000* (New York: Wiley, 2007), p. 151.
8   Roland, *The Way of the Ship*, p. 157.
9   Roland, *The Way of the Ship*, p. 156.
10 Tucker, *Diary of a Voyage*, Kindle Locations 63–65.
11 Mark Hopkins, *Letter to Brother, Moses*, March 3, 1849; Huntington Library manuscript, HM 26036.
12 Mark Hopkins, *Letter to Brother*.
13 Charles Warren Haskins, *The Argonauts of California: Being the Reminiscences of Scenes and Incidents That Occurred in California in Early Mining Days* (New York: Fords, Howard & Hulbert, 1890), pp. 16–17.
14 Haskins, *The Argonauts of California*, pp. 16–17.
15 Roland, *The Way of the Ship*, pp. 153–154.
16 Willard Thompson, *Going For The Gold: By Sea to the California Gold Rush* (Chronicles of Western Pioneers) (Rincon Publishing. Kindle Edition), Kindle Locations 104–194.
17 Roland, *The Way of the Ship*, p. 157.
18 See J. S. Holliday, *The World Rushed In: The California Gold Rush Experience* (New York: Touchstone, 1983), pp. 45–79; also Roland, *The Way of the Ship*, p. 151.
19 Holliday, *The World Rushed In*, p. 95.
20 Holliday, *The World Rushed In*, p. 105.
21 Charles E. Rosenberg, *The Cholera Years: The United States in 1832, 1849, and 1866*, 2nd edition (Chicago: University of Chicago Press, 1987), pp. 2–3.
22 Dolnick, *The Rush*, pp. 130–137.
23 Elliott West, *The Way to the West: Essays on the Central Plains (Calvin P. Horn Lectures in Western History and Culture Series)* (Albuquerque: University of New Mexico Press, 1995) pp. 33–37.
24 John D. Unruh, *The Plains Across: The Overland Immigrants and the Trans-Mississippi West, 1840–1860* (Urbana: University of Illinois Press, 1993), p. 306.
25 Unruh, *The Plains Across*, pp. 303–308.
26 Holliday, *The World Rushed In*, p. 253.
27 Holliday, *The World Rushed In*, p. 80.
28 Holliday, *The World Rushed In*, p. 83.
29 Holliday, *The World Rushed In*, p. 339.

CHAPTER 4

Rushed Foundations

Before the gold discoveries at Sutter's Mill and Mormon Island, only a handful of non-native peoples ever visited the region, and then usually only on a temporary basis, hunting or gathering wood or other resources. In 1848, approximately 5,000 men and women set out for the foothills of the Sierra Nevada, looking for "placer" gold—the gold resting on or very near the surface. As the summer ended, Colonel Richard Mason toured the gold camps and worried that the region did not have the resources and infrastructure to support a major mining boom, and that the region was already growing impossible to regulate or police.

One year later, the situation was far worse than even he could have imagined. As a result of the great rush, over 100,000 men and women were now working in the foothills. For the most part, the primitive conditions Mason described a year earlier still prevailed, but with the huge influx of new miners, the conditions grew far worse. Food, shelter, mining equipment, medicine, and law enforcement were all severely limited. Merchants tried to get goods to California's gold camps, but the long distances from eastern suppliers to California limited their ability to operate effectively in the region. Meanwhile, the difficulty in finding men willing to work for mere wages as teamsters, tradesmen, and manufacturers when a golden fortune could be easily gathered from the ground further stymied efforts to set up the infrastructure needed to support the miners.

A potential catastrophe awaited the gold rushers. Even if gold could be found, miners could not eat it. The lack of any real support services for the miners meant that food would be in short supply and offered at high prices. Newly arrived miners already suffering the effects of the long trip to California would be even less likely to recover, given the lack of medicines and shelter. And many of the miners soon found themselves threatened by personal violence and banditry. The gold camps in 1849 were not so much mining settlements as vast, largely unsupported refugee camps, far from the support of any organized society. Indeed, it has been estimated that one in five miners who reached California died within the first six months.[1] This would place the deaths from the unsettled state of the region at over 20,000—a figure larger than the total non-native population of the state only two years earlier.

The story of early mining in California has two interlocking elements. There was the struggle to find and get the gold out of the ground and return home again with that fortune; but there was also the struggle to provide food, clothing, shelter, medical services, legal protections and a whole host of other services. Providing these services required a far-flung and developed urban infrastructure in California. This infrastructure needed to develop simultaneously with the mining camps.

The historian Gunther Barth described San Francisco as an "instant city," an urban commercial headquarters that essentially sprang to life fully formed in service of the gold rush.[2] In fact, it was not just San Francisco, but an entire urban hierarchy, reaching from San Francisco Bay to the smallest of the mining camps, that was forged in the early days of the gold rush. To support a large mining population, California needed a social, political, economic, and technological foundation in place from the beginning. What it needed, in other words, were cities. The gold rush miners not only needed to dig up their fortunes, but they needed to lay the foundations of a complex urban infrastructure if they had any hope of succeeding.

ROARING CAMPS AND BOOMING TOWNS

As noted before, once they arrived in California most of the mining associations created before the journey broke up. Anxious to get their own fortunes in the face of the vast crowds of competitors, individuals set out for the gold camps as quickly as possible. Yet, on arrival in the foothills, the would-be miners quickly discovered that gathering a fortune would not be so easy after all. Mining was hard, exhausting, and lonely. Even in a crowded mining camp, the daily work consisted of digging, carrying water, panning, and more digging. "The labor of gold-digging is unequalled by any other in the world in severity," noted Edward Buffum. "It combines, within itself, the various arts of canal-digging, ditching, laying stone-walls, ploughing, and hoeing potatoes."[3] The vast majority of men in the gold rush were completely unprepared for this level of physical labor. Issac Lord noted

> Cramp is so common that a person can hardly hold his hand
> tightly closed for a moment and open it again, without a violent
> effort to overcome the spasm which is almost sure to follow a
> strong contraction of a muscle.[4]

Nor was the work easy to sustain, especially given the poor diet and malnutrition common throughout the mining camps in the early years of the rush.

> Worse still, none of the effort guaranteed success. "The fever and
> uncertainty of mining made the people grow old and haggard,"
> Luzena Wilson lamented, remembering the early years. They
> might dig, dig, dig, fruitlessly for days, making scarcely enough to
> keep body and soul together, and then disheartened, sell the
> worthless claim for enough provisions to last till they struck
> another camp. Perhaps the first day's work on the old claim by
> the new owner would yield hundreds of dollars.[5]

Most miners quickly came to see that mining was a lottery, with a heavy cost in money and labor as the price for a chance.

The odds of making a fortune quickly diminished. The miners soon discovered that most of the easy to find surface, or "placer," gold had already been taken in 1848. Not only was the gold becoming harder to find, buried under streambeds or ancient gravel banks, but the numbers of miners—competitors in the lottery—were increasing daily. As one miner wrote to a friend in the summer of 1850,

> I thought the country full to overflowing some time ago, but they
> still come. There are a thousand per day arriving by the overland
> route. They come into the country strapped and have no place to
> strike a lick, for all the diggings are claimed that can be worked.[6]

The solitary, physical activities left the miners alone with their thoughts— and their fears. After having set off with high expectations, few miners found it easy to face mining's realities. For many of the disillusioned, the thought of returning home empty-handed was the most bitter disappointment of all. At the end of a hard day's work, Joseph Bruff confided that he "laid down with considerable fever, slept uncomfortably, and dreamt that I was abandoned by my family, my friends, and the whole world, because I had not found a gold mine."[7] Failure for many miners led to depression, and a life of wandering the West in search of a fortune they could never find. Throughout the 1850s, the suicide rate for miners was high.

New gold finds were still being made, but by the time rumors of these sites spread across the region and hopeful miners showed up to try their luck, the placer gold was usually already depleted. As early as 1848, mining rockers and cradles were in use in the mines, introduced by experienced miners from Sonora. Working these basic tools was best managed by teams of two, three, or four miners. Miners also quickly saw other advantages of teamwork—of working more gravel and sharing the risks and rewards, of taking turns having someone in the group go gather mail or supplies while the others worked, or of having someone else to help guard a claim or nurse a sick miner back to health. Despite their individual goals, most miners realized early on they had to organize and co-operate with their neighbors to succeed.[8]

Fortunately, the men had experience in this. Forming and living in associations on the way to California gave many practical experience in creating new associations now. Miner J. D. Borthwick believed that the Americans had an edge in this activity, that they were "prompt to organize and combine to carry out a common object. They were trained to it from their youth in the innumerable, and to the foreigner, unintelligible caucus-meetings, committees, conventions, and so forth."[9]

Most of these new partnerships and associations were basic and limited. Miners agreed to share the work and share the rewards equally. If a partner wanted to leave to try a new camp, a quick settling of accounts usually ended the matter. They were, in essence, "gentlemen's agreements," since there was almost nothing in the way of a legal system to adjudicate contracts anyway.[10]

The basic labor agreements miners worked out for themselves also provided an example and a basis for more extended camp agreements. Each mining camp agreed to these according to the men actually in the camp. Miners in the camps agreed to these rules, or were forced to move on. Everyone in the camp was expected to enforce the informal compact, though rules might change when the population of the camp changed. Each camp had its own rules, but in general these camp rules were remarkably similar in their composition. At the heart of each set of rules was an agreement regarding mining itself. Miners were allowed as individuals to work a limited area, usually only about twelve by twelve feet, as their claim. No one else was to trespass on another's claim, and simply leaving a pick or shovel on the ground was notice that the spot was being worked. Miners were required to work their claims steadily, in some districts at least twenty days a month, or their claim was considered abandoned and open to a newcomer.[11] Theodore Hittel noted,

All men who had or expected to have any standing in the
community were required to work with their hands, labor was

dignified and honorable; the man who did not live by actual physical toil was regarded as a sort of social excrescence of parasite.[12]

Other mining camp laws were both limited in extent and in the penalties to be meted out to offenders. Stealing was considered one of the most heinous of crimes, as might be expected in a region with limited resources and few secure buildings, and theft of any kind, whether food, equipment, or gold, was prohibited, and often carried a brutal, physical punishment. Since there were no jails—and no one who wanted to spend their time in the camps acting as a guard—detention was not an option. Historian Gordon Morris Bakken noted that

> The practice of the mining camps was to give the criminal accused a trial by jury, and if the accused were found guilty, to sentence the criminal ("enemy deviant," in modern parlance) to whipping, banishment, or death. The sentence was carried out immediately.[13]

Gold and Wage Values, 1848–1860

Year	Amount of gold mined	Value at time($)	Average wage in mines ($)
1848	11,866	245,301	20.00
1849	491,072	10,151,060	16.00
1850	1,996,586	41,273,106	10.00
1851	3,673,512	75,938,232	8.00
1852	3,932,631	81,294,700	6.00
1853	3,270,803	67,613,487	5.00
1854	3,358,867	69,433,931	n/a
1855	2,684,106	55,485,345	n/a
1856	2,782,018	57,509,411	3.00+
1857	2,110,513	43,628,172	3.00+
1858	2,253,846	46,591,140	3.00+
1859	2,217,829	45,846,599	3.00
1860	2,133,104	45,846,599	3.00–

Compiled from Mary Hill, *Gold: The California Story* (Berkeley: University of California Press, 1999), p. 263; and Paul Rodman, *California Gold, California Gold: The Beginning of Mining in the Far West* (Lincoln: University of Nebraska Press, 1947), pp. 349–350.

The harshness of the sentencing was meant to be a warning to others.

Other than these few rules, mining camps were generally sprawling, unorganized and transient. They usually lasted as long as the gold in the area lasted. Miners might make a trip down to Sacramento or town for supplies, but needed to insure that they returned quickly or their claim was considered abandoned. Miners in partnerships thus took turns going for supplies and mail, while their partners guarded the claims and kept the work progressing.

It did not take long for many of the miners to grow weary of the back-breaking and often unrewarding work. Some soon realized that, in bringing up supplies from Sacramento, they could bring extra goods to sell at a profit. "I found I could make only about my expenses in mining," frustrated miner Alonzo Hill wrote his parents, "and I did not come here to mine for my expenses. SO I just set my face again toward Sacramento City as I knew I could get some wages there."[14] Meanwhile, merchants in Sacramento and elsewhere, seeking to get their goods up to the mining camps, hired teamsters at high wages or offered to let them carry some goods of their own to sell in the camps.[15]

Historians would later refer to this as "mining the miners," conjuring up an image of merchants and others taking advantage of the miners and their fortunes without participating in the hard labor and risk of mining. Yet while accurate, the phrase is also misleading. Many of the merchants and teamsters were themselves miners, either seeking a bit of money to buy their own supplies, to supplement their mining returns, or shifting away from mining to a more certain and lucrative field of work. Furthermore, without these services, the "pure" miners could not possibly have sustained themselves in the foothills for the months it took to search for their dreamed-of fortunes.

Furthermore, mining camps that proved especially large and long-lasting, or were located centrally to many smaller mining camps, soon attracted a more permanent merchant, dealing in equipment, groceries, tents and clothing, medicines, and a wide range of needed commodities. Gambling tents and other services soon located nearby. With little clear planning, some mining camps became developed into towns. By 1851, more than 500 mining camp towns had formed in the gold fields.[16] Each was tied to teamsters and merchants supplying goods to the camps from the new booming cities of the Central Valley, such as Sacramento, Stockton, or Marysville. Each of these cities, in turn, was supported by wholesale merchants and teamsters headquartering in San Francisco. As each new camp and town was formed in the foothills, the power and size of San Francisco and the Valley cities grew as well.[17]

The peculiar nature of daily life in these gold rush camps and towns was often remarked upon by the miners. Gold rush society was heavily composed of men—often reaching as much as 90 to 95% of the population. Often these men, the greatest numbers were in their young twenties. Their behavior has been the subject of both comedy and moral rebuke. They were largely seen as bachelor societies—vast encampments of young, unattached men, often behaving badly. Their character seemed much like that of young men in a fraternity, or young soldiers away from home and on leave in a foreign place. They were rowdy, boisterous, reckless, and free to give in to their least civilized impulses.

The rowdy behavior was stunning. Vincente Perez Rosales captured the sense that California was a new Tower of Babel. "Most people here speak English, good or bad," he noted.

> But you find, at the side of a lean Yankee in tight pants, others recognizable by their clothing or accent. There is a stocky John Bull, a Chinaman, a Hindu, a Russian, and a native *Californio*, all trying to converse. A Chilean and an Oregonian are watching each other suspiciously. A Frenchman and an Italian are winking at a Hawaiian girl crowned with flowers and clad in a blue dress and red shoes. In short, you can find whatever you like in terms of oddities and extravagances in this land of promise. It is like a masquerade ball of gigantic proportions.[18]

Yet this image hides as much of the reality of gold rush society as it reveals. William White was one of the early recorders of the rush that was able to see through the surface image.

> To look at the returned miners in those days in San Francisco the first impression you would get was that they were all of a rough cast of men, uneducated and savage. Their uncut hair, their long beards, their red flannel shirts, with flashy red Chinese scarfs around

THE BEST BAD THINGS

Hinton Helper summed up the temptations precisely: "I have seen purer liquors, better seegars, finer tobacco, truer guns and pistols, larger dirks and bowie knives, and prettier cortezans, here in San Francisco than in any place I have ever visited; and it is my unbiased opinion that California can and does furnish the best bad things that are obtainable in America."

Hinton Helper, *The Land of Gold, Reality versus Fiction*, Baltimore, Published for the Author, By Henry Taylor, Sun Iron Building, 1855, p. 68.

their waists, the black leather belt beneath the scarf, fastened
with a silver buckle, to which hung the handsome six-shooter and
bowie-knife, the slouched, wide-brimmed hat, the manly, bold,
independent look and gait of the man as he walked along, made
each one look the chief of a tribe of men you had no knowledge
of before. Get into conversation with this man, and you will find,
to your surprise, in nine cases out of ten, a refined, intelligent,
educated American, despising the excesses of the idle and the
dissipated. You will find his whole heart on his old home and
those he has left there.[19]

Unlike many frontier movements, this one was made up primarily of middle class men. Many had college degrees. Most miners had traveled to California within companies, among neighbors, and often with family members. They sought letters and many wrote piles of them in return. Miners reported on their behavior and that of their companions regularly. They were rarely as cut off from home and family as we might think. Writer Tom Coles estimated that there were actually more college graduates in San Francisco in the 1850s than in any other town in America, and the California historian Hubert Howe Bancroft believed that by 1853, when the city had twelve newspapers, there were over 1,000 journalists busy throughout the state.[20] Reading—whether books or newspapers—and writing letters home were popular pastimes.

When not hard at work digging under the hot sun, these young men sought relief in diversions. In an age when music was a participatory activity, singing was also popular, and a number of songs specific to the mining camps were soon heard in the camps, day and night. Drinking helped ease aching muscles, and alcohol, though initially in short supply, could be easily brought up to the mining camps.

Gambling was one of the most popular forms of entertainment, probably because it spoke so directly to the miners' experience. Josiah Royce recalled

Gambling in the big saloons, under the strangely brilliant lamplight,
amid the wild music, the odd people, the sounding gold, used to
be such a rapturous and fearful thing! One cannot express this
odd rapture at all! Judges and clergymen used to elbow their way.
. . to the tables and play with the rest. The men in San Francisco
who did not thus gamble were too few to be noticed.[21]

Gambling seemed a perfect metaphor for mining. Picking out a claim, turning over its gravel to see if it held gold or not found a direct parallel

Resting with the Miners

Sometimes four of them might be seen about a stump, intent on reviving their ancient knowledge of "poker," and occasionally a more social group, filling their tin cups from a kettle of tea or something stronger. . . . The fragments of conversation . . . were narratives of old experiences on the Plains; notes about the passage of the mountains compared; reminiscences of the Salt Lake City and its strange enthusiasts. . . . The conversation, however, was sure to wind up with a talk about home—a lamentation for its missed comforts and frequently a regret at having forsaken them. The subject was inexhaustible.

Samuel Upham, quoted in Mark A. Eifler, *Gold Rush Capitalists: Greed and Growth in Sacramento* (Albuquerque: University of New Mexico Press, 2002), p. 107.

in anteing up, dealing out cards face down, and turning them over to see if they were a winning hand or not. Card playing condensed the whole experience into a few moments—and could be endlessly repeated, as if to assure the miners that, though they had no luck today, they might have a fortune tomorrow![22]

As camps became towns, one of the first and most elaborate buildings to be built were gambling saloons. Built specifically to attract the miners, they were large, well-lit, luxurious and festive buildings. By making their profits directly from the miners, they could afford to make their halls grander and more welcoming than any other building in town. In a town composed mostly of tents, with a few perhaps sporting false wooden facades facing the street, the gambling saloon was in effect a cultural temple.[23]

Another building that was built to impress was the bank. With few safeguards or police to enforce security, bank buildings were designed to impress the depositor that they were solid and impervious to robbery. Built of brick and stone, with imported iron or steel safe boxes or vaults, they promised protection even from the fires that periodically swept mining towns. These designs worked. Though Hollywood later suggested that western banks were easily robbed, in fact there were no successful robberies on western banks before the 1920s.[24]

Robbery and violence, however, was not uncommon in the more remote mining fields or along unprotected roadways. Given the harsh punishments for theft in mining camps, bandits tended to attack teamsters or other travelers between camps or in isolated locales. Violence could break out almost anywhere, especially given the crowds of young men

A MINER'S WARNING

"Have your pistol loaded and keep the middle of the street at night," cautioned Alonzo Delano.

Tom Cole, *A Short History of San Francisco* (Berkeley: Heyday Books, 2014), p. 51.

already pushed to the edges of physical work, emotional competitiveness, and anxiety for the future. Most men did not interfere if two men engaged in a fight between themselves. When they erupted in violent drunken sprees, or started organizing in gangs of toughs, towns and cities formed vigilante committees to establish a rough form of law and order. Most mining towns experienced only a single instance of vigilante justice, though San Francisco experienced two major outbreaks.

Town populations were remarkably cosmopolitan, given the international appeal of the gold rush itself. However, a social order rapidly developed. Americans, usually in the majority, tended to cast non-Americans as a distinct under-class. This was especially true if non-American miners collected in groups. For example, Chilean miners, most coming from Valparaiso in the early days of the rush, were assaulted and cast out of the mines—though goods from Chile such as flour and beef were vital necessities. French miners, who tended to travel in associations and work in camps together, also found themselves subject to discrimination. Perhaps the non-Americans most discriminated against in the mines were the Hispanic and Chinese miners who were charged a "Foreign Miners Tax" in order to drive them from the mines.[25]

Yet this kind of domination was not universal. The northern mines were too close to the overland trails and San Francisco, which brought in a steady stream of American miners. Mexican and Asian miners were easily harried out of the northern mines, but tended to find more refuge in the southern mines, east of Stockton and centered on the town of Sonora, which were somewhat off the beaten paths and closer to Mexico. Here the American population was not in the majority, placer mining lasted longer, and a far more mixed society emerged. Susan Lee Johnson's study of this area shows a higher number of Native, French, Mexican, and Chilean men and women in the mines and camps. Though Anglos and their wives did attempt to recreate American mores in the mines within a few years, the arrival of Chinese women as prostitutes undermined many of these efforts. As a result, society in the southern mining region was far more complex and creative in social dealings than the northern mines, and the period of social mixing lasted far longer.[26]

Yet even in the northern mines and the cities of the central valley and the coast, American miners found it nearly impossible to create dominant class or social distinctions even among themselves. Clothing, accent, birthplace, education all seemed irrelevant. As Tom Cole noted, "The man who carried your bags might be a bored Pennsylvania judge; the saloon fiddler, the scion of some worried Eastern family."[27] Bayard Taylor also observed this confusion of social position in a restaurant. "There are cries of 'Steward!' from all parts . . . the word waiter is not considered sufficiently respectable seeing that the waiter may have been a lawyer or merchant's clerk a few months before."[28]

Larger towns might try to sort out the population mix in interesting ways. Sacramento, for example, had various hotels named after eastern states, such as the Kentucky House or the Illinois House, which tried to attract residents to sort themselves by birthplace. Yet, for the most part, the greatest distinctions came down to whether or not you had gold, and whether you were newly arrived or heading home.[29]

INSTANT CITIES

California before the gold rush had nothing like a regional urban structure capable of supporting the rush that arrived in 1849. What towns and marketplaces existed at the beginning of the rush were centered along the coast, from the San Francisco Bay region down to San Diego. The Spanish missions had been set up roughly a day's ride apart along the coast, and by 1848 these early settlements provided the only basis of a regional infrastructure, tied together now by small settlements and ranches, and with a tentative extension into the Central Valley centered on Sutter's Fort. The administrative headquarters of California under both Mexican and then US military authority was Monterey, but its port could not possibly accommodate the rush of ships heading to California, and it was not easily accessible to the mining fields. Los Angeles was even further remote, and was also lightly populated.

San Francisco Bay had potential in being located by the most important natural harbor on the North American west coast. A small town, originally named Yerba Buena, had sprouted at the tip of the peninsula on the western side of the bay, near where Spanish padres had established a mission and Spanish soldiers had constructed a preside to guard the mouth of the bay from intruders. Though the cove was a natural site for a port, the land around the cove was crowded by steep hills, and the peninsula itself was rather remote from the "mainland" of the state, across the bay. In 1848, the population of its small bay-side settlement was only a few hundred, of which the majority were either soldiers waiting to be discharged from the Mexican War, or Mormons preparing to leave for Salt Lake City.[30]

San Francisco had two advantages, however. First, its large bay and cove were capable of handling the press of ships that would soon be coming to northern California. Second, San Francisco Bay connected to the Delta, a tule-covered maze of streams and rivers draining from the central valleys. Though the delta was confusing and difficult to navigate in the early years, it was possible for ships to travel up the delta as far as the mouth of the American River, only a few miles from Sutter's Fort. From there it was a straight line up the American River to the gold fields. At the same time, the overland trail also crossed the Sierras to the east of Sutter's Fort, and for many of the gold seekers, the end of the trail was Sutter's Fort. The Bay, the Delta, and the overland trail almost dictated the rise of an urban network centered on Sutter's Fort and San Francisco Bay. Sacramento City, built on the site of Sutter's Fort, would become the supply center for the foothill mining camps. Marysville was set up to the north to supply the northern mining areas, while Stockton was established to service the southern mines. The mountainous California coastline, however, insured that San Francisco Bay alone would remain the main international port feeding all three areas.

That Yerba Buena Cove would be the obvious bay-side city was not geographically obvious. There were alternative city sites to San Francisco. Across the bay, the small settlements that would eventually become Oakland and Berkeley would have allowed goods unloaded there to be sent overland directly to the mines. However, the eastern side of the bay was disadvantaged by extensive mud flats, making it more difficult to dock and unload shipments, especially for the deep keels of the clipper ships. Perhaps the best site in the bay would have been at or near Benicia, at the mouth of the delta. It had a deep-water frontage, as well as an extensive landed area for the rise of a city, and goods landed there could make an overland trip to the mining districts relatively easily. It lacked a sizable cove, however, and in 1849 was simply less well known to arriving captains.[31]

That San Francisco emerged as the metropolis by the bay was as much a quirk of the recent war as it was the timing of the gold rush. US military authorities set their base in San Francisco during the war in order to defend the bay and its entrance from foreign attackers. This drew the attention of merchants and suppliers, who started their small outposts near the military, who were both their earliest customers as well as their protection. The gold rush happened so quickly on the heels of the California conquest that merchants, though they might have seen the advantages of a more inland site like Benicia, felt safer committing to their original locations. Given the press of migrants and shipping, San Francisco became the port of call more by default than due to careful planning.[32]

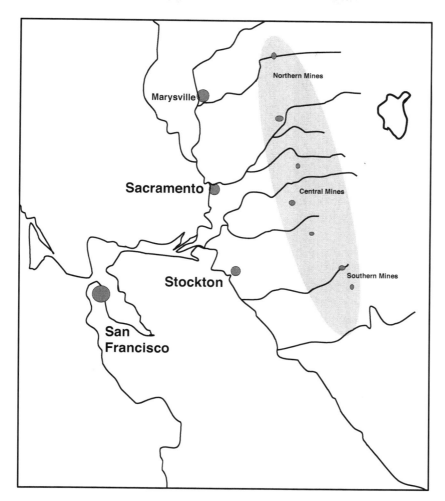

Figure 4.1 Map, Northern California. The urban hierarchy of Northern
California was tightly tied to the flow of commerce. San Francisco
was the great warehouse of the gold rush, while Marysville,
Sacramento, and Stockton were the distribution centers for the
northern, central, and southern mining camps, respectively.

At the same time, the urban structure of the Central Valley and the
mining camps was emerging. During the winter of 1849, the mining camps
were largely abandoned as miners flocked to Sacramento for the long, wet
winter. Increasingly men started looking for work, to support them during
their winter hiatus, and often to raise money to start anew in the gold
fields in the coming months. With the now largely captured labor pool,

Sacramento now began to see the rise of more permanent buildings. However, the oversupply of workers also meant that wages dropped precipitously, while the cost of food and equipment remained high. By the spring of 1850, the miners rushed back up to the mines, joined again by newly arrived immigrants. This year, miners and merchants increasingly spent time building more secure camps and log cabins in the mining camps themselves. Sacramento, Marysville, and Stockton, however, saw a new basis of stability in merchants and teamsters who used these cities as distribution centers for the mining camps. Indeed, many of these merchants were themselves miners who had given up on mining and were looking for other ways to either earn enough money to return home or to raise a new stake for another attempt at mining. Many, however, saw the profits to be made from business in these inland cities. Many switched from mining to supplying the needs of the booming mining camps, towns, and cities. By the summer of 1852, the relationship between the three major inland cities and the gold country mining camps was well established.

Like San Francisco, these inland towns were erected in a rush to serve the miners, and not always with an eye to geography. Sacramento, for example, was planned to take advantage of its known location near Sutter's Fort and its accessibility to the Delta. The Mormon entrepreneur Samuel Brannan deserves perhaps the greatest credit for the location of this city. After inspecting the gold mining at Mormon Island, and before announcing the finds in San Francisco, Brannan realized that potential miners would need supplies, and established a store and warehouse near Sutter's Fort at the mouth of the American River. Within a few months, he had convinced John Sutter's son to donate and organize a city for merchants, including himself, who would build on the site. In commercial terms, it was perfectly chosen. It was as far as an ocean-going ship could sail up the delta toward the mining camps, and it was near the known landmark of Sutter's Fort. It was also, however, a point that underwent periodic flooding, a feature Sutter had noticed when he placed his fort several miles away from the site. But, like San Francisco, Sacramento would grow rapidly to support the press of the mining rush, despite its geographical limitations.[33]

The rise of these cities awed the rushing miners. As they came to need supplies, they made multiple trips to Sacramento to gather goods, returning quickly to the gold camps. Each time they returned the city at the mouth of the river seemed to have doubled in size, though at least for the first couple of years it seemed more an enormous tent camp rather than a city. As the overlanders reached the area in the fall of 1849, they also congregated around the city, giving the tent city an even more disorderly and mobile appearance. Newly arrived miner Charles Glass Gray wrote

Sacramento City should be called, *Ragdom,* as almost all the dwellings are built of slender joists of wood, covered over with canvas or cloth. Many tents were also in use and they gave the place the look and air of *an immense camp.*[34]

The growth of cities like Sacramento were chaotic and often brutal, in part because they were erected so quickly and without basic planning. For example, in the late fall of 1849, thousands of miners in the foothills retreated to Sacramento to wait out the cold, wet winter. Others, newly arrived overland, sought to recover from the hardships of the trail. Overcrowding and poor conditions there sickened and killed many of the wintering miners. Then, in January, 1850, heavy rains raised the level of the American and Sacramento rivers and flooded the new city, in some areas inundating the city under twelve feet of water. Residents lost their tent shelters, and even several more substantial buildings were washed away. The loss of goods was devastating to the new town, and the loss

Sacramento Rises

Alonzo Delano visited Sacramento in the spring of 1850, and noted:

Before returning to the mines, I visited Sacramento, and the improvements not only in the city, but in the country around, which a few months had produced, astonished me. Along the road hotels and dwellings had been erected at convenient distances; and where we had traveled the previous fall without seeing a human habitation, was now the abode of civilized man. . . . Sacramento City had become a city indeed. Substantial wooden buildings had taken the place of the cloth tents and frail tenements of the previous November, and, although it had been recently submerged by an unprecedented flood, which occasioned a great destruction of property, and which ruined hundreds of its citizens, it exhibited a scene of busy life and enterprise, particularly characteristics of the Anglo-Saxon race by whom it was peopled. An immense business was doing with miners in furnishing supplies; the river was lined with ships, the streets were thronged with drays, teams, and busy pedestrians; the stores were large, and well filled with merchandise; and even Aladdin could not have been more surprised at the power of his wonderful lamp, than I was at the mighty change which less than twelve months had wrought, since the first cloth tent had grown into a large and flourishing city.

Alonzo Delano, *Life on the Plains and Among the Diggings: An Overland Journey to California, 1849* (Auburn and Buffalo: Miller, Orton & Mulligan, 1854), p. 287–288.

of life shocked many of the city's residents. Its commercial advantages notwithstanding, the booming city of Sacramento now began a decades-long struggle to keep itself above flood level.[35]

Meanwhile, San Francisco's development also struggled against the limitations of its physical site. The small cove was quickly overrun. Ships from the Pacific and then from the Atlantic sailed into the bay on a daily basis, but when their crew abandoned their stations for the gold fields, the cove was filled with hundreds of abandoned ships. By the summer of 1849, San Francisco's streets were one giant bottleneck in the supply system to the mines and the disadvantages of the site suddenly became critical. Without a spacious hinterland, goods tended to be dumped in the streets, or even left aboard abandoned ships, where they often spoiled. The hills of San Francisco, which provide romantic vistas today, hemmed in the burgeoning city.[36]

Desperate to establish organization from the chaos, San Franciscans creatively dealt with the reality confronting them. With a severe lack of warehouses, or laborers willing to work in the city, merchants simply used the abandoned ships as temporary storage. Several ships were drawn up to the shoreline and repurposed as warehouses, hotels, saloons, and offices. Wharfs were built out into the cove to extend streets out to abandoned ships. The cove was soon completely filled in with wharves and ships, leaving newly arrived ships to dock at the ends of the wharves in the bay. Meanwhile, dirt, garbage, spoiled goods, and other debris was added to the cove or washed down from the surrounding hills, filling in the cove until it essentially disappeared, buried under, as one observer described it, "conglomerate layers of cook stoves, boxes of tobacco, Chilean flour, barrels of spoiled beef, rolls of sheet lead, gold-washing machines, tons of wine sieves, discarded clothing [and] a slight covering of earth."[37] Forty square blocks of flat land of today's financial district in the city—the home of its landmark office buildings such as the Transamerica Tower—are built atop this filled in cove.

Meanwhile, San Francisco residents also spread out from the cove, especially to the north, towards the opening of the bay. Telegraph Hill was named due to its function as a place where newly arrived ships would be spotted first, alerting the city of newly arrived goods. Despite the hills, tents of residents as well as transient gold seekers lined the shores and covered the hills. William Taylor observed the magical effect the rising city produced at night.

The appearance of San Francisco at night, from the water, is
unlike anything I ever beheld. The houses are mostly of canvas,

Megquier's Boarding House

I should like to give you an account of my work if I could do it justice. We have a store the size of the one we had in Winthrop, in the morning the boy gets up and makes a fire by seven o'clock when I get up and make the coffee, then I make the biscuit, then I fry the potatoes then broil three pounds of steak, and as much liver, while the woman is sweeping, and setting the table, at eight the bell rings and they are eating till nine. I do not sit until they are nearly all done. I try to keep the room warm and in shape as we put it on in small quantities after breakfast I bake six loaves of bread (not very big) then four pies, or a pudding then we have lamb, for which we have paid nine dollars a quarter, beef, and pork, baked, turnips, beets, potatoes, radishes, salad, and that everlasting soup, every day, dine at two, for tea we have hash, cold meat bread and butter sauce and some kind of cake and I have cooked every mouthful that has been eaten excepting one day and a half that we were on a steamboat excursion. I make six beds every day and do the washing and ironing you must think that I am very busy and when I dance all night I am obliged to trot all day and if I had not the constitution of six horses I should [have] been dead long ago.

Polly Welts Kaufman, ed., *Apron Full of Gold: The Letters of Mary Jane Megquier from San Francisco, 1849–1856*, 2nd edition (Albuquerque: University of New Mexico Press, 1994), pp. 68–69.

which is made transparent by the lamps within, and transforms them, in the darkness, to dwellings of solid light. Seated on the slopes of its three hills, the tents pitched among the chapparal to the very summits, it gleams like an amphitheatre of fire. . . . The picture has in it something unreal and fantastic; it impresses one like the cities of the magic lantern, which a motion of the hand can build or annihilate.[38]

As the import center for the California mines, San Francisco exploded as a business center. Over 50,000 people came to the city in the first years of the rush. "One knows not whether he is awake or in some wonderful dream. Never before have I had the difficulty in establishing satisfactorily to my own sense, the reality of what I saw and heard."[39] Writer Tom Cole noted that, "In 1851, only two years after the Gold Rush began, San Francisco ranked fourth in the nation in foreign trade (after Boston, New York, and New Orleans)."[40]

Bayard Taylor captured the speculative frenzy that characterized San Francisco for his readers:

The crowd in the streets is now wholly alive. Men dart hither and thither, as if possessed with a never-resting spirit. You speak to an acquaintance-a merchant, perhaps. He utters a few hurried words of greeting, while his eyes send keen glances on all sides of you; suddenly he catches sight of somebody in the crowd; he is off, and in the next five minutes has bought up half a cargo, sold a town lot at treble the sum he gave, and taken a share in some new and imposing speculation. It is impossible to witness this excess and dissipation of business, without feeling something of its influence. The very air is pregnant with the magnetism of bold, spirited, unwearied action, and he who but ventures into the outer circle of the whirlpool, is spinning, ere he has time for thought, in its dizzy vortex.[41]

San Francisco businessmen were desperate to acquire goods to send to the miners. Anything could be sold profitably, as everything was needed. Merchants sometimes rowed out to incoming ships, offering to purchase their cargos before they even knew what was being carried, certain they could make a profit off whatever items they brought. At the same time, merchants first around the Pacific and then from the Atlantic were sending ships full of goods they hoped to sell to, or ordered by, California emigrants for the mines. The city handled goods coming into California, and soon was the center of western transportation—whether by the Pacific Mail Steamship Company, by Wells Fargo and Company, or later by the Central Pacific and Southern Pacific railroads. The city also handled California's exports—returning miners as well as thousands of pounds of gold, sent to families and businesses in the United States, Europe, and Asia. Express companies took on banking functions, and San Francisco quickly became the center of capital investment, first for northern California, but later stretching to Nevada, Southern California, Oregon, and around the Pacific Rim. San Francisco bankers and businessmen poured money into Nevada mining stocks, hydraulic mining, and California agriculture and real estate.[42]

San Francisco also became a manufacturing center, especially in iron making. Initially support- ing the manufacturing of mining

EASY COME, EASY GO

Bayard Taylor wrote, "If a person lost his all, he was perfectly indifferent; two weeks of hard work gave him enough to start on, and two months, with the usual luck, quite reinstated him."

Bayard Taylor, *Eldorado, or Adventures in the Path of Empire*, 18th edition (New York: G.P. Putnam, 1861), pp. 91–92.

equipment, San Francisco's Union Iron Works soon supported not just the manufacturing of mining machinery, but also pipe for mining and irrigation, and gave rise to the city's US Navy shipyards. By 1860, San Francisco was the ninth-largest manufacturing center in the nation, and a powerful center of capital, business, and manufacturing on the Pacific Rim.[43]

RUSHED STATEHOOD

The sudden influx of miners, the new economy based on gold dust, the opening of businesses and the building of towns all demanded the law, order, and organization of a state. California had been a quiet Mexican province only a few months before. It had recently been ruled by martial law under the US occupation forces. With the formal end of the Mexican War, both Mexican law and martial law ended. Under normal circumstances, the US Congress would then have established a territorial government for California, and US law would have provided a legal and political infrastructure for the region. But, like so much with the gold rush, "normal circumstances" were impossible to find.

This time, however, the root cause of the difficulty was not just the gold rush, but the politics of expansion and slavery in the United States. Since 1787, under the provisions of the Northwest Ordinance, western territories were to be drawn up and established by Congress with appointed governments. These territories would effectively be wards of the federal government until their populations reached 60,000, at which point they could write their own state constitutions and petition Congress for admission as an independent state, equal to any other state. The Northwest Ordinance had also prohibited slavery in the five territories that would become Ohio, Michigan, Indiana, Illinois, and Wisconsin. The ordinance thus set up Congressional oversight into the expansion of the United States through newly organized territories.

This process worked well until 1819, when Missouri petitioned to become a state, and included the legalization of slavery within its borders. The US Senate deadlocked, with eleven states in favor of slavery and eleven states opposed. In the Compromise of 1820, Congress admitted Missouri as a slave state and Maine as a free state at the same time, thus maintaining the sectional balance of power in the Senate. It also drew a "compromise line" across the Louisiana Territory along the 36°30′ latitude line, and agreed that territories south of that line would be organized with slavery and north of that line would be organized without it. Territorial expansion would not proceed along this given blueprint.

The Mexican War and the new acquisitions in the Southwest which this brought dramatically complicated this blueprint. Northern leaders, led by David Wilmot, argued that slavery could not be introduced in these new territories as Mexico had already outlawed slavery there nearly twenty-five years earlier. Southern leaders argued that the old Missouri Compromise had kept the peace for nearly thirty years, and should be extended through the Southwest to the Pacific. Unable to reach an agreement as the Mexican war was winding down, Congress was thus unable to establish an official territorial government in California.

Before the gold rush, this would have been a difficult situation for California, but not an impossible one. California residents, most of them native *Californios*, had lived comfortably under Mexican legal institutions and were generally prepared to continue doing so, even if informally, until the Congress finally acted. The gold rush, however, brought in a massive new population, the majority Americans who viewed Mexican laws and legal institutions with suspicion and contempt. They brought with them expectations of legal and political rights that they insisted be maintained, but they also brought with them conflicting ideas of what American rights actually were. Newly arrived Americans looked at the large grants of land made to local *Californios* as illegal and immoral land grabs. They disputed the ability of California *alcaldes* to make law and decide legal questions on what was now American soil. Gold mining introduced a new industry to the region, which needed regulating, and there was very little precedent to guide them. As miners shifted to other businesses, they demanded the legal protections and institutions that were most familiar to them. Under these circumstances, Congressional delay meant chaos for California.

One example of the chaos could be found in Sacramento. When John Sutter Jr set up the city and began selling town lots, some Americans questioned Sutter's initial ownership of the site. His land grant boundary was poorly described and, in any case, many Americans felt that the vast size of the grant was improper. By the fall of 1849, a Settlers Association had come into being, challenging Sutter's title, and thus the very legal basis of land in Sacramento. Merchants, led by Samuel Brannan, backed Sutter's claim, and thus their subsequent ownership of city lots. Both groups believed they had US law and principle on their side, but without an official territorial government to look into the matter, no resolution could be found except a resort to force. For several months in 1850, the Settlers Association set up their own land title office, and recorded land titles that directly conflicted with the titles being recorded by the city's merchants. In August of 1850, a demonstration by the Settlers Association sparked a riot that lasted two days and resulted in the deaths of half a dozen people, including Sacramento's mayor and sheriff.[44]

With the rising potential for chaos in California, and the continuing delay in Congressional action in setting up a territorial government, Colonel Mason, his replacement Bennett Riley, and the newly-elected President Zachary Taylor suggested that Californians meet independently to draft their own constitution and petition Congress for statehood directly, skipping the territorial phase and thus its congressional obstacles.

California leaders met in Monterey in the fall of 1849 to draft a constitution. The new constitution prohibited slavery in California. Though a few Southern miners had brought their slaves to California, the lack of a strong legal system discouraged most Southerners from bringing slaves west, where they could more easily escape. Miners themselves rejected slavery in the mines—in part because it gave some miners an unfair advantage, but also because it would have put their work on the same level as that of slaves. The introduction of slavery into California, therefore, was a non-starter. There was simply no one in the mines willing to enforce such a measure. Mining camps quickly outlawed the use of Indian, Mexican, or Black servants or slaves in the gold fields.[45]

President Taylor and many northern officials backed California's immediate admission as a free state. Southern leaders in Congress were furious. Most believed that the compromise line should have been extended to the Pacific coast, thus bisecting California, creating two territories, one free and one slave, dividing the gold fields in two. Since Californians themselves rejected this, President Taylor and most northern political leaders argued that California would become a free state through the action of "popular sovereignty." Their argument was that Congress could legislate law for the territories, but not for a state, and if a state chose not to allow slavery, Congress had no right to interfere. The argument had originally been made in 1847 by Lewis Cass, and had essentially been used by Texas, which had skipped the territorial stage and entered the Union as a full (and slavery allowing) state. Moreover, in encouraging *Californios* to overthrow the Mexican government at the beginning of the recent war, American policy had in effect promoted popular, locally elected home rule all along.[46]

In the Compromise bills of 1850, Congressional leaders tried to salvage what they could of the Missouri Compromise, admitting California as a free state, and creating two large territories (Utah and New Mexico) in the Southwest, one north and one south, in effect extending the older compromise line west to California's border. This time, instead of determining that these two territories would be free or slave, the idea was introduced that they would be determined by popular sovereignty. Thus California's entry as a single, free state essentially repealed the principle of the Missouri Compromise line, and reinforced the concept of "Popular

Sovereignty," the idea that settlers in a territory would determine for themselves whether the territory would allow slavery or not.[47]

California's instant statehood, like its instant cities, grew directly from the need to quickly regulate the hundreds of thousands of people rushing to California. Like its cities, which soon encountered the drawbacks of their settings—San Francisco's hills, Sacramento's floods—California's statehood imposed difficulties for federal policies on slavery and expansion that would very soon come back to trouble the nation.

FORGING CONNECTIONS

The transformation of the gold fields and California's urban and commercial infrastructure also depended on developing instant communications and transportation systems between California and the rest of the world, but most especially with the United States. By 1849, it was clear that the migration to California was massive and would continue for years to come. The 1849 rush had shown not only the strength of the interest in California, but also the weakness of communications and transportation between California and the rest of the Union. People demanded easier and safer ways to get to and from California, to send and receive mail from family and loved ones, to import manufactured goods, and to send home gold.

Had the gold rush occurred in a region contiguous to the eastern states, the extension and strengthening of roads, trails, freighting, and shipping would have been dramatic but comparatively easy. Establishing such services for California was far more difficult. The region was distant. Any extension of services to California would be a giant leap, not a short one. From a business perspective, the extension of a shipping service to a nearby eastern city might require adding perhaps ten or twenty miles of routing to an established and paying route. The expense of this longer route could be borne by the overall profitability of the company's shipping routes or network. Adding California would require thousands of miles of service. In addition, for the majority of that route, there were no profits; all costs and expenses of operating the extensive route had to be recouped in California. Thus companies seeking to extend transportation or communications services to California needed to think on a huge scale: they would be regularly crossing continents and/or oceans, and their operations would be enormously expensive. California held potential fortunes, but companies attempting to reach it faced equally high costs and potentially enormous failures. Nor would the routes be easy to create and maintain, given the mountains, deserts, and oceans to be crossed. Binding California to the nation would not be for the faint of heart.

Perhaps the first to try to create transportation services for miners were coach lines that promised fast and easy travel to California, beginning in 1849. Companies such as the Pioneer Line promised that passengers and their baggage would travel faster, more comfortably, all for only $200. Tickets were relatively cheap, compared to ocean traveling. None of these companies actually succeeded in getting their passengers to California as promised in 1849. Exhausted draft animals died en route. Trails suitable for wagons barely existed, and either bogged down in rain or disappeared on rocky ground. Axels broke. Passengers were told to walk, then to abandon their baggage. Nor was a stagecoach any protection from trailside disease. Some may have been angry that the lines had made promises they could not deliver upon, but once out in the middle of the far West, there was no choice but to walk on and hope to make it to California.[48]

Miners in California demanded a mail service. The US Post Office set up stations in San Francisco and Sacramento, and eventually in a few other towns. However, it took a while to develop a system for distributing letters. Making matters worse, the Federal government refused to pay postal workers the high wages demanded in California, and thus for several months in the summer of 1849 mail in the region was simply delivered to San Francisco and left to be sorted and distributed by the miners.[49] Miners had to leave the gold fields, wait in a line, often for hours, to see if anything had come in for them or not. Maintaining connections to families, sweethearts, wives, and children back home was critical. Miners who did not receive letters worried that something had happened to their families at home. Cholera was raging in eastern cities in 1849, not just on the trails and in mining camps. Though everyone understood that some letters were lost or not forwarded properly, the lack of a letter provoked worries about the health and safety of distant loved ones.

In the absence of reliable mail service, express companies such as Adams Express and Wells, Fargo & Company found an opportunity. Though carrying the mail was illegal, these companies offered to transport gold and goods—and letters—for a fee. To get around the postal service laws, Wells Fargo had envelopes already stamped with both their own fees and US postage available to miners. Congress worried that rival companies could put the postal service out of business, which was a serious concern in the East, where mail service was also expensive and unreliable. But, in the far West, there was often simply no other option. By taking on gold shipments, Wells Fargo and the other express companies took on the role of bankers, laying the foundations of a financial system for the new state.[50]

Shipping lines were the premier vehicle for transportation and communications in the early years of the rush. The rush coincided with the

Hopkins Gets a Letter

Brother Moses,

The great mail from New York arrived at our Post Office the 26th inst and was ready for delivery in twenty hours after. On the evening of the 29th I went to the Office and found a great crowd there, more than could be possibly be served before sunset, so I came back to the store without getting my letters. Next morning I went down again and found the crowd was larger still. There are two delivery windows, one "from A to K" and the other "from K to Z." The window from A to K where the Hopkins' should look for their letters was besieged with one hundred and eighty persons, packed close together one behind the other in a string reaching down the walk almost the entire block. I entered the line as the 181st, and stood it a while in the sun and heat. Soon I heard a fellow offer to sell out his chance for $3 which was taken. This suggested to me the idea of getting my letters, if there should be any, at a cheaper rate than spending two hours time there in the sun and heat. So I, being at this time about twenty from the tail end of the line, offered my chance for one dollar and readily found a taker. Then I offered $4 to any man who would enter the line & get my letters and deliver them to me at the store before 12 o'clock. I readily found my man, which delivered me from that procedure and enabled me to go home and sell a wagon load of goods to a man who I knew would be there. A good arrangement for me.

Before 12 o'clock up came my man with your letter. I paid him $4.40 and on opening it I found it contained just six lines. Such a letter would be considered dear in the states, but I thought it no way unreasonable under the circumstances.

Mark Hopkins, *Letter to Brother, Moses,* September 30, 1850; Huntington Library manuscript, HM 26046.

creation of the fastest sailing vessels to sail the seas. American ship builders had already been improving the design of sailing ships in the years before the gold rush to better utilize the North Atlantic trade and the growing Pacific market. The culmination of these efforts was the clipper ship, with its long narrow hull and massive clouds of sail. Gathering tremendous power from the wind, these sleek ships seemed to barely touch the water, and seemed more nearly aircraft than sailing ships. The clippers set record times around South America to California, records that would not be broken for over a century. However, even the clippers were dependent on the winds and they traded cargo space for the narrow hulls.[51]

Yet if the gold rush coincided with the zenith of sailing ships, it also arrived as more powerful steam-powered vehicles were beginning to appear, and the gold rush in many ways further powered that movement. Ocean-going steamers were still ungainly, most often side wheelers, which sometimes dragged the ship's speed down in rough weather almost as much as it propelled them forward. In calm waters they could essentially ignore the wind, as they operated under their own power. Though still somewhat rare in oceanic routes in 1849, they would grow increasingly popular and numerous through the course of the gold rush, dominating the routes by 1860. Such ships also connected California with Asia and Europe.[52]

As an international movement, the gold rush also had ramifications far outside the United States. Steamers made the first big impact carrying passengers to and from Panama. To Panamanians, the rush of gold seekers seemed at first to promise a golden future. Before the gold rush, only about a dozen people crossed the Isthmus on a monthly basis. Beginning in 1849, that number went up dramatically, first by hundreds, then by thousands. The US government inadvertently created some of the traffic by giving mail contracts to two steamship companies—the US Mail Steamship Company, and the Pacific Mail Steamship Company—to insure regular service between New York and California and Oregon. The companies were just in the process of setting up the steamship lines when they were overwhelmed by the gold rush. A handful of ships designed to carry a few dozen passengers were suddenly swamped with demands to carry hundreds, then thousands of emigrants.[53]

Transporting rushers across Panama became an industry in its own right. Local boatmen and muleteers came out to transport passengers and their goods across the Isthmus, while local women in the transit zone set up cooking and washing services. To cash in on the rush, people from Central and South America and around the Caribbean came to Panama to provide services. For locals, especially the poorer people of the transit zone, California gold spurred their own local fortune seeking.[54]

★ ★ ★

When gold was discovered in California early in 1848, there had been no infrastructure to support a major new mining industry. The rise of camps, towns, cities, a state, and transportation and communications infrastructure to facilitate an international rush of hundreds of thousands was critical to the success of the dreams of individual wealth of the many miners. California's rushed foundations were a wonder of social, political, and technological engineering. The instantaneous nature of the transformation awed those who saw it. Yet it came with costs that would bring bitter results in coming years. The question remained to be asked: Was it worth it?

NOTES

1   Mitchel Roth, "Cholera, Community, and Public Health in Gold Rush Sacramento and San Francisco," *Pacific Historical Review*, 66, no. 4, (November, 1997). Cited in Edward Dolnick, *The Rush: America's Fevered Quest for Fortune, 1848–1853* (Boston: Little, Brown and Company, 2014), p. 338.

2   See Gunther Barth, *Instant Cities: Urbanization and the Rise of San Francisco and Denver* (Albuquerque: University of New Mexico Press, 1975).

3   Quoted in Dolnick, *The Rush,* p. 223.

4   Quoted in Dolnick, *The Rush,* p. 238.

5   Quoted in Dolnick, *The Rush*, pp. 232–233.

6   Dolnick, *The Rush*, p. 280.

7   Quoted in Dolnick, *The Rush,* p. 274.

8   Malcolm J. Rohrbough, *Days of Gold: The California Gold Rush and the American Nation* (Berkeley: University of California Press, 1997), p. 125.

9   Maureen A. Jung, "Capitalism Comes to the Diggings: From Gold-Rush Adventure to Corporate Enterprise," in James J. Rawls and Richard J. Orsi, eds., *A Golden State: Mining and Economic Development on Gold Rush California* (Berkeley: University of California Press, 1999), p. 58.

10 Rohrbough, *Days of Gold*, pp. 125–127.

11 Rohrbough, *Days of Gold*, pp. 125–127; Jung, "Capitalism Comes to the Diggings," pp. 56–59.

12 Jung, "Capitalism Comes to the Diggings," p. 58.

13 Gordon Morris Bakken, "The Courts, the Legal Profession, and the Development of Law and Race in California, 1848–1878," in John F. Burns and Richard J. Orsi, eds., *Taming the Elephant: Politics, Government, and Law in Pioneer California* (Berkeley: University of California Press, 2003), p. 75.

14 Quoted in Mark A. Eifler, *Gold Rush Capitalists: Greed and Growth in Sacramento* (Albuquerque: University of New Mexico Press, 2002), p. 92.

15 Eifler, *Gold Rush Capitalists*, pp. 168–170.

16 Tom Cole, *A Short History of San Francisco* (Berkeley: Heyday Books, 2014), p. 36.

17 Carl Abbott, *How Cities Won the West*, (Albuquerque: University of New Mexico Press, 2008), p. 61.

18 Malcolm E. Barker, ed., *San Francisco Memoirs, 1835–1851: Eyewitness Accounts of the Birth of a City* (San Francisco: Londonborn Publications, 1994), p. 138.

19 Barker, *Memoirs*, p. 152.

20 Cole, *Short History*, p. 50.

21 Cole *Short History*, p. 49.

22 Eifler, *Gold Rush Capitalists*, pp. 192–194.

23 Gary Kurutz, "Popular Culture on the Golden Shore," in Kevin Starr and Richard Orsi, eds., *Rooted in Barbarous Soil: People, Culture, and Community in Gold Rush California* (Berkeley: University of California Press, 2000), pp. 287–289.

24 Larry Schweikart and Lynne Pierson Doti, "From Hard Money to Branch Banking: California Banking in the Gold Rush Economy," in James J. Rawls, and Richard J. Orsi, eds, *Golden State: Mining and Economic Development in Gold Rush California* (Berkeley: University of California Press, 1999), p. 218.

25 Rohrbough, *Days of Gold*, pp. 223–229.

26 See Susan Lee Johnson, *Roaring Camp: The Social World of the California Gold Rush* (New York: W.W. Norton, 2000); also Susan Lee Johnson, "The Last Fandango," in Owens, *Riches for All*.

27 Cole, *Short History*, p. 43.

28 Bayard Taylor, *Eldorado: Adventures in the Path of Empire* (Berkeley: Heyday Books, 2000), p. 95.

29 Eifler, *Gold Rush Capitalists*, pp. 112–114.

30 Mel Scott, *The San Francisco Bay Area: A Metropolis in Perspective*, 2nd edition (Berkeley: University of California Press, 1985), pp. 23–24.

31 Scott, *The San Francisco Bay Area*, p. 28; Roger W. Lotchin, *San Francisco, 1846–1856* (Urbana: University of Illinois Press, 1997), p. 38.

32 Barth, *Instant Cities*, pp. 110–112, 134; Scott, *The San Francisco Bay Area*, p. 24; Lotchin, *San Francisco*, p. 37.

33 Eifler, *Gold Rush Capitalists*, pp. 53–55; Steven M. Avella, *Sacramento: Indomitable City* (Charleston, South Carolina: Arcadia Publishing: 2003), p. 31; Nathan Hallam, "The Stability and Permanence of the Place," in Christopher J. Castaneda and Lee M. A. Simpson, eds., *River City and Valley Life: An Environmental History of the Sacramento Regions* (Pittsburgh: University of Pittsburgh Press, 2013), p. 62.

34 Quoted in Eifler, *Gold Rush Capitalists*, p. 105.

35 Eifler, *Gold Rush Capitalists*, pp. 95–96.

36 Scott, The San Francisco Bay Area, pp. 24–26.

37 Cole, *Short History*, p. 42.

38 Taylor, *Eldorado*, p. 96.

39 Cole, *Short History*, p. 33.

40 Cole, *Short History*, p. 46.

41 Taylor, *Eldorado*, pp. 93–94.

42 Abbott, *How Cities Won the West*, pp. 61–64.

43 Abbott, *How Cities Won the West*, pp. 61–64; David St. Clair, "The Gold Rush and the Beginnings of California Industry," in James J. Rawls and Richard J. Orsi, eds., *A Golden State: Mining and Economic Development in Gold Rush California* (Berkeley: University of California Press, 1999), pp. 203–204.

44 Eifler, *Gold Rush Capitalists*, pp. 131–161.

45 Rohrbough, *Days of Gold*, pp. 125, 211–215; Neal Harlow, *California Conquered: The Annexation of a Mexican Province, 1846–1850* (Berkeley: University of California Press, 1982), p. 342.

46 David M. Potter, *The Impending Crisis, 1848–1861* (New York: Harper & Row, 1976), pp. 93, 99–100.

47 Potter, Impending Crisis, p. 91; Harlow, California Conquered, p. 317; Robert V. Remini, At the Edge of the Precipice: Henry Clay and the Compromise that Saved the Union (New York: Basic Books, 2010), p. 58.

48 Patricia Nelson Limerick, *The Legacy of Conquest: The Unbroken Past of the American West* (New York: W.W. Norton, 1987), pp. 100–102.

49 Richard T. Stillson, *Spreading The News: A History of Information in the California Gold Rush* (Lincoln: University of Nebraska Press, 2006), p. 142.

50 Philip Fradkin, *Stagecoach: Wells Fargo and the American West* (New York: Simon and Schuster, 2002).

51   Lincoln Paine, The Sea and Civilization: A Maritime History of the World (New York: Knopf, 2013), pp. 520–521.
52   Paine, *Sea and Civilization*, pp. 520–521.
53   Paine, *Sea and Civilization*, pp. 520–521.
54   Aims McGuinness, *Path of Empire: Panama and the California Gold Rush* (Ithaca: Cornell University Press, 2008), pp. 35–38, 50–51.

CHAPTER 5

Reckonings

In 1854, the bottom fell out of the stock market on California mining stocks. Most were held in San Francisco, New York, and London. The gold rush had promised quick wealth not only to miners, but also to investors, especially of industrial mining equipment. There seemed many ways to make money on the rush, not only for miners, and merchants, but even for stock holders in San Francisco and London. The collapse of these mining stocks was a rude awakening. British investors especially withdrew from the market in droves. Though they would eventually come back years later, once the region had matured and mining practices were more standardized, the early rush among investors was over.

Similarly, the rush of miners was ending. Over 100,000 people rushed to California by sea and overland in 1849. By 1854, that number reached over 300,000. Yet as early as 1849, the easy-to-get surface or placer gold was rapidly disappearing. The daily average miner's take does seem to have dwindled sharply in 1854, to roughly what a daily wage would be for work back in the eastern United States—or less. Workmen's wages in California also dropped, as mining became less popular and men started looking for work in cities, swelling the availability of workers and thus depressing wages. By 1852, miners were increasingly using machines, dams, and large scale hydraulic works to get to the gold. By 1854, to be a miner in California was largely to be a wage earner in a corporate mine. The days of easy fortunes were gone.

Had it been worth it? One way to look at this is in economic terms. Had the miners made fortunes? Had any of them? Had most of them? The miners themselves quickly realized that there was no easy answer to this. They might mine a small fortune in gold, but given the costs of getting to and from California, as well as the high prices charged for everything in new state, their fortunes were in fact worth much less than it appeared, and they often disappeared as rapidly as they were found. When looking at the success or failure of the gold rushers, we need to consider the balance sheet of profits versus expenses that gave the true reckoning of the value of a bag of gold dust. We also need to include the human costs of the rush, not only for the miners themselves, but for their families, as well as for others who were directly affected by the rush. Only by looking at all the costs of the rush can we determine the ultimate success or failure of those who participated.

THE MINERS' CALCULATIONS

For the miners who rushed to California to find a fortune, the daily question was: "Have I succeeded?" To a historian years later, the question might be: "How much gold did the ordinary miner find?" Or to put it another way: "Did the majority of miners strike it rich, or did they fail to find and hold on to their dreamed of fortunes?"

It is relatively easy to estimate the answer in a broad and ultimately abstract way. Just under $346 million of gold was mined in California between 1848 and 1854. During the same years, at least 300,000 people came to California. If it were all distributed equally, each miner might have gathered about $1,150 in gold over the course of these seven years, or about $165 a year.[1]

This figure suggests that the gold rush ultimately did not pay off for most emigrants. In the 1840s, a farmer in the United States might bring in around $350 per year. Common laborers were usually paid $1 a day, while skilled workers or craftsmen might make $1.50 to $2.[2] Over time, it would seem to make more sense to simply have stayed home.

Reports from the early years of the rush, 1848–1849, show that many miners did find around $20 a day in a good location, making more in a few weeks than they might have made in a whole year at home. However, not everyone found that much gold, and fewer still managed to gather that much on a continual, daily basis. Ultimately, mining was a gamble. Bernard Reid, who arrived in California in 1849, judged the situation starkly: "Some of the miners are making good wages—others barely make expenses. All seems a lottery."[3]

Another way to calculate gold rush success is to look at the wages men earned in California for work other than mining. Securing laborers was difficult, and thus most were paid high wages if they were willing to turn their backs on mining, even temporarily. As mining returns dwindled, however, more and more prospectors looked for work outside the mines, and wages fell. Gold rush historian Rodman Paul calculated that wages in the gold regions were as high as \$16 a day in 1849, but had fallen to \$5 a day by 1853, and less than \$3 a day by 1860.[4]

Compared to eastern wages, California wages were high throughout the 1850s. Yet, while wages were high, the costs of living in California were even higher. A miner who decided to bring home \$10,000 in gold (a typical goal) might, in the long run, have to save several times that much in order to cover the expenses of getting to and from California, as well as the high cost of basic necessities while in the gold fields. The longer it took to gather gold, the longer the miner needed to pay these high costs, and the longer his family struggled without him at home. Ultimately, it took a *real* fortune to seek a *possible* fortune.

The fortunes of the gold rush, however, were not distributed evenly. Experiences in the mining camps ranged from great success to nightmarish failure. When reckoning an individual's success or failure, it is helpful to consider the extremes on both ends: the heights that could be reached and the depths that could bring disaster. The stories of two California emigrants—Mark Hopkins and Samuel Nichols—set out the extremes of gold rush possibilities. Both set out for California in 1849 to make a quick fortune and then return home. One would be remembered as a shining historic success; the horrific failure of the other would destroy him and his family.

MARK HOPKINS AND SAMUEL NICHOLS

Mark Hopkins represents gold rush success, even years before he became famous for helping create the Central Pacific Railroad. Hopkins set out for California from New York City on January 22, 1849 as a founding member of the "New England Mining and Trading Company," with his brother Augustus and his cousin William. He promised to write regularly to his brother Moses, who stayed behind in New York to manage the family business. Hopkins also promised to keep him informed of his progress, including advising whether and when Moses should join his brothers in California. This arrangement would be one of the keys to Mark's eventual success. The Hopkins brothers as a family made sure to secure their business interests in New York while exploring the opportunities in California.

After arriving in the mines, Hopkins quickly got his fill of mining. He wrote home to his brother Moses:

> Since I have been in California I have worked in the mines six days—six of the hardest days work I ever performed any where.

> I was reasonably rewarded. But I shall probably dig my gold some other way. It is outright folly for merchants, clerks, mere in-door men, to think of working with their hands in the mines. The daily tasks of the Irish laborer on your canals and railroads is very easy work compared with it.[5]

Leaving mining behind, Mark looked for a new opportunity.

> I have been an ox teamster or perhaps it would sound softer & pleasanter to say a traveling merchant. I have until recently been driving from six to twelve oxen in my team, buying my load here [Sacramento] & selling in the mines 50 to 100 miles distant, and such roads and hills and rocks and gullies to run a wagon over would astonish you. Although I never drove an ox until I came here, I believe I can perform the most difficult feats in that sort of navigation.[6]

Hopkins next opened a grocery in Sacramento with E. H. Miller, whom he first met on the voyage out from New York, and the two were quickly making a fortune. "Hopkins and Miller, without anybody but themselves to do the work, have sold since the first of July over $13,000 worth of goods all for cash. A few goods at California prices amount to a heap of money."[7] Only a few months later, Hopkins updated his report to his brother.

> You will believe when I tell that myself and Mr. Miller, with no help, not even an hour's labor in doors or out, in buying or selling goods, have turned out over twenty-two thousand dollars worth of goods this month. Our sales have steadily increased every month since we commenced, exceeding up to this time $70,000 since the first of July. How many more than seven hours we get to sleep, out of twenty four you may guess, but I will tell you we sleep well, and feel quite well.[8]

After only a couple of years in California, Mark Hopkins returned home briefly in 1854 to marry his first cousin, Mary Frances Sherwood, then returned to California, where he resided for the rest of his life. His business successes in the gold rush as a merchant made him a leading merchant in Sacramento, and ten years after he first arrived in California he would join with several other Sacramento businessmen to invest in the building of the Central Pacific Railroad, the western half of the first railroad to cross the continent.

By nearly any measure, Mark Hopkins's gold rush experience was a dazzling success. However, like many if not most of the gold rush success stories, it involved not just going to California, but shifting to business pursuits other than mining. It was not that mining was always a failure— Hopkins himself acknowledged that some men did work hard, save their gold, and return home with modest fortunes—but the odds for success were always much better supplying the miners than digging in the hard ground.

If Mark Hopkins represents the dazzling power of gold rush success, Samuel Nichols represents the true horror of gold rush failure, and its terrible consequences, often extending far beyond California. Samuel Nichols set out for California in the spring of 1849, like many other adventurers, with a mixed sense of hope and real economic need. Samuel ran a feed and seed store near Buffalo, New York. He was also a plaintiff in several cases of real estate title theft. He and his wife Sarah had three sons—George, Austin, and Charles. The details of his finances are not precisely known, but surviving letters suggest they were not good, and perhaps had not been for some time.

Samuel Nichols decided to take his son George and head to California and rescue his fortunes in the gold fields. Before leaving, he decided to purchase enough seed to allow the store to continue—under his wife Sarah's management—while he was gone. He also decided to visit several lawyers on a detour at the beginning of his trip, to make sure that they were continuing to press forward his claims.

In a hurry to buy and sell seed before leaving, he admitted to his wife that his profits on the transaction were "as high a price as could be expected considering it was necessary to make a hasty sale."[9] The legal cases also seemed mired in limbo, and though he had the assurances of his lawyers that the cases would proceed, nothing was actually moving toward a resolution.

Furthermore, these side trips had delayed his departure. By the time Samuel and George reached the Missouri River, the bulk of the migration had already set out across the plains. Cholera had already broken out along the route. While traveling up river by steamer, George became sick. Despite Samuel's desperate efforts to find a doctor, George died within a day.

Samuel turned back to New York and brought his son's body home. George's death devastated the family. Sarah's father blamed her for the death, claiming she should have prevented Samuel and George from setting out at all. The broken family dealt with the loss and recriminations for most of 1849. By the end of the year, Samuel was on his way to California again. The financial problems that drove him to go in the first place were not resolved, and the tensions at home likely made staying home unbearable.

Samuel went to California this time by way of Panama, and arrived in San Francisco in the spring of 1850. He sent letter after letter to Sarah, and noted in his letters that he was not getting any letters from her. One can only wonder what must have been going through his mind: Had they been ravaged by cholera, too? Or had Sarah simply dismissed Samuel from her life? Finally, in late August, Samuel received a letter from his wife.

Overjoyed to be back in touch with his wife, Samuel immediately wrote back that he was finding some success, had already mined "eight to ten hundred dollars," and hoped to come home soon. He sent Sarah a few nuggets of gold, and asked her to have them made into jewelry for herself. Sarah, however, in a measure of her family's poverty, needed to use the nuggets to pay the taxes on the home and business. Shortly after

POST OFFICE, SAN FRANCISCO, CALIFORNIA.
A FAITHFUL REPRESENTATION OF THE CROWDS DAILY APPLYING AT THAT OFFICE FOR LETTERS AND NEWSPAPERS.

Figure 5.1 Post Office. Californian's demanded letters from home, and post offices to allow them to keep in touch with family. The Federal government's attempts to meet these demands fed the growing need for efficient communications and transportation systems, such as stagecoach companies, the pony express, telegraph lines, and the transcontinental railroad.

this, Sarah got a letter from Luther Cleaves, who claimed to be Samuel's partner, informing her of Samuel's death from cholera.

Sarah was still grieving the loss of her son George when the news of her husband's death arrived. Now she was left with two children, a failing business, and a father who still seemed to blame her for the disaster. When she and her father tried to get Cleaves to send the eight to ten hundred dollars that Samuel had mentioned, Cleaves wrote back that Samuel had no such fortune. Sarah now had to determine from a distance what had really happened in California. Had Cleaves robbed Samuel? Had Samuel boasted of a fortune that he really did not have, to impress his wife after the long silence? Had Samuel been honest about how much he had found, but neglected to point out that his expenses had been equally high?

Sarah and her father hired a lawyer to interrogate Cleaves when he returned with a small fortune to Boston shortly after this, but could not shake him from his story that Samuel had died penniless. Sarah then tried to find the physician who had examined her husband and to find out where he was buried, only to be told that neither the physician nor Samuel's burial site could be found. Foul play could not be ruled out. Perhaps, neither could the suspicion that Samuel had simply changed his name and walked away from his family—it was known to happen in California.

In the end, the character at the center of this story is not Samuel, but Sarah. Though she never left for California, her world was tremendously changed by it. She lost her husband and son, had the bonds of affection between herself and her father strained, and was left in a very precarious financial position. Perhaps worst of all, she was left without even a clear sense of what had actually happened. While she had the letters from Samuel and Cleaves, she clearly also had suspicions and doubts, which must have nagged at her poisonously for years.

Sarah's experience was not atypical. For many families, when

WHAT REALLY HAPPENED?

When Luther Cleaves returned to Boston, Sarah's family sent a lawyer to interrogate Sam's partner, trying to see if there had been any foul play. "He appears to be a respectable young man (say 35 years old) and gave me reason to think he had nothing to conceal. . . . I tried hard to make a good impression on Mr. Cleaves by representing the desolate condition of Mrs. Nichols etc. etc. . . . I am sorry, my dear sir, that I cannot do more to dry the widow's tears. This is another melancholy instance of the folly of leaving a good home to encounter every hardship & even death itself in a land of savages, white and colored."

L. Kingsley, Esq., *Letter*, April 5, 1851; Huntington Library manuscript, HM 48296.

news stopped coming from California, there remained nothing but silence. While many young men wrote home, many did not, or did not write regularly. As the silence stretched into years, families were left to wonder if their husbands, fathers, and sons had died along the way, come to a foul end, or simply abandoned them. In 1899, when a celebration was held in California for the fiftieth anniversary of the gold rush, the coordinating committee received hundreds of letters from families still trying to find news of their absent loved ones, even fifty years on.[10]

Hopkins and Nichols suggest the extremes of gold rush experience, but for most miners the gold rush was neither a complete success nor a complete failure. Still, reckoning the line between success and failure involved weighing many factors, both financial and personal. There were no simple answers, and those who participated were often left unsure of their success, and could be haunted by the question for years. The experiences of William Carpenter and Mary Jane Megquier represent the more ambiguous and uncertain nature of the gold rush that most of the miners experienced.

WILLIAM CARPENTER'S DILEMMA

In the spring of 1850, William Carpenter left his rural home in up-state New York, in the company of several friends, heading for the crowded wharves of New York City to book passage to California. Carpenter was twenty-six years old, and engaged to Lucretta Spencer. Unable to support himself and his fiancée, William planned to gather enough gold to return and buy a farm.

Carpenter's story seems to follow the pattern of thousands of other gold rush emigrants. He set out eagerly, writing home about the poor food served on the ship, the sights of Havana, and his journey through Panama, including a gun battle between "the Yanks" (including himself) and local thieves.

In his letters to Lucretta, Carpenter reveals himself as someone who is determined to stay morally pure and above the sordid world of the gold rush, but also someone very attracted to the region and its opportunities. He looks with disdain on California, but also sees its beauties. He describes California's climate as "first rate. Cloudless days and nights. Air pure, but what a place for a woman to be in! I pity those women here." The problem as he sees it are those who have rushed to California merely to make a quick fortune. Carpenter criticizes the men who have created "a barbarous land for vice of every kind, dissipation, sloth and crime, men of every nation, rank and station, name, shape, color and hue abound."[11]

After several months in the gold fields, William confessed to Lucretta that he was only an average miner, not making as much as he had hoped, and his dream of a quick fortune was fading.

> I know that if I had been in possession of a competence I should never have come to this place, and now with my knowledge I can advise no one person to come to this barren country, though there is gold enough; yet but few get it; and as for the farming country in California, well, I had rather have one good county in York State than all the farming country in this barren land.

Like many other gold seekers, William discovered the hard way that mining was a lottery. By the spring of 1851, he was looking for other ways, including teamstering, to get himself on firmer ground.

Before the year was over, William had formed a partnership with two other men and opened a store in Sacramento. To his delight, it was a success. California, he wrote home,

> is a country to make money in. It is a fast country, a very fast one. A year here is worth four at home. . . . I can tell you our amount of business by saying that I have paid out for the last three months from eight to fifteen hundred dollars every week for goods in gold dust.

Soon William was also partners in an iron foundry and speculating in land titles. His future was suddenly bright.

With business success, William's descriptions of California began to change.

> It seems to me now, from being accustomed to this beautiful clime and genial skies, as though it were impossible to feel as well in that cold bleak country [ie, New York] as we do in this sunny clime. Oh! It is a beautiful climate to live in; scenery which none

THE NEW M.D.

"I have got an M. D. attached to my name," William Carpenter wrote playfully to Lucretta, "but it stands for quite a different thing in California than it does at home. I have turned Mule Driver and am in the city every week buying goods to take in to the mines."

William Carpenter, *A California Pioneer of the Fifties,* no date. Edited by Frederic Ives Carpenter; Huntington Library typewritten manuscript, HM16777.

> can surpass. Would you see nature in all its grandeur, it is here.
> . . . California is bound to be a great state.

Not only did his opinion of California change, but he also begins raising a topic that must have shocked Lucretta.

> If you were only here I could live contented for three or four years
> at least. If you should come to me we can be married
> immediately on your arrival. . . . (Then) I should not be obliged to
> keep Bachelors Hall as I do now. Answer me as your own good
> sense and feelings dictate.

William had set off for the gold fields as a temporary sojourner with a promise that he would return home soon. Now, two years in, he had begun to see himself as a permanent resident of California, and as a businessman instead of a farmer. This was not what his family and Lucrettta had agreed to. Worse still, by writing earlier of California in such disparaging terms in order to enhance his virtuous constancy, he had made it impossible for Lucretta or her family to imagine California could ever be their new home.

In his letters, William seems engaged in a debate not only with his family and his fiancée, but also with himself. He alternates between praising the climate and opportunities available in California and condemning its get-rich-quick ethic—and inadvertently tangles himself up rather than selling a coherent vision of a California future to his family. Unable to win his case through his letters, William returned home in the late fall of 1852, and promptly married Lucretta. Yet he had not yet given up on California. Rather than sell his business in Sacramento, he had arranged for his brother to manage it in his temporary absence. He clearly returned home not only to marry Lucretta, but also to convince her to return to California with him.

During his short visit, Lucretta became pregnant, and argued that she could not make the journey to California safely. William returned to California in the summer of 1853 anyway, possibly arguing that, with the coming child, they needed the profits from his store in Sacramento more than ever. Before leaving, he promised his father-in-law that he would return within two years, but his letters from this second trip make it clear that he still hoped to convince Lucretta to come to California instead. He wrote to her in May

> If you should ever come to California be sure to procure if
> possible an upper Saloon State-room. . . . (I will) send for you or

come to you as soon as possible, although . . . it would be a hard journey for you, very hard. Yet there are women not half as capable as you are that have come alone.

Lucretta did not rise to the bait. A full year passed with William in California, while Lucretta in New York gave birth to their son, and struggled to raise him on her own. William continued trying to convince her to join him in 1854, incredibly claiming that if she came out in the fall "the danger of health to you and the little one . . . will be nothing."

Lucretta refused, and by the following year, William finally resigned himself to returning home. But before at last leaving California in 1856, William wrote several defensive letters to Lucretta.

Do not blame me for thinking it best for you to come here, for consider how hard it is to start in business at home; prostrated as it is with you, can you wonder I deem it best to stay where a man can know how much he makes and get his pay in gold that does not fail as banks do with you.

And again, in a bit of poetic fancy, William would write words that would come back years later to haunt him.

We may well look at one of the greatest enterprises of the day with marked interest, the Pacific Rail Road, for it is one of vast magnitude to all the earth, and to America's sons in particular, and perchance to you and me . . . for it may be our wish to travel over it in the course of time . . . I more particularly look at it with great interest, for have I not seen California in its infant days, and now fast verging into strong and vigorous manhood? What she will be with this road is not distinctly seen, but that it must be of great utility to her is plain. That I should think of this state as much more than of any other is a natural result of being with her in her infant days and having seen her progress to its present state.

THE MISTAKE

William's son Frederic later edited his father's letters and sent a copy to the Huntington Library. He recorded that his father thought it had been a mistake to leave California. Frederic does not comment on this, but given that his father's return was at least in part to care for his children, William's confession must have been troubling to his son.

As Lucretta was raising their son in New York, William compared his own efforts to hers as raising a great new state in the far West.

Decades later, William returned to California, traveling there quickly and comfortably by railroad. He traveled this time with his son and daughter-in-law, and pointed out to them the places he had worked, the sights he had seen, and the many ways California had changed since he had been there. In a troubling insight, he told his son during the trip that he should never have left California. Though he had returned with a modest fortune and managed to keep his family together, William Carpenter judged that leaving California had been a mistake.

CROSSROADS: MARY JANE MEGQUIER

The decision to return or stay in California forced men and women to decide where their goals were ultimately taking them. The story of Thomas and Mary Jane Megquier shows that California sometimes offered personal freedoms as well as financial rewards, but that these freedoms came with a cost.

Thomas Megquier held a medical degree from Bowdoin College, and practiced medicine in Winthrop, Maine. Unable to raise enough money to build his family a home, Thomas and several companions planned to relocate to Hawaii in 1848, where a family friend worked in the US Consulate office. News of the gold rush caused them to consider California instead. In January, 1849, Thomas and his associates set out for San Francisco to open a drug store and practice medicine, "for the purpose of getting the gold after it is coined, not to dig,"[12] as his wife explained. Thomas was in his late forties, older than most of the gold rush emigrants. Compared to them, Thomas was a rock of stability and experience.

At the last moment, the party decided that Thomas's wife, Mary Jane, should accompany them. Mary Jane was nearly a dozen years younger than her husband, and fully supported her husband's temporary relocation to the West, in order to secure a better living for the family. However, she was surprised when he decided to bring her along. As she explained to a friend, they were "very anxious for me to go with him, as it is very difficult to get any thing done in the way of women help."[13] Mary Jane never saw her role in California as only being one of profit. As she explained to a friend in a masonic lodge, "When I found out how much the ladies were appreciated in the far west, be assured I was ready to start, (not only for their help, but for their good influence upon society. What do you think of that?)."[14]

While Mary Jane was willing to go, she was also unhappy about leaving her three children behind in Maine. The children—Angeline, 17 years old; John, 15 years old; and Arthur, 9 years old—were farmed out to live with relatives and friends. Mary Jane would write regularly to her daughter "Angie" in the coming years, in a manner that historian Polly Welts Kaufman described as "frank and straightforward. . . . As one would correspond with a sister and confidante more than as if she were writing to a daughter."[15]

The Megquiers shipped out of New York in February, crossing Panama in March, and (after a long delay waiting for a steamer) reached San Francisco in June 1849. The couple were amazed at the high costs of goods and services in the city, but still liked their chances at getting ahead.

> At the rate we have to pay for board it amounts to about four thousand dollars a year . . . money is plenty as dirt if you have any means of getting hold of it, but we have not been here long enough to tell whether we can make any thing or not, but if your Father can get practice there will be no doubt but we can get money enough in a year or two to come home.[16]

By the end of the first year, the couple was pleased with their progress. "We have made more money since we have been here than we should make in Winthrop in twenty years," noting that their income came from Thomas's practice and her income running a boarding house.[17]

Mary Jane was proud of her accomplishments, calling her home above their pharmacy

> the most comfortable place in California (so all say that come to see me) though there are many that have better furniture, but we keep it warm and decently clean, a very rare thing where the gentlemen do their own work.[18]

She added, "I have starched twenty shirts this evening. I tell you this to give you an idea of the amount of work I do."[19] At the same time, Mary Jane reported on the developing social scene in San Francisco:

> A few weeks ago I could have left without regret, but we are beginning to live like civilized beings, we have two theaters one of which we attended last week. . . . There was a dozen ladies which is very rare to see so many at any public place of amusement.[20]

Mary Jane also found the openness of California society liberating. "There is no such thing as slander known in the country, no back biting, every ones neighbor is as good as himself, that you know is to my mind."[21] In San Francisco, she was quickly meeting a much wider range of people than she ever would have met in Maine. "We have a young lad living with us from Hungary, he was one of the students that took an active part in the rebellion and was obliged to flee for his life."[22] Unquestionably, Mary Jane's world was opening up in new ways, and she found the new experiences enlightened compared to her old life in New England. She confided to her daughter,

> Mother has not written but once. . . . I suppose she thinks I am very wicked but no one respects the pure religion more than myself which is to do as you would be done by. But that which says, I am more holy than thou, has no resting place in my bosom.[23]

The couple returned home in the spring of 1852 for a visit, and Thomas bought eighteen acres of land in Maine and began construction of a new house for his family to move into when their California sojourn was over. They remained in Maine that spring to attend the marriage of their daughter. However, their San Francisco real estate investments were disputed by one of Thomas's associates, and the couple needed to return to San Francisco to sort out the problem. Arriving in San Francisco in May, 1852, Thomas' problems grew even more complicated and prolonged due to his partner's sudden death. Mary Jane opened another boarding house, and tried to keep the family economically afloat. However, by 1854, something had changed in the relationship between Thomas and Mary Jane.

Money was certainly one of the couple's problems. The mortgage in Maine, the legal complications in San Francisco, and the rise of competing medical practices in California strained their resources. Mary Jane worked long hours to make the boarding house

---

MARY JANE'S SOCIAL LIFE

Mary Jane reported to her daughter, "We had a nice little dance the other [night] at the store of one of our boarders. I was engaged four dances ahead, isn't that smart? I suppose you will have a good laugh to see your Mother tripping the light fantastic toe."

Polly Welts Kaufman, ed., *Apron Full of Gold: The Letters of Mary Jane Megquier from San Francisco, 1849–1856,* 2nd edition (Albuquerque: University of New Mexico Press, 1994), p. 54.

profitable during this stretch. But she was growing restless with the work schedule, and frustrated with Thomas's ongoing legal woes. News that her daughter had given birth to a baby girl made her miss her children and grandchild even more. Yet the freedoms and excitement of California continued to beckon Mary Jane.

> I have seen so much of things a little more exciting I fear I shall never feel perfectly satisfied with [the] quiet ways again. Here you can step out of your house and see the whole world spread out before you in every shape and form. Your ears are filled with the most delightful music, your eyes are dazzled with every thing that is beautiful, the streets are crowded the whole city are in the streets.[24]

Mary Jane left Thomas in San Francisco in the spring of 1854, his legal affairs still unsettled, and returned to Maine alone to be with her family and supervise the building of the new house. Thomas joined her a few months later. With the San Francisco estate still not settled, Mary Jane returned to California for the third time in 1855, again leaving Thomas behind. Her letters indicate that by this time she was unhappy in her marriage and that she and Thomas had become estranged. Mary Jane's letters also suggest that she found a freedom in California that was unavailable to her in New England. She immersed herself in the parties and entertainments of the city, running a boarding house, and tried to get her children to move to California—despite the investment in land and the new house she and her husband had made in Maine.

Shortly after she arrived in San Francisco, Mary Jane learned that her husband had died in Maine. She was making good money running her boarding house, the legal problems were wrapping up, and she was surrounded by friends and the open world of San Francisco.

Mary Jane thus found herself at a crossroads. She had made a good life in California, and she loved the freedom of city life and the latitude women had in the largely male city. Her journey in the gold rush went from wife and mother, to California businesswoman, to becoming the economic mainstay for her family. Along the way, she enjoyed the independence and society that California offered, but she also missed her children and grandchildren. She wanted to do right by her sons. In the end, she could not have both.

> I am anxious to be square with the world, and place the boys above want. But for myself I do want to be with you, but if I am obliged to work hard for a living, I would rather do it here than at

> home. I look to my home in Winthrop as my final home but not
> until I can procure for my children the reasonable comforts of life
> without intruding upon any ones generosity but my own.[25]

By the spring of 1856, Mary Jane realized she had to make a final decision. "I have been turning my whole attention to thoughts of making a comfortable home here," she confessed to her daughter, "but as it is impossible to have all here, I turn to make my arrangements to go home." She was under no illusions that she would be able to live a California lifestyle in Maine. "I dread that thought of returning. California life suits me, there is not a day I do not receive kind words and wishes of friends which are so very unlike what I will meet at home, excepting my children."[26]

Mary Jane returned to Maine in 1856, and lived over four decades in the large new house paid for by her income from California, surrounded by her family. She died in 1899, fifty years after she had first set sail for California. Little is known about her later years. For Mary Jane Megquier and her family, as for many other gold rush sojourners, the great California rush could not be easily defined merely by the accumulation of gold.

LOSS AND FORFEITURE

If the measure of gold rush success was complicated for white American miners, the meaning of success was further complicated for non-white miners during the 1850s. Perhaps as many as 25% of the miners were not from the United States, but from other nations.[27] If anything, the difficulties of making the gold rush a success for these men was more difficult. Being more distant from the home, it was harder if not impossible to get mail from loved ones. While the absolute numbers of missing men may have been highest among the Americans, the percentage of lost men by national groups was likely much higher among European, Asian, and Central and South American miners, who potentially faced more ethnic violence. Beyond the possibility of death, other obstacles often prevented a return home. Most Chinese miners, for example, needed to stay to work off their original transportation contracts, and many European miners were fleeing political persecution.[28] For these men, the hurdles blocking a return home could be insurmountable. Throughout the world, the experience of the gold rush was often marked by the permanent loss or disappearance of a loved one, and the resulting emotional and financial crises that followed. For many, what had started as a golden dream had become a brutal nightmare.

The overwhelming American attitude towards people they deemed as "foreign" made the gold rush more brutal. The roots of this attitude were diverse and deep. American society already condoned racial slavery, and had experienced decades of bloody battles with Native Americans over land claims. The recent war with Mexico had played up the racist attitudes by portraying Americans as generally superior to Mexicans, a superiority they also saw as approved by God's "Manifest Destiny" for the American people.[29] Furthermore, the competitive nature of the gold rush made it easy to ascribe devious motives to other groups in the gold fields, and rationalized attempts to control or expel them. California's distance from the East, its inefficient political regulation, the sudden appearance of so many people from other cultures, even from within the United States, all lent an aura of crisis to Americans in the mining camps. The step toward legalized racist violence was a short one.

Ironically, legal mechanisms had been drafted to prevent this just months before the gold rush began. The Treaty of Guadalupe Hidalgo, which ended the Mexican War, was signed on February 2, 1848, only nine days after Marshall had found the first flakes of gold on the American River. The negotiators, of course, had no idea that gold had been discovered, and were mainly concerned with creating the conditions that would end the war peacefully. Since the United States would acquire a vast amount of Mexican land in the treaty, the question of legal rights for Mexican citizens in the newly conquered lands needed to be addressed. Articles VIII and IX of the treaty had promised that Mexican citizens in California and the Southwest would have full US citizenship rights. This included the right to vote, the secure right of previously owned property, and legal rights. This provision would seem to be straightforward. There were very few US citizens already in the area. To not extend full citizenship to the people who already had such rights under Mexico would certainly have created rebellion and resistance.

Yet in the chaos of the gold rush, these calculations of citizenship and legal rights shifted dramatically. Two new laws suggest the new orientation of California's leaders: the Foreign Miners Tax, and the Land Act.

In 1850, the California state legislature passed a Foreign Miners Tax Law, charging non-American citizens a $20 per month mining license. The Foreign Miners Tax was selectively enforced. Though it could have been used against European miners (and sometimes was), it was primarily enforced against Hispanic and Asian miners. Hispanic miners represented a large group in the early mining camps, as Mexico was close and Mexican miners understood mining practices better than most American miners. Having just fought a war against Mexico, American war jingoism had already raised anti-Mexican racism to a high level. Yet the Foreign Miners

Treaty of Guadalupe Hidalgo, 1848

ARTICLE VIII

Mexicans now established in territories previously belonging to Mexico, and which remain for the future within the limits of the United States, as defined by the present treaty, shall be free to continue where they now reside, or to remove at any time to the Mexican Republic, retaining the property which they possess in the said territories, or disposing thereof, and removing the proceeds wherever they please, without their being subjected, on this account, to any contribution, tax, or charge whatever.

Those who shall prefer to remain in the said territories may either retain the title and rights of Mexican citizens, or acquire those of citizens of the United States. But they shall be under the obligation to make their election within one year from the date of the exchange of ratifications of this treaty; and those who shall remain in the said territories after the expiration of that year, without having declared their intention to retain the character of Mexicans, shall be considered to have elected to become citizens of the United States.

In the said territories, property of every kind, now belonging to Mexicans not established there, shall be inviolably respected. The present owners, the heirs of these, and all Mexicans who may hereafter acquire said property by contract, shall enjoy with respect to it guarantees equally ample as if the same belonged to citizens of the United States.

ARTICLE IX

The Mexicans who, in the territories aforesaid, shall not preserve the character of citizens of the Mexican Republic, conformably with what is stipulated in the preceding article, shall be incorporated into the Union of the United States. and be admitted at the proper time (to be judged of by the Congress of the United States) to the enjoyment of all the rights of citizens of the United States, according to the principles of the Constitution; and in the mean time, shall be maintained and protected in the free enjoyment of their liberty and property, and secured in the free exercise of their religion without restriction.

Tax was also used against *Californios*, who were anything but foreign in California, and who, under the Treaty of Guadalupe Hidalgo, had full US citizenship rights. Few tax collectors in California, however, made much of that distinction.[30]

Many Hispanic and Asian miners paid the Foreign Miners Tax and took their receipts to mean that they essentially had a permit, and thus a right, to mine alongside the white miners. Many white miners disagreed.

Some white miners posed as tax collectors, getting a tax payment and pocketing it, without ever turning in the money to the state. A revolt in the southern mines led by Mexicans, Chileans, and Peruvians, as well as French and German miners, led to the repeal of the law in 1851. The tax was re-enacted in 1852, however, and the rate was later set at $4 per month.

The tax succeeded in its true intended effect: it drove most of the Hispanic and many of the Asian miners out of the mining camps. Most of the Hispanic miners left the northern and central mining regions, and many Mexican miners returned home.[31] While Hispanic miners might turn to ranching in California or return to Mexico, Chinese miners did not have an easy return or out from mining. As such, they stayed in California, in the mines, and through hard work and sheer necessity, managed to gather gold, even from areas that American miners had already worked over and abandoned as unproductive. Chinese miners tended to work together, both for protection against whites but also to fulfill the contracts that helped pay their passage to America. Their success only further aggravated race relations, as white miners now believed that the Chinese miners would eventually replace them in the mines because they were willing to live such meager lives there. The institutionalized racism of the mining tax took its toll, however, and many Chinese miners turned to other jobs—as cooks, launderers, or merchants—taking jobs that either whites did not want, or that directly served the Chinese community.[32]

The Land Act of 1851 further attacked the rights of *Californios* under the Treaty of Guadalupe Hidalgo. According to the treaty, California's original Mexican property owners would be secure in their land ownership. However, white Americans entering California in the gold rush were astounded by California ranches. Spain and Mexico had granted large land grants of nearly 50,000 acres each to California settlers, in part to entice settlers to the underpopulated region, in part because ranching required vastly more acres than farming. Few Americans believed they should respect these huge grants made to people who, only months before, were considered the nation's enemies. Worse still, many of the land grants seemed to have been filed sloppily, with carelessly drawn maps and descriptions of boundaries.

Few of these grants covered any of the major gold mining areas, but as miners started setting up commercial cities such as Sacramento or establishing ranches and farms of their own, these earlier land grants seemed both "foreign" and capricious. In 1849, H. W. Halleck, as California's Secretary of State, had reported to Col. Mason that the majority of California's Mexican land grants were actually invalid. In response, the US government sent William Carey Jones, a lawyer and son-in-law of the prominent expansionist Missouri Senator, Thomas Hart Benton, to conduct an investigation into the land grants. After several months of careful research in California, Jones reported in 1850 that the grants were "mostly perfect titles."[33]

To sort out this perceived confusion, California Senator William Gwin introduced a bill to establish a Public Land Commission in California to determine if the grants were truly valid. It was passed on March 3, 1851. Under the Land Act of 1851, land holders in California from before the American conquest had to prove to the Commission that their titles and paperwork were legal and proper. Furthermore, every case, no matter what was determined by the Commission, was automatically reviewed again by the United States District Court.

The court procedure was stacked against the original owners. Land titles were filed in Mexico, and were written in Spanish. Owners needed not only their own copies of the land titles, but proof that they had been filed correctly in Mexico. Lawyers and judges in these cases were not required to read Spanish—owners needed to provide translations, and prove the translations were accurate. It took owners years to prepare these cases, working with teams of lawyers every step of the way—who, of course, charged high fees for their services. After making their case to the Commission, every grant holder then had to repeat the proceedings again at the district court.

The result of all these actions was a false victory for the owners. As it turned out, the vast majority of the grants were in fact legal, proper, and clear, but few owners enjoyed the final decision. The costs of defending their lands were usually so high that they were required to sell the lands in the end to pay off the lawyers. Very little of the land that was guaranteed to the original owners by Articles VIII and IX of the Treaty of Guadalupe Hidalgo in 1848 was actually in the hands of the owners fifteen years later.[34]

The effect of the Foreign Miners Tax and the Land Act of 1851 was to secure California as a white outpost on the Pacific coast. Walter McDougall notes that California was essentially engineered as a white state, and that early miners-turned-residents understood that they were creating a privileged white bastion on the Pacific Rim, a strongly American foundation in the Pacific.[35] It was not a natural development, it was a calculated step toward an ultimate goal. Despite the promises made in the 1848 treaty, the profits of the gold rush would be American, the losses would be borne by "foreigners," defined racially, and despite legal protections.

If this was true of California's Asian and Hispanic residents, it was especially true of its Native peoples.

THE DESTRUCTION OF CALIFORNIA'S NATIVE PEOPLES

Before the arrival of the Spanish in the late 1760s, California's Native peoples were among the most diverse and numerous in the nation. The region's varied landscape led to many different environmental niches, and Native peoples fit these places in unique ways. Before European settlement, it is estimated that over 300,000 natives in over 100 tribes, lived in California.[36] However, these numbers are misleading. Most California natives lived within closely bounded worlds, and sub groups of tribes often had little contact with others within the larger tribe, even developing distinct dialects. California's Native peoples were, in many ways, a vast mosaic of separate and nearly independent peoples.

The arrival of the Spanish shattered at least part of that world along the coast. Missionaries insisted on converting California's diverse peoples into a single Catholic and Spanish population. Natives resisted, but without large native tribal structures, they were rarely effective. Diseases carried by the Spanish killed coastal natives from San Diego to the San Francisco Bay area by the hundreds of thousands. Survivors had little choice but to seek shelter with the Spanish missionaries, or to flee to the interior tribes—facing an uncertain welcome while also spreading the disease epidemics further.

When Mexico won its independence from Spain, California and its peoples went through a major change. In 1833, the old Spanish missions were secularized, and most of their resources divided up among the *Californio* ranchers who remained. Native peoples in these areas had become dependent on the missions, and were viewed as a resource by the ranchers, who claimed their labor in much the same manner they claimed mission cattle or lands. Former mission Indians now became indentured servants on these ranches, held in a state of virtual slavery. Newcomers to California before the gold rush understood and used this system eagerly. John Sutter, for example, built and ran his pioneering outpost almost entirely through enforced native labor.[37]

By the time of the American conquest during the Mexican War, California's Native peoples were still very much divided. The greatest affects of the Spanish and Mexican periods had been along the central and southern coastal tribes. The interior tribes of the Central Valley had also suffered the effects of disease, but faced fewer settlements, and braced by the runaways from the coast, were making a more effective fight against Spanish and Mexican expansion there. Again, this is partly why John Sutter was allowed land in the interior: to help control growing Native resistance. Meanwhile, most tribal people in the Sierra foothills and mountains and in the northern reaches of California had only limited contact with Euro-American settlers.

The American conquest was bound to change the world of California's Native peoples, but, as the war ended, the exact nature of that change was uncertain. As harsh as Spanish treatment had been, Spain had always seen natives as potential citizens and laborers within society. Mexico had further taken the step of outlawing slavery, and, at least officially, this applied to the natives as well. Americans, however, had predominantly viewed Native peoples as a threat and an obstacle to expansion. Federal policy had not been to incorporate natives but to remove them. Only ten years before the gold rush, the Federal government had overseen the removal of the "civilized tribes" of the Southeast—those most integrated into American culture—to the permanent "Indian Territory" of the Great Plains. Rather than integrating Indians as laborers, Americans wanted them eliminated.

However, the acquisition of California, and the almost immediate gold rush, challenged even that policy. The idea of "permanent" Indian Territory in the plains could no longer stand, as Americans now demanded permanent trails and passageways through that territory to the west coast. The Treaty of Guadalupe Hidalgo, at least in theory, promised the Southwest Indians the legal protections of citizens that it had promised Mexican citizens in the area. Clearly, California challenged the existing federal policy toward western natives. Further, the debate that erupted over slavery in the Southwest in the aftermath of the war provided at least the possibility that Indian legal rights might shift as well if slavery were indeed prohibited. As a result, federal Indian policy was undergoing change, but the outline of that change could not be easily foreseen in 1848.[38]

The gold rush, however, powerfully forced many of these issues into a brutal course that few policy makers could direct, much less control. Between 1848 and late 1850, the debate in Congress left California virtually ungoverned, free to make up its own laws locally. As noted before, these laws were usually designed for the convenience of the miners and tended to be harsh. While people from around the world rushed into the area, the majority were Americans, who brought with them cultural ideas of white racial dominance, and the belief that Indians could not be integrated into white society. The result was virtual genocide.

Initially, during the first days of the gold rush, *Californio* ranchers brought their Indian laborers to the foothills to work as indentured miners. During the first months of surface mining, the "take" was generally good, and those with Indian laborers stood to make huge fortunes. However, as Americans began arriving in California, they demanded an end to the practice. *Californios*, they argued, already had taken huge tracts of land, and now these "beaten foes" from the war were monopolizing the gold fields unfairly. Miners in 1848 from Oregon—the first substantial body of American settlers to reach California—attacked Indian workers in the mines. When James Marshall, who used Sutter's Indians to mine the region near the mill, tried to defend his workers, he had to flee to the foothills due to death threats against his own life. After a massacre of eight workers at Coloma, the site of Sutter's mill, the practice of using Indian laborers in the mine quickly ended.[39]

Native peoples did try mining as individuals, especially after seeing the value whites put on the flakes of gold, but natives found themselves endangered in the crowded mining camps, and tended to mine on the outskirts of these camps, or sifted through the tailings already processed by the white miners. Even when successful, Indian miners found few whites who would give them full value for their gold in trade.[40]

As Indian miners were pushed out of mining camps, the white miners themselves pushed into Native worlds. Mining camps destroyed the natural environment Native peoples depended on. Camps on the rivers disrupted trails used by original peoples and the migratory patterns of the animals they hunted. Forests were cut down to build camps, provide firewood, and to build rockers, dams, water flumes, and tunnel braces. Rivers were diverted to get at underlying gold, and hydraulic mining washed away whole hillsides, choking streams in normal times and creating destructive floods in the wet season.[41]

Natives who depended on the natural systems of the foothills and interior valleys saw these systems destroyed, often within the space of a few months. Some tried to fight back, but the rush of people into the foothills overwhelmed them. Given the cultural predisposition to see Indians as an implacable enemy, white miners quickly organized raiding parties against native villages, and often attacked villages that had not been part of any resistance to the miners. Seeing themselves as heroic manly heroes, off on a western adventure, many miners engaged in these raids as simply a part of the gold rush experience. In many raids, miners rejoiced at having "wiped out" entire villages—men, women, and children.[42]

It is perhaps questionable if any other course of action could have prevented the slaughter. Col. Mason had noted in 1848 that federal control in the mines was and would likely be ineffective in the face of the massive rush, but the Congressional debate over the fate of California that lasted until 1850 unquestionably made the situation worse. The delay in establishing a territorial government left local Californians to develop their own government and to address the matter of Indian policy on their own. Since the very beginning of the US government, it was understood

Terrible Vengeance

SACRAMENTO NEWS [PER ADAM'S & CO.'S EXPRESS]

Exciting News from Tehama—Indian Thefts—Terrible Vengeance of the Whites

Mr. Lurk of Adams & Co., furnished the Union with the following exciting news.

The Indians have committed so many depredations in the North, of late, that the people are enraged against them, and are ready to knife them, shoot them, or inoculate them with small pox—all of which have been done.

Some time since, the Indians in Colusa county destroyed about some $ 5,000 worth of stock belonging to Messrs. Thomas & Toombe; since which time they have had two men employed, at $ 8.00 per month' to hunt down and kill the Diggers, like other beasts of prey. On Friday, the 25th ult., one of these men, named John Breckenridge, was alone, and armed only with a bowie knife, when he met with four Indians and attacked them. They told him to leave, and commenced shooting arrows at him; but, undaunted, he continued to advance, and succeeded in killing one, and taking one prisoner, while the other two escaped. He immediately proceeded to Moon's Ranch, where the captured Indian was hung by the citizens.

On Friday, the 25th Feb., stock was stolen from Mr. Carter of Butte county, to the value of $ 3,000. Mr. Carter went forthwith to the camp of the well known stage proprietors, Messrs. Hall & Crandall, and the men started with a party of twelve men in search of the Indian depredators. After a fruitless search in the vicinity of Pine and Deer Creeks, the party became impatient and dispersed in Sunday evening and returned home, one detachment of the party discovered a half-breed by the name of Battedou, and took him prisoner. The man, fearing for his own life, agreed to show the cave where the Indians were concealed, if they would release him. Notice was sent round and the people assembled again at Oak Grove on Monday, from which they started at midnight for the cave.

Arriving there at early daylight on Tuesday morning, rocks were rolled into the cave, and the wretched inmates, rushing out for safety, met danger a thousand times more dreadful. The first one that made his appearance was shot by Capt. Geo Rose, and the others met the same fate from the rifles of the Americans. Altogether, there were thirteen killed; three chiefs of different rancherias, and three women. Three women and five children were spared; and it is but doing justice to say, that the women who were killed were placed in front as a sort of breast-work and killed either by accident or mistake. Capt. Rose took one child, Mr. Lattimer another, and the others were disposed of in the same charitable manner among the party.

Daily Alta California, March 6, 1853.

that Indian policy must be handled by the federal government. Local governments, it was agreed, had too much of a personal stake in Indian treaties and dealings, and would likely take too much land, and mistreat Indian peoples so badly that warfare was bound to break out. Leaving Indian policy to be formulated by California's white miners was a certain recipe for disaster. Perhaps the only thing that prevented a major retaliatory war by Native peoples against the miners was the fragmented nature of California's tribes, and the deluge of miners that invaded the region.[43]

The resulting California policy towards its Native peoples thus sprang from a variety of influences: from a federal policy that was already shifting and not even in place in the state; from a Hispanic history of native exploitation, and an American history of removal and extermination; from a period of local mining rush governance in the face of social chaos; and from the broken environments of the native world and its traditionally fragmented basis. At first, the California legislature adopted the miners' worst cultural biases as law. Bounties were offered for native scalps, and the state helped organize military raids on Indian villages. Governor Peter Burnett declared that California's Indians needed to be exterminated.

This was quickly followed in 1850 by a more formal and permanent policy, a bill entitled the "For the Government and Protection of the Indians." The title was bitterly and brutally misleading. Under the act, Indians were to be protected by the state by being assigned to individuals who would protect them in exchange for their labor. In effect, Indians would be made available as slaves for California miners, ranchers, farmers, etc., or they would continue to face the raiding parties of miners organized by the state. Native villages now faced new attacks, as Californians raided them for enslaved workers as well as to remove them from the mining regions.[44]

The impact of the gold rush on California's Indians was enormous. In 1848, it was estimated that 150,000 natives lived in California. Twelve years later, that number was estimated at only 30,000. Nor would the immediate effect of the gold rush be the end of the story. As we shall see, the gold rush left a lasting legacy on both California and federal Indian policy in the coming years.

★   ★   ★

The California gold rush enriched the economy of the United States in the mid-1850s, established the foundations of the State of California, and provided a remarkable experience for hundreds of thousands of gold rush migrants. Accessing the success of these miners, however, is difficult. For many, like William Carpenter and Mary Jane Megquier, a clear sense of success was elusive. While many made fortunes in California, others found only disappointment or death. However, the balance sheet of gold rush success needs to take into account more than just the miners. When George and Samuel Nichols died during their California adventure, it was Sarah Nichols and her family that needed to deal with the aftermath. The balance sheet also needs to consider the unwilling participants in the rush: the native *Californios* and Native peoples, who did not rush to California, but were rushed by the gold seekers. For many *Californio* families, the gold rush transformed them from natives in their homeland into strangers in a strange land. If the story of George and Samuel Nichols shows us the devastation caused by two gold rush deaths, how are we to balance the deaths of 120,000 Native peoples?

NOTES

1 See Mary Hill, *Gold: The California Story* (Berkeley: University of California Press, 1999), p. 263; and Rodman W. Paul, *California Gold: The Beginning of Mining in the Far West* (Lincoln: University of Nebraska Press1947), pp. 349–350.

2 Malcolm J. Rohrbough, *Days of Gold: The California Gold Rush and the American Nation* (Berkeley: University of California Press, 1997), pp. 3, 205–206.

3 Quoted in Patricia Nelson Limerick, *The Legacy of Conquest: The Unbroken Past of the American West* (New York: W.W. Norton, 1987), p. 101.

4 Paul, *California Gold*, pp. 349–350.

5 Mark Hopkins, *Letter to Brother, Moses,* July 10, 1850; Huntington Library manuscript, HM 26040.

6 Mark Hopkins, *Letter to Brother, Moses,* July 10, 1850; Huntington Library manuscript, HM 26040.

7 Mark Hopkins, *Letter to Brother, Moses,* July 30, 1850; Huntington Library manuscript, HM 26041.

8 Mark Hopkins, *Letter to Brother, Moses,* October 27, 1850; Huntington Library, HM 26045.

9 Samuel Nichols, *Letter to his Wife, Sarah,* March 19, 1849; Huntington Library manuscript, HM 48265.

10 Rohrbough, *Days of Gold*, p. 282.

11 William Carpenter, *A California Pioneer of the Fifties*, no date. Edited by Frederic Ives Carpenter; Huntington Library typewritten manuscript, HM16777.

12 Polly Welts Kaufman, ed., *Apron Full of Gold: The Letters of Mary Jane Megquier from San Francisco, 1849–1856*, 2nd edition (Albuquerque: University of New Mexico Press, 1994), p. 4.

13 Kaufman, *Apron Full of Gold*, p. 4.

14 Kaufman, *Apron Full of Gold*, p. 6.

15 Kaufman, *Apron Full of Gold*, p. xv.

16 Kaufman, *Apron Full of Gold*, p. 35.

17 Kaufman, *Apron Full of Gold*, p. 43.

18   Kaufman, *Apron Full of Gold*, p. 47.

19   Kaufman, *Apron Full of Gold*, p. 48.

20   Kaufman, *Apron Full of Gold*, p. 50.

21   Kaufman, *Apron Full of Gold*, p. 56.

22   Kaufman, *Apron Full of Gold*, pp. 66–67.

23   Kaufman, *Apron Full of Gold*, p. 68.

24   Kaufman, *Apron Full of Gold*, pp. 120–121.

25   Kaufman, *Apron Full of Gold*, p. 145.

26   Kaufman, *Apron Full of Gold*, p. 153.

27   Mark A. Eifler, *Gold Rush Capitalists: Greed and Growth in Sacramento* (Albuquerque: University of New Mexico Press, 2002), pp. 85, 108.

28   Sylvia Sun Minnick, "Never Far From Home: Being Chinese in the California Gold Rush," in Kenneth N. Owens, ed., *Riches for All: The California Gold Rush and the World* (Lincoln: University of Nebraska Press, 2002), p. 150; Malcolm J. Rohrbough, " 'We Will Make Our Fortunes—No Doubt of It' The Worldwide Rush to California," in Owens, *Riches for All*, p. 63.

29   Martin Ridge, "Disorder, Crime, and Punishment in the California Gold Rush," in Owens, *Riches for All*, pp. 185–187; Manuel G. Gonzales, *Mexicanos: A History of Mexicans in the United States* (Bloomington: Indiana University Press, 2000), p. 85.

30   Gonzales, *Mexicanos*, p. 86.

31   Michael J. Gonzales, " 'My Brother's Keeper': Mexicans and the Hunt for Prosperity in California, 1848–2000," in Owens, *Riches for All*, p. 124., Gonzales, *Mexicanos*, p. 86; Rohrbough, *Days of Gold*, pp. 224–229.

32   Minnick, "Never Far From Home," pp. 145–146, 151–152.

33   W. W. Robinson, *Land in California* (Berkeley: University of California Press, 1979), pp. 91–95.

34   Robinson, *Land in California*, pp. 100–109; Harlow, *California Conquered*, pp. 331–332.

35   Walter A. McDougall, *Let the Sea Make a Noise: Four Hundred Years of Cataclysm, Conquest, War and Folly in the North Pacific*, (New York: Avon Books, 1993), pp. 288–97, 344–53.

36   James J. Rawls, *Indians of California: The Changing Image* (Norman: University of Oklahoma Press, 1984), p. 6.

37   Albert L. Hurtado, *Indian Survival on the California Frontier* (New Haven: Yale University Press, 1988), pp. 55–71.

38   Albert L. Hurtado, "Clouded Legacy: California Indians and the Gold Rush," in Owens, *Riches for All*, pp. 104–107; Robert M. Utley, *The Indian Frontier of the American West, 1846–1890* (Albuquerque: University of New Mexico Press, 1984) pp. 37–43.

39   Hurtado, "Clouded Legacy," in Owens, *Riches for All*, p. 101.

40   Hurtado, "Clouded Legacy," p. 100.

41   Hurtado, "Clouded Legacy," pp. 98–99.

42   Rawls, *Indians of California*, pp. 171–201.

43   Hurtado, "Clouded Legacy," p. 108.

44   Hurtado, "Clouded Legacy," pp. 102–103.

CHAPTER 6

California Changes the Nation

The influence of the California gold rush continued to affect the nation and the world for decades to come. Like a stone thrown into a still pond, the ripples sent out carried far from the initial impact. The sudden arrival of hundreds of thousands of people in California gave rise to a new and powerful American outpost in the far West and on the Pacific Rim. The gold rush advanced the development of transportation and communications systems in the United States and the Pacific Rim. It affected critical social trends, from the debates over slavery and federal Indian policies, to shaping the ethnic make-up of the United States for decades to come. The real pay-off of the gold rush was not the amount of gold that was mined and added to the nation's economy. The prize was California itself, but that prize came with costs. The gold rush changed California, but California in turn changed the nation.

NEW RUSHES

The California gold rush was not the only mineral rush of the mid and late nineteenth century. After the California discoveries, gold was discovered in Colorado, Montana, and the Black Hills. Silver was discovered in Nevada. Each of these discoveries led to sudden rushes similar to the California gold rush, if on a somewhat lesser scale. In each case, the region was suddenly invaded by prospectors and miners who dramatically transformed the landscape, setting up transportation links and instant cities, dispossessing Native peoples and creating strong new political realities on the ground in the West. The discovery of silver in Nevada, so close to the California gold fields, essentially expanded the transportation, urban, and financial systems of California eastward. In some cases, such as in

Colorado, the conditions of the rush allowed for the rise of a powerful new city at the center of regional transportation and power: Denver.

These mining rushes disrupted the lives of Native peoples throughout the West, but the tension was not one sided. The Colorado rush brought miners over the plains on the southern boundary of the expanding Sioux confederation, which in turn made it much harder for the Sioux expansion to continue. On the other hand, the Black Hills rush of the 1870s was located in the Sioux heartland, and faced much stiffer Native resistance than had been the case in California, Colorado, and Nevada. In addition, the national financial environment of the 1870s was more difficult. The depression of the mid-1870s drastically curtailed railroad construction, halting work on the Northern Pacific Railroad which would have connected the northern plains mines to Chicago and Seattle. By the time the financial conditions were improved and the Sioux reduced to reservations, the days of easy placer mining in the Black Hills had passed, and the rush was much reduced. Ultimately, the region did not develop as intensely as Northern California or the area around Denver.

In each case, though, the California gold rush had pointed the way. Each area essentially repeated the cycle of development that had emerged in California: a fevered rush by an eager population, the shift from placer mining to rockers and eventually to deep rock mining, the sudden appearance of boom towns, attempts to incorporate the region into national and international transportation and communication systems, and the legal chaos and dispossession of Native peoples.

Nor was it just the pattern of development that these rushes shared. In each case, many of the miners had come from the California mines, eager to recreate opportunities elsewhere that were slipping away in California. In some cases, the California mines actually started the new rushes. It was California miners who made the original discoveries of silver in Nevada and the reach of miners with California experience was wide. In 1851, Edward Hargraves believed that the hills and valleys of Australia looked enough like California that he decided to prospect there. His discovery of gold there set off a gold rush to Australia. A similar story occurred in New Zealand. The California gold rush was not only the first of the nineteenth century mineral rushes, but it also deeply shaped the many rushes that occurred in the following years.

The discoveries of gold in these previously remote places were not simple events. In each case, it was not the *gold* discovered, but *the rush of people* coming into the area, that had the greatest potential power for change. The California experience sparked not only dreams of profits for miners, but nightmares of administration and law for home governments.

These considerations can be best seen in the case of Alaska. Russian fur hunters and traders had begun settling Alaska in 1784, but the great isolation of Alaska had always strained the Russian American Company's resources. The Russian government had always known it was greatly over-extended in Alaska. Indeed, the transportation system in central and eastern Russia and Siberia was primitive and largely unreliable. In an age of imperial power projection, with the US and Britain gaining more influence over China and Japan, Russia understood that its own interests in Asia and Siberia were extremely vulnerable. Alaska was simply too far away to be adequately defended.[1]

Alaska's vulnerability, however, was further underscored when Russian officials became aware of scattered gold discoveries on the Stikine River in Alaska. Should news of these discoveries leak out, and Americans rush to Alaska, Russia would be in no position to keep the Americans out. As in the California gold rush, Americans would rush in and Russian authority soon be overwhelmed. Not only would Russia be saddled with the impossible job of governing the chaos of the gold fields, but when it failed in this task it would make Russia look weak in the Pacific, just as it needed to project an image of power there. Russia was thus put in the awkward position of trying to sell Alaska to the US, knowing that gold deposits were there, but keeping it secret in order to have any negotiating power at all.[2]

In the end, the model of the California gold rush played out in Alaska in its own unique way. The Russian government began offering to sell Alaska to the United States in the 1850s, and hoped particularly to entice William Seward as Lincoln's Secretary of State. However, the Civil War delayed American interest in the Great North. Russian sold Alaska to the United States for $7.2 million in 1867.

Russia used much of that money to build its own Trans-Siberian Railroad, to strengthen its hold on its Pacific coast and central and eastern Russia. When Americans did discover gold in the Klondike and in Nome, Alaska in 1896, a rush of over 100,000 predictably overwhelmed the regional population and environment. This time, however, due in part to the improved transportation systems of the Pacific (in themselves greatly due to the California gold rush), the urban infrastructure reached not only from the mining camps to the coast, but then down to Seattle,

THE ALASKA KICKBACK

When it came time to purchase Alaska, Seward and the Russians discovered that the only way to get the US Congress to agree to the deal was to provide cash kickbacks to those who voted for it—thus the extra $200,000 in the purchase price!

which quickly took on the role San Francisco had played in the California rush.[3]

British Columbia was another case in point. Gold was discovered on the Frazer River in 1858, drawing thousands of California miners to the region. Within a few years, the region was inundated with gold rushers—over a quarter of them from California and the United States, and British Columbia found itself economically more a satellite of California and Oregon than of Canada or

THE COSTS OF MINING

Every miner who participated in a gold rush needed to spend money on transportation, equipment, supplies, and food to get to the strike and engage in mining. Often the amount mined did not equal the initial outlay. In the Klondike Rush, it is estimated that the miners as a whole spent ten times more to get to the mining fields than the fields actually contained.

Britain. It appeared that the United States might soon acquire the remaining section of the west coast between Alaska and Washington State.[4]

Thus when British and Canadian politicians attempted to set up the confederation of Canada in the 1860s, the fate of British Columbia was far from settled. Corralling the eastern provinces into a new union was a challenge, but to survive and prosper Canada would need a port on the Pacific. As a trans-continental power, Canada could trade both in the Atlantic and the Pacific, and transport goods between the two oceans within the structure of the British Empire. In 1868, Victoria residents voted to join Canada if they could be connected to the east by railroad. The Canadian government quickly voted to sponsor construction of a trans-continental line, the Canadian Pacific Railroad, to insure the province's loyalty. American Secretary of State, William Seward, joined with the financier Jay Cooke to raise funds for a Northern Pacific Railroad that could connect the region to the United States. However, the Americans' effort was slow to organize, and in 1870 the British Columbia council voted to join Canada.[5]

The California gold rush was a powerful force in the American West and throughout the Pacific Rim in the latter half of the nineteenth century. The power of the strikes was not in the gold they mined, but in the vast mobile populations careening from one strike to another, and threatening to shift geopolitical power. As historian, Douglas Fetherling, has suggested, the California gold rush was not an isolated event, but the start of what might be seen as "The Gold Crusade," a fifty-year movement that transformed the West and the Pacific.[6]

THE GOLD RUSH AND THE CIVIL WAR

Only a dozen years after the gold rush, the United States erupted into civil war. The heart of that struggle was the institution of slavery, and whether it would expand or shrink, to eventually encompass the entire nation or none of it. However, the California gold rush had an important role to play in the coming of the war, as well as in the way it was fought.

The Compromise of 1850 had been pushed through Congress by Illinois Senator, Stephen Douglas, who quickly came to tout the "popular sovereignty" idea to western territories. The Compromise had dealt with the lands acquired from Mexico, but the vast northern extent of the Louisiana Purchase was still unorganized territory. It had originally been believed that this territory was unfit for cultivation or American settlement, and could be permanent Indian Country, at least for generations to come.

California and the gold rush forced a reassessment of this policy. Clearly overland transportation was needed to link California to the eastern states. Douglas hoped for a railroad connection, especially one that might link Chicago to California's golden marketplaces. As chairman of the western territory committee, Douglas needed to now organize part of the Louisiana Territory on the central plains, roughly along the Republican and Platte Rivers, in order to provide protection and legal standing to a transportation system on the plains, whether it was wagon trail, stagecoach roads, or a railroad.

Douglas's plans, however, ran into the objections of southern, slave-state politicians, still smarting from the Compromise of 1850. They demanded that Douglas rescind the Compromise line of 1820, and open the central plains to slavery. Douglas obliged, at least as far as to end the determination that the old 36°30' compromise line still determined whether a territory would allow slavery or not. With the California experience in mind, Douglas argued for "popular sovereignty" in the newly created plains territory. The settlers themselves, he argued, could decide if they wanted slavery or not. Accommodating southern wishes still further, however, Douglas also divided his proposed territory into two: Kansas and Nebraska. What was not determined was when these settlers would actually decide.

The result became known as "Bloody Kansas." Slaveholders, especially from Missouri, rushed into Kansas to force free soilers out and to demand that the "popular" vote of Kansas be pro-slavery. Northern free soil settlers—who actually outnumbered slaveholders anyway, also pushed for a moral "rush" into Kansas to save the territory for the North. The Kansas rush was a perverse parody of the California rush of 1849. California had suffered a great deal of chaos for nearly three years without Congressional direction. In Kansas, the chaos was a result of Douglas's political plans—while Californians were largely united in their opposition to slavery in the mines, Kansas settlers were violently split on the issue of slavery.

Gangs of both free and slave soil settlers attacked each other in raids that quickly took on the aspects of formal warfare. Most historians agree that, for all intents, the Civil War had now begun. In the midst of Bleeding Kansas, John Brown first became a terrorist, but with backers in the north. A southern congressmen beat a northern congressman bloody and senseless on the floor of the Senate, and an until then rather obscure Illinois congressman, Abraham Lincoln, started working to organize the new Republican Party. California, in many ways, represented the ideal West of the Republican Party—a West where men could get ahead by their own efforts, possibly spectacularly, without the interference of slavery. Meanwhile, Stephen Douglas, who had pushed through the Compromise of 1850 and the Kansas-Nebraska Act became so wedded to the idea of "popular sovereignty," that southerners doubted his devotion to their goal of the expansion of slavery. Douglas's fall from the leadership of the Democratic Party would help not only create a vision for the Republican Party but also to divide the Democrats in the 1860 election, which would elevate Lincoln to the Presidency.

LIBERTY. THE FAIR MAID OF KANSAS...IN THE HANDS OF THE "BORDER RUFFIANS".

Figure 6.1 The Kansas-Nebraska Act. The sudden rush of miners to California suggested that the West could be settled quickly by settlers who could decide on their own whether slavery would be legal. This idea underlay the logic of "Popular Sovereignty" and the Kansas-Nebraska Act of 1854. In reality, however, the rush of settlers became a bloody, political struggle.

Filibusters

Kansas was not the only region that bled as a result of "popular sovereignty." If California could enter the Union as a free state as a fait accompli based on a rush by early settlers, many Southern leaders believed slaves states beyond Kansas could be created under the same circumstances. A number of southern "filibusters" set out to create rushes into Central America and the Caribbean in order to create new slave states. And California was a popular base for such activity. The gold rush seemed to validate the power of a private stampede to a coveted area, that could be then quickly acquired by the US government. The Tennessean William Walker was particularly prominent in these attempts. Though ultimately none of these attempts succeeded, they were, like the rush into Kansas, attempts to use a population rush to acquire new territory.

After the war began, the California gold rush still had lasting consequences. Historian, Robert Remini, writing about the Compromise of 1850, noted that even as a failure it still delayed the start of the war by ten years and that the North was in a much better position to win that war then than it would have been in in 1850.[7] California cast its votes for Lincoln in both the 1860 and 1864 elections, and over 17,000 volunteers fought for the Union cause in the war.[8] Perhaps even more important were the millions of dollars' worth of California gold and Nevada silver that bankrolled the development of northern enterprise, technology, and industrialism during the 1850s.

The California gold rush had itself prepared both business and the government for the Civil War in an important way. The huge armies of the Civil War demanded logistical support and quick transportation and communications over a vast area—precisely the kinds of operation that the California gold rush had also required. As William Carpenter and Mark Hopkins noted, the California business scene was like nothing they had ever experienced before. Whether they stayed in California with Hopkins, or returned home like Carpenter, they carried the lessons and outlooks of the scale of gold rush business with them. When the Civil War broke out, with its sudden demands for large-scale organization, it would have looked familiar to many who had participated directly or indirectly in the gold rush.

Businesses that served to ship large amount of goods to distant California, or to create industrial goods for mining, found themselves prepped for the same tasks as during the gold rush. Managers in these companies had also gained experience in supplying the needs of a massive migration useful in supplying the large Union and Confederate armies. The profits to be made in the mining business also suggested the profits to be made in the civil war, and this, too, played its role in the war.

One example of this echo was the war bond drives organized by Jay Cooke to help pay for the war effort in 1862. Historians have noted that this was a remarkable event, in which hundreds of thousands of ordinary Americans were introduced to bond investments. Cooke made the bond prices low enough so that the middle class could participate, and sold it as a patriotic drive with a future pay off.[9] Yet the gold rush had, in many ways, prepared the way by promising much the same thing: the chance to experience a historic experience and gain a financial pay off. To miners who had gone to California, and to the many who had stayed home but had supported California migrants with loans, letters, and substitute work, Cooke's bond drives offered another chance to participate in a historic adventure. The sale of Cooke's war bonds was a familiar experience to Californians and eastern Americans who had already dabbled in California mining stocks.

Historians who look at the period after the Civil War as a period of big business growth, as the rise of an era of Robber Barons, correctly note that the vast effort of the Civil War gave this mentality and its associated economic environment a strong boost.[10] Yet economic studies of the American economy suggest that the Civil War did not create these practices or start these trends. The California gold rush had already produced an economic boom, both in supplying the rush and in supporting it logistically. A number of new entrepreneurs started lasting American businesses catering to the gold rush—including Levi Strauss, Wells Fargo, Studebaker, and Spreckels. The railroads, which provided the stage for political corruption and vast fortunes, were built to connect California to the East, not to further the war effort. It is perhaps revealing that the name that is given to the era after the Civil War—the Gilded Age—comes from a novel by Charles Dudley Warner and Mark Twain which is largely set in the West and in Washington, DC. It features business, speculation, railroad building, and corruption, themes that were all introduced on a grand scale by the California gold rush. If we imagine an American past *without* the brutality of slavery and the Civil War, but *with* the gold rush, it is possible to see the roots of much of the Gilded Age in the California experience.

TRANSPORTATION

The California gold rush spurred a world-wide demand for new, efficient, reliable, and cheap transportation systems to and from California. Because of the international participation in the gold rush, the construction of these new routes changed migration and trade patterns worldwide. The rush coincided with new developments, particularly in steam-powered engines, which were already quickening international travel. The California gold rush provided a powerful early incentive for this development to reach out across the American West and throughout the Pacific.

The global system of transportation that was being created at the time of the gold rush aided world travel, but it also redefined political, economic, and social order. One of the places to experience this change in a concentrated form was Panama. From the first days of the rush, American entrepreneurs extended steamship lines to both the Caribbean and Pacific coasts of the region, and dreamed of constructing a railroad that crossed the isthmus.

With the backing of New York investors, the Panama Railroad Company began construction of a railroad linking the Atlantic and Pacific shores of Panama. The work was one of the engineering marvels of the mid-nineteenth century, but as historian Aims McGuinness points out, the biggest problem was finding labor. Local residents refused the dangerous and grueling work that paid less than they could make transporting miners and goods themselves. In fact, transporting goods and supplying the California-bound emigrants paid so well that thousands left their workplaces throughout Panama, raising wages to impossible levels throughout the region. Unable to get local workers, the railroad imported workers—from the Caribbean, the United States, Ireland, China, and India.[11]

Meanwhile, relations between the emigrants and Panamanians grew strained. Emigrants believed they were being charged exorbitant costs for services, and forced to use these services while the backlog in steamships left thousands stranded for weeks or months in Panama. Many Americans were also troubled by the racial inversion of Panama. To most American emigrants, people of color were considered to be racially inferior; yet here in Panama, whites found themselves dependent on the *genre du color* for vital services. Already puffed up from the recent victory over Mexico and with visions of racial superiority dancing in their heads, Americans often treated Panama as if it was the next nation to be conquered.[12]

This attitude was also shared by the railroad company. In 1852, it established a new town in Limon Bay as the Atlantic terminus of its railroad line. Though the government gave the company the right to found the town of Colón, company officials renamed the town Aspinwall after the company's leader, William Aspinwall. The company ran the port not only as a company town but as an American satellite. When labor troubles interfered with their plans, the company simply organized its own police and court system, and dealt with its opponents in vigilante fashion.[13]

The railroad was opened in February, 1855, and until the completion of the American transcontinental railroad in 1869 it quickly became the main avenue of people and goods going to or from California. Yet while local elites had hoped the completion of the railroad would bring prosperity to Panama, it brought ruin instead. Between the steamships and the railroad, it was possible for a passenger to step directly from a steamboat to a railroad car, and then a few hours later to step back on a Pacific steamer—having bypassed any local merchant or services in Panama at all. Money spent by the passengers went to the New York-based steamship companies. Instead of prosperity, the railroad brought a severe depression.[14]

The construction of a railroad across the American West remained elusive in the 1850s. The public demand for a transcontinental railroad remained high, but the political struggle over the extension of slavery bedeviled any easy solution. The dream of a railroad reaching from the East to the Pacific coast had been promoted in the 1840s. The technical problems of such a route were still extreme, as was finding a way to make it profitable. Construction of a western railroad also ran into sectional controversy. Before the Civil War, it was beyond Congress's ability to find any agreement over the path of a western route—especially whether it should connect a northern or a southern city to the gold fields. Hoping that western geography would suggest an obvious solution, Congress authorized four expeditions to map out the best possible route to the

The Coming of the Railroad

William Carpenter, to his wife, Lucretta:

We may well look at one of the greatest enterprises of the day with marked interest, the Pacific Rail Road, for it is one of vast magnitude to all the earth, and to America's sons in particular, and perchance to you and me . . . for it may be our wish to travel over it in the course of time, yet not very probable. I more particularly look at it with great interest, for have I not seen California in its infant days, and now fast verging into strong and vigorous manhood? What she will be with this road is not distinctly seen, but that it must be of great utility to her is plain. That I should think of this state as much more than of any other is a natural result of being with her in her infant days and having seen her progress to its present state.

William Carpenter, *A California Pioneer of the Fifties,* no date.
Edited by Frederic Ives Carpenter; Huntington Library
typewritten manuscript, HM16777.

Pacific. The hope was that only one would be suitable, thus letting Nature force the sectional deadlock. Instead, five routes were found to be viable. The deadlock remained.[15]

In the meantime, then, land travel to California moved at the pace of oxen, mules, horses, or human pedestrians. Yet even this mode of transportation saw significant innovation. Stagecoach lines sought to connect California with the Mississippi and Missouri river valleys, despite the early overland coach failures. Stage companies such as Adams Express and Wells Fargo and Company sought opportunities in transporting goods, especially gold, between California and the eastern states. One of the most important freighters was Russell, Majors, and Waddell, which began by supplying goods to Army posts in the Southwest after the Mexican War and then throughout much of the far West. The cost of operating a stage line, however, was enormous. Stations were established approximately every twenty miles, so that draft animals could be changed out, and rested. Traveling by stagecoach was a bone-jarring affair. Trails were rough and passengers were jostled unmercifully. Thick dust filled the coach, making breathing difficult, unless window shades were drawn, which then often left the passengers sweltering in the heat. Food and some minimal level of service were provided at some of the stations along the way. In order to cover expenses, Russell, Majors, and Waddell received subsidies from the federal government for carrying the US Mail.[16] Though useful for passengers over short trips, stagecoach travel was a brutal ordeal over the long distances of the West.

With the outbreak of the Civil War, the deadlock over a western railroad route in Congress was finally broken when the South walked out. Railroad construction was finally authorized by the Pacific Railroad Acts of 1862 and 1864. The dream of connecting California by rail to the eastern states was finally completed in 1869, when the Union Pacific and Central Pacific railroads met at Promontory Point, Utah. The California gold rush, though now nearly fifteen years after its peak, still played a prominent part in the construction. The Central Pacific was organized by four Sacramento merchants who had no idea how to build a railroad—Leland Stanford, Collis Huntington, Charles Crocker, and Mark Hopkins. Each had made their fortunes in the gold rush, and their gold rush money and experience laid the groundwork for their taking on the construction of the railroad. Further, their railroad was largely constructed by Chinese workers, most of whom originally came to California for the gold rush. Crocker hired them because they were hard working, and willing to work for less. While this got the railroad built, it made the Chinese even more of a target for white laborers in the West.[17]

Meanwhile, California's Central Pacific Railroad directors clearly understood they were at the center of west coast transportation, and moved to join their railroad to the steamship lines that entered California—much as Aspinwall was doing in Panama and the Caribbean. After reorganizing the Central Pacific as the Southern Pacific, the railroad operators dominated shipping in, into, and out of California. Their power was widely hated, and the conglomeration despised as "The Octopus" whose many tentacles grasped and controlled all activity in the state and beyond.

By the 1870s, California was tied into a powerful transportation system that connected it directly to the eastern states, Asia, and Central and South America. The ability of this system to transport people and goods reshaped the West and the world. At the same time, it equalized costs and prices dramatically. Ironically, California itself fell into an economic depression, as prices fell from "gold state" standards to more nationally comparable levels. Yet while it brought a deep depression to the golden state, the economic adjustment was in itself a powerful sign that California was now firmly within the national economy. Previously isolated and remote, California's economy had been subjected to the high costs of imported goods and the abundance of local gold. Now firmly tied into the economic mainstream of the nation, California's wages and prices began to reflect nationwide levels.[18]

CALIFORNIA AND FEDERAL POLICIES

The California gold rush created unique technological and social problems. Ideally, these problems would have been solved with due consideration and in line with other federal policies. However, the chaos of the gold rush demanded instant solutions, and the federal government in the 1850s and 1860s was struggling to survive and define its relationship within the eastern states. Torn over ideas of popular sovereignty, states' rights, and the ultimate authority of the federal government, leaders in Washington DC faced the collapse of the Union, a Civil War, and then the problem of Reconstruction as California struggled to deal with issues related to mining, the environment, and society that had little precedence in US development.

In all these cases, miners and rushers looked to California, not the federal government, for technological expertise, including policies towards resource development. California's solutions, as we have seen, were rarely made with an eye to anything other than the immediate place and time. Later, many of these solutions became de facto national policy because they had been given such force by the California gold rush years. Even when the federal government took a more active role in policy making at the time, such as in Indian affairs, the California gold rush was a powerful example that could not be ignored. California's policies towards water use, mineral exploitation, and basic civil rights took place in this context. As a result, policies developed in direct response to the California gold rush would generate powerful precedents for national policies.

Resource Law

California's early miners quickly altered the landscape by diverting rivers and streams, casting gravel into the rivers, and felling trees for a variety of uses from building to heating. As time passed, the environmental transformation expanded. With the decrease in placer mining, hydraulic and hard rock mining emerged, creating ever greater environmental devastation. Mountains were literally washed away, and mining debris rose around the new mines. The results were increased run-off and flooding, spreading destruction to the Central Valley and the farms and ranches of Central California.[19] At the same time, the number of newcomers to the state continued to rise, though for many the trip to California was seen as a sojourn, not a permanent relocation. The booming population, in other words, had little interest in creating a sustainable society or industry, but only in getting their fortunes as quickly as possible before leaving. Efforts to control this attitude, to create a more stable society and economic order, faced a get-rich-quick-by-any-means cynicism.

Two new legal customs emerged in the California gold rush that would later have national implications: water law and mining law. American water law had before the gold rush been based on riparian rights, which essentially gave anyone with land beside a river or stream rights to use the water, but not to pollute or impede the flow of water to downstream users. The gold rush required the relocation and damming of rivers, and used the flow to wash away mining debris. Downstream users had their water polluted, interrupted, or even entirely stolen. What quickly emerged in California was a new type of water law, known as "prior appropriation." Under this system, the first settler on a stream or river had first use rights, independent of other users. Not only did this water law system facilitate mining in California, but also in other places in the West. It became a model for water use throughout the West, where water was already in shorter supply and where irrigation and damming were required to plan the use of water in a semi-arid land.

California mining law also challenged federal law regarding mineral rights. As Colonel Mason had noted in 1848, minerals on or under federal land technically belonged to the federal government. It was in the people's interest to insure that the federal government retained these rights. These lands could be leased or sold to miners or mining companies, of course, and their sale would go toward public expenditures by the government. Miners could be allowed to take a major percentage of a mineral, with the government retaining a small percentage of the "take" toward public programs. This was ancient and accepted mining practice.

> **THE KING'S FIFTH**
>
> Even early Spanish explorers and conquistadors from the 1500s onward reserved 20% of their gold and silver finds, the "king's fifth," for the home government.

California, however, faced the outbreak of the gold rush with two handicaps. First, because its mineral laws were not well developed before the rush, it was not really prepared to extend a systematic body of laws and regulation over the California mines. Second, even had such laws existed, there was really no way to enforce them in the isolated and chaotic gold fields of California. The establishment of mining law in California thus faced much the same situation as the establishment of free vs slave labor laws: a kind of "popular sovereignty" regarding mining practices and law. The powerful precedent of California's mining customs could not be easily changed once they had become widespread. US mineral rights laws thus followed the California experience, rather than shaping it.

Mineral law in essence grew out of the small camp laws of the rush. Miners were allowed to work public lands without paying for a license or even for the land itself. They were allowed to take what they found. When finished, they simply moved on. In 1872, California and then the US government finally legislated these customs into a body of formal law, which was used in other mining rushes, even eventually in non-precious mineral mining. Though more formalized and regulated, mining companies have not been required to share their finds with the original landowners, the federal government, and until recently have also had very limited responsibility for environmental cleanup. Further, this policy suggested a model for western lumber and ranching interests, demanding the nearly free use of public forest and grasslands with limited federal supervision. In its influence on western extractive industries, the California gold rush cast a long and dark shadow.

Indian Policy

If the gold rush recast the western natural environment, it also recast the human environment. The gold rush caused a significant change in American Indian policy, both in California and far beyond. Before the gold rush, Native Americans were expected to relocate to the West, to vacate lands desired by white settlers. With the purchase of the Louisiana Territory in 1803, Thomas Jefferson believed that the Great Plains could be the uninterrupted home of Native Americans for generations to come, allowing them to either gradually assimilate to American culture, or to die out. However, the conquest of California and the Southwest, and especially the press of gold rush immigrants crossing the plains, demanded a new Indian policy. There was no further west to push tribes towards, and the "Indian Territory" of the Great Plains also needed to be redefined to establish trails and future railroad lines.[20]

In the aftermath of the Mexican war, and with the rush of overland miners already growing, Congress attempted to secure safe passage across the plains by Americans to and from California. Congress called for a great intertribal conference at Fort Laramie to work out clear and permanent boundaries on the plains.[21]

The Fort Laramie Treaty of 1851 attempted to secure a right to trail use across the plains as well as define specific lands set aside for each of the Plains tribes. Intertribal warfare, it was feared, could quickly close the trail and might also involve Americans in a general Plains Indians war. The American agents scolded the natives not to make war on each other and to obey these boundaries. The Sioux, the rising power on the plains, scoffed at such lecturing. They reminded the Americans that, in taking lands from their weaker neighbors, they were doing just as the US had done against Mexico only a few years before. Furthermore, the Sioux used their power at the conference to keep their enemies away and to make separate agreements with their allies. The treaty of Fort Laramie, designed to secure American overland trails, instead secured the growing power of the Sioux. The trail itself, in other words, would soon be an arena of confrontation.[22]

The attempt to impose specific boundaries for the Plains tribes could not be easily enforced. However, within California establishing such boundaries was a humanitarian necessity. With the destruction of California's Indians,

THE PLAINS INDIAN WARS BEGIN

In 1854, only three years after the Fort Laramie Treaty, members of the Brulé band of Sioux under Conquering Bear found and butchered a stray cow along the overland trail. American officers demanded repayment, and when the Sioux refused, US soldiers attacked the Sioux village. The Sioux in response killed nearly the entire regiment of soldiers. Peace returned uneasily, but it was the first major confrontation of the Plains Indian Wars.

Ralph K. Andrist, *The Long Death: The Last Days of the Plains Indian* (New York: Collier Books, 1964), pp. 23–26.

attempts were made to "save" Native peoples from the destruction. California Indian Superintendent, Edward Fitzgerald Beale, tried creating isolated pockets of land where California Indians could live away from the mining camps. Envisioned initially as a humane reserve where Indians could live unmolested, these reservations were a new idea being tried throughout the West. Despite Beale's best efforts, the system did not work in California. Because the state government allowed whites to use native laborers in a state of peonage, California's reservations more accurately became Indian refugee camps, which whites often raided for Indian labor. They eventually rejected the system for California. Though it was largely a failure, it was a model to be applied again elsewhere.[23]

Racial Discrimination

Though California's population would remain largely white and "American," it had a far larger portion of residents from many different corners of the world. Northern California, and San Francisco in particular, was a much more cosmopolitan society than most of the rest of the nation. It also had a lasting sense of competition and isolation, born of the gold rush itself. Californians increasingly felt uneasy about the large populations within the state that were not traditionally present on the eastern states. Hispanic residents, many having been born in the state as opposed to the newly arrived miners and settlers, were increasingly seen as foreign and undesirable. Though somewhat acceptable politically in the early days of the rush, especially in Southern California, they were largely discriminated against in the gold camps, and soon also found themselves excluded from political participation in much of northern California.[24]

Even more alarming to Californians was the increasing inflow of Chinese workers and miners. From only 500 miners in 1850, annual migration from China exploded to 20,000 in 1852, and maintained a level of approximately 8,000 new immigrants each year for the next decade. The Chinese seemed especially threatening to white miners for a number of reasons. Chinese workers came to California, like their American counterparts, largely as young men and as sojourners. They came in associations—much like American miners—but unlike the American miners, these associations tended to be more cohesive and longer-lasting, partly because of the nature of the associations themselves, which provided both direct services and home connections, but also due to white racism which made it more difficult for Chinese miners to integrate into California society. Chinese dress, language, and customs struck white Californians as strange and foreign, further cementing their identity as outsiders. Worse still, Chinese miners working together seemed to succeed even where white miners had already given up. In an age of a dawning sense of Social Darwinism, the Chinese seemed more fit and successful than white miners. As competitors, they were increasingly seen as undesirable competitors who might themselves eventually overwhelm the white population.[25]

The Chinese had another gold rush related strike against them: they were imported and used by the Central Pacific Railroad to do the difficult and dangerous construction of the railroad from Sacramento to Utah. Again, the railroad was a direct product of the gold rush, and its construction by "Orientals" seemed to affirm the ability of the Chinese to thrive and succeed in an environment that white Californians believed too degrading for themselves.

Before long, the Chinese had become "the indispensable enemy," in the words of historian Alexander Saxton. In the cosmopolitan politics of San Francisco, it was hard to use nationalist or racial appeals that could tie enough voters together to carry a political party to power. However, by using the Chinese as a scapegoat, it became easier to rally San Francisco's multi-varied population around a political party.

As the railroad's power grew in California, and began to be resented by white Californians, the railroad's use and protection of its Chinese workers only furthered the open discrimination of the Chinese and calls for new legislation to counter the "yellow peril."[26] In 1879, California's new state constitution prohibited Chinese immigrants from entering the state. California thus defied the 1868 Burlingame Treaty, which had promised free immigration between the US and China.[27] By any measure, this provision in the constitution should have been illegal, as immigration law was subject to federal, not state, law.

In 1882, however, the federal government enacted its own version of the California restriction. California's political power had by this time grown too large to ignore. In the bitter clashes between the states during and immediately after reconstruction, California had played a major part in electing six presidents and had become a powerful broker in congressional legislation. Ironically, California's anti-Chinese stance—born of the gold rush—further enhanced the power of the South in creating Jim Crow laws in the late nineteenth century. Before the Civil

"THE CHINESE MUST GO!"

San Francisco politicians often found it hard to appeal for votes across all the great variety of citizens and interests in their city. The Workingman's Party, however, quickly adopted a tag line, used at the end of nearly every speech: "But whatever else happens, the Chinese Must Go!"

War, the Dred Scott decision declared that blacks could not be citizens; the 14th Amendment then declared that US citizenship could not be denied based on race—with the intention of affirming the core value of US citizenship. The Chinese exclusion act now limited Chinese from American citizenship, opening a loophole in what was supposed to be a definitive constitutional point.[28]

Anti-Chinese legislation grew directly from the gold rush experience, and affected US citizenship laws nationwide for decades to come.

★ ★ ★

The sudden rush of people into California required the state to develop a massive infrastructure overnight. As we have seen, miners and merchants constructed instant towns and cities, and assembled a complex infrastructure of trade, transportation, and communications almost overnight. They also rapidly developed advanced technological innovations in mining, and experimented in social order and political organization. The result was a powerful new state, an imperial American outpost on the Pacific coast, and a new force in American politics. Yet the challenge remained to more fully tie the far western state into the Union. Over the next few decades, by building railroads and developing steamship lines, California was fully incorporated politically and economically within the United States.

Yet at the same time, California faced new problems, especially regarding mining and resource use, for which the federal government had little experience. With the crisis of the Civil War, the very role of the federal government was in turmoil and its policies undergoing redefinition. California developed as a powerful state in the 1850s to 1870s as a result of the gold rush, and it was also left to define broad policies towards resources and social rights on its own. By 1870, when California was firmly embedded within the nation by new railroad ties, it was also a Pacific colossus that now defined mining law, water use, and social rights that would shape the nation. The United States had created a giant on the Pacific that now took its place in international affairs, and ironically, now changed and redefined many of the policies and institutions of the United States. The world had rushed into California and created it; in return, California recreated the nation and the world.

NOTES

1   Walter A. McDougall, *Let the Sea Make a Noise: Four Hundred Years of Cataclysm, Conquest, War and Folly in the North Pacific*, (New York: Avon Books, 1993), pp. 300–306.

2   McDougall, *Let the Sea*, p. 306.

3   McDougall, *Let the Sea*, pp. 412–413.

4   McDougall, *Let the Sea*, pp. 323–324.

5   McDougall, *Let the Sea*, p. 325.

6   See Douglas Fetherling, *The Gold Crusades: A Social History of Gold Rushes, 1849–1929* (Toronto: University of Toronto Press, 1997).

7   Robert V. Remini, *On the Edge of the Precipice: Henry Clay and the Compromise that Saved the Union* (New York: Basic Books, 2010), pp. 157–159.

8   Glenna Matthews, *The Golden State in the Civil War* (New York: Cambridge University Press, 2012), pp. 1, 3.

9   Melinda Lawson, *Patriot Fires: Forging a New American Nationalism in the Civil War North* (University Press of Kansas, 2002), pp. 51–57.

10   James M. McPherson and James K. Hogue, *Ordeal by Fire: The Civil War and Reconstruction*, 4th edition, (New York: McGraw-Hill, 2010), p. 403.

11   Aims McGuinness, *Path of Empire: Panama and the California Gold Rush* (Ithaca: Cornell University Press, 2008), pp. 70–71.

12   McGuinness, *Path of Empire*, pp. 42–52.

13   McGuinness, *Path of Empire*, pp. 73–77.

14   McGuinness, *Path of Empire*, pp. 77–79.

15   David Haward Bain, *Empire Express: Building the First Transcontinental Railroad* (London: Penguin Books, 1999), pp. 13–55.

16   See J. V. Frederick, *Ben Holladay: The Stagecoach King* (Lincoln: University of Nebraska Press, 1968).

17   Bain, *Empire Express*, p. 208.

18   McDougall, *Let the Sea*, p. 322.

19   Todd Holmes, "Rivers of Gold, Valley of Conquest: The Business of Levees and Dams in the Capital City," in *River City and River Life*, pp. 122–123. See Raymond F. Dasmann, *The Destruction of California* (New York: Collier Books, 1975), pp. 67, 98; Andrew C. Isenberg, *Mining California: An Ecological History* (New York: Hill and Wang, 2006).

20   Robert M. Utley, *The Indian Frontier of the American West, 1846–1890* (Albuquerque: University of New Mexico Press, 1984), p. 37; Ralph K. Andrist, *The Long Death: The Last Days of the Plains Indian* (New York: Collier Books, 1964), pp. 2–10.

21   Utley, *The Indian Frontier*, pp. 39–43; Andrist, *The Long Death*, pp. 16–17.

22   Utley, *The Indian Frontier*, p. 61; Andrist, *The Long Death*, pp. 18–20.

23   James J. Rawls, *Indians of California: The Changing Image* (Norman: University of Oklahoma Press, 1984), pp. 148–158. p. 119, 129–133.

24   Michael J. Gonzales, "'My Brother's Keeper': Mexicans and the Hunt for Prosperity in California, 1848–2000," in Owens, *Riches for All*, pp. 119, 129–133.

25   Malcolm J. Rohrbough, *Days of Gold: The California Gold Rush and the American Nation* (Berkeley: University of California Press, 1997), p. 228.

26   See Alexander Saxton, *The Indispensable Enemy: Labor and the Anti-Chinese Movement in California* (Berkeley: University of California, 1975).

27   McDougall, *Let the Sea*, p. 349.

28   McDougall, *Let the Sea*, pp. 349–351.

CHAPTER 7

Fools' Gold

The California gold rush did not begin with flakes of gold laying in a cold water stream in the Sierra Nevada. It did not begin when James Marshall and Henry Bigler first picked up those flakes, rolled them between their fingers, and gazed at them wonderingly. It began in the mind. It sparked to life in the imaginations of Marshall and Bigler and Samuel Brannan and others living in California in 1848. Then in the minds of merchants and adventurers around the Pacific Rim who heard of the news even before seeing any gold. And by 1849, those sparks had become a feverish vision that gripped hundreds of thousands worldwide.

What animated the California gold rush was the hunger for a better life, available to anyone willing to travel to California to grasp it, and thus to turn it into reality. The gold rush itself had a sense of unreality about it from the beginning, however. For many of the miners, perhaps for most of them, grasping that ambition proved elusive, even when they did succeed in collecting their bags full of dust. Gold, it turned out, was not always the answer to family stability, future happiness, or satisfied expectations. Individual and even national greatness based on embracing piles of gold in California led to industrial and social transformation, but also increased racism, promoted genocide, and contributed to a civil war. As we have seen, the reach of gold rush consequences wove itself into the fabric of American resource law and foreign policy, and encircled the globe in the experiences of individual families from Ireland to China, Australia to Chile, France to Mexico.

Gold is finite, and the amount that could be found easily in California quickly diminished. But dreams are not easily deterred by hard realities. Despite disappointment, destruction, and even death, dreams have sources in the human psyche, in longings and yearnings—not merely in gravel banks and quartz rock. The California gold rush was based not on the reality of gold but on the desire to get ahead, to gamble one's energy and efforts in pursuit of a dazzling prize. Dreams like these have the power to forget what is not glittering, to overlook the brutal truth in favor of a yearned for future. The addictiveness of the dream feeds a kind of amnesia, a reset button for unpleasant memories. As a result, the dream has endured, long after the miners and their families have turned to dust.

CALIFORNIA DREAMING

America began as a country out to make a new society in the world, a nation where everyone was created equal. It was, in many ways, a dramatic gamble in 1776, in a world filled with class and monarchic rule. By the 1840s, the French Revolution had essentially failed, and the governments of Europe were becoming more repressive. And the American economy was calcifying, and seemed to be heading towards a nearly permanent class system. Slavery and the aristocracy of the South suggested that future could emerge in America as well. Then came the gold rush. Suddenly opportunity seemed open to anyone willing to reach for it. The fact that some did find fortunes secured that dream in reality. For many others, the fortunes made on merchandising, or investments, or in developing transportation and communications systems simply furthered the idea that the gold rush could break down class restrictions by promising the possibility of social mobility.

The gold rush reinvigorated the American dream. It gave reality to the hope that social and economic rise was still possible. That it was not a reality for all was not critical. It was not the individual success that mattered but the way it gave at least some truth to the dream of the possible. The impossible dream, in other words, was sometimes possible.

From the beginning, the gold rush was proclaimed in popular culture as a grand adventure. "O California," a song popular with the miners themselves, spoke of the adventures they would have, the fortunes they would gather up, and the new status they would enjoy when they returned. Tellingly, the song was actually written in Boston, and was sung by the would-be miners *before* they ever reached California.[1] Songs and depictions of the gold rush as a grand adventure remained strong even as the realities of the rush began to dawn on many in the nation.

Yet at the same time, ministers and public leaders warned against the greed and immorality of a mad pursuit of wealth at the expense of health and family. Gold rushers were seen by many as fools—in both positive and negative senses of the word. Henry David Thoreau decried the moral obscenity of the rush. "It makes God to be a moneyed gentleman," he wrote, "who scatters a handful of pennies in order to see mankind scramble for them. Going to California. It is only three thousand miles closer to hell."[2] To many, the gold rush was a disaster propagated by fools; to others, it was a foolish romp of an adventure for young men eager to make their mark in the world. These contrasting attitudes towards the rush have never completely disappeared.

Nineteenth century writers Bret Harte and Mark Twain had a particular influence on the creation and perpetuation of the gold rush dream. Harte, a writer out to make a name for himself, traveled to California in 1854, and after being hired as editor for the *Overland Monthly* started writing short stories about the miners and the gold rush in comic terms. His most famous works were *The Luck of Roaring Camp* (1870), *The Outcasts of Poker Flats* (1869), and *The Heathen Chinee* (1870). His stories created many western fictional stereotypes, such as the western gambler, the schoolmarm, the stage driver, the prostitute with a heart of gold. As Wallace Stegner noted, his stories were neither realistic nor penetrating, but they captured American archetypal myths.[3] In his tales, Bret Harte found humor in the topsy-turvy world of class and social relations that the gold rush helped create.

Both Harte and Mark Twain tended to portray miners as innocents abroad, comically encountering a strange new world on the shores of the Pacific. Their humorous stories softened the real pain and tragedy of the gold rush, while at the same time spotlighting its quirky, social freedoms.

The Minister's Lament

Reverend James Davis at the First Congregational Church of Woonsocket, Rhode Island:

This excitement is become truly appalling, and reaching not our cities alone, but our villages and towns and shaking every family. There never has been any excitement equal to it within the remembrance of our oldest citizens—War, Pestilence, Famine, the most astonishing discoveries in the arts and sciences . . . the advancement of civilization and Christianity in the subjugation of heathen lands—all these have never filled our land and the minds of our young men with such intense excitement . . . the gold pestilence which is more terrific than the cholera, threatens to depopulate our land of those whom we had looked upon as the morning stars and bright hopes of future times.

Quoted in Malcolm J. Rohrbough, *Days of Gold: The California Gold Rush and the American Nation* (Berkeley: University of California Press, 1997), p. 30.

But Twain's characterization tended to be more complex on further examination. Mark Twain, sought to show the foolishness of the miners as both comic and tragic, as both light-hearted and darkly self-destructive. Like Mary Jane Megquier, Samuel Clemens saw in the gold rush dream not just an economic dream, but also a golden social order—or disorder—which promised its own sense of new opportunities. The gold rush, he suggested, was not merely about finding flakes, but finding and living in a new kind of social order. Perhaps significantly, it was a social order without slavery, one not tainted with the bloody stain of the Civil War, and in many ways a kind of new resting place for the dream of the American future. But for all that, it was a society that seemed to have lost its moral compass, that had substituted greed and intemperance for generosity and self-restraint. As Twain wrote in *Roughing It*,

> It was a splendid population that gave to California a name for getting up astounding enterprises and rushing them through with a magnificent dash and daring, and a recklessness of cost or consequences, which she bears unto this day—and when she projects a new surprise, the grave world smiles as usual, and says "Well, that is California all over."[4]

Mark Twain Remembers the Miners

It was a driving, vigorous, restless population in those days. It was a curious population. It was the only population of the kind that the world has ever seen gathered together, and it is not likely that the world will ever see its like again. For, observe, it was an assemblage of two hundred thousand young men—not simpering, dainty, kid-gloved weaklings, but stalwart, muscular, dauntless young braves, brim full of push and energy, and royally endowed with every attribute that goes to make up a peerless and magnificent manhood—the very pick and choice of the world's glorious ones. No women, no children, no gray and stooping veterans—none but erect, bright-eyed, quick-moving, strong-handed young giants—the strangest population, the finest population, the most gallant host that ever trooped down the startled solitudes of an unpeopled land. And where are they now? Scattered to the ends of the earth—or prematurely aged and decrepit—or shot or stabbed in street affrays—or dead of disappointed hopes and broken hearts—all gone, or nearly all—victims devoted upon the altar of the golden calf—the noblest holocaust that ever wafted its sacrificial incense heavenward. It is pitiful to think upon.

Mark Twain, *Roughing It*, (Berkeley: University of California Press, 1972), p. 370.

Of course, Twain and Harte were not alone in portraying California. Frank Norris wrote a remarkable portrait of life in late nineteenth century San Francisco in *McTeague* (1899). In this novel the title character lives in post-gold rush San Francisco, but is fatally influenced by the search for an easy, wealthy rise in California society. Perhaps Norris's most direct representation of the survival of the California Dream came in his epic *The Octopus* (1901), in which his character Magnus Derrick is described as a ruthless, exploitative rancher and politician, out to gain his own profits regardless of consequences.

> At the very bottom, when all was said and done, Magnus remained the Forty-niner. Deep down in his heart the spirit of the Adventurer yet persisted. . . . Magnus remained the gambler, willing to play for colossal stakes, to hazard a fortune on the chance of winning a million. It was the true California spirit that found expression through him. . . . When, at last, the land worn out, would refuse to yield, they would invest their money in something else; by then, they would all have made fortunes. They did not care. "After us the deluge."[5]

Like Twain, Norris did not so much celebrate the gold rush mentality as warn against its continuing destructive influence. But even Twain had seen as much, in the book that became the symbol of the late nineteenth century, *The Gilded Age* (1873). As in the case of Norris, but with more irony and humorous satire, Twain and his co-author Charles Dudley Warner point to the destructive, greedy side of the gold rush mentality that survived long after the gold rush itself had ended.

Indirectly, perhaps one of the most significant writers to keep the gold rush dream alive, while also shaping its meaning, was the historian Frederick Jackson Turner. In his famous thesis on the frontier in 1893, Turner saw the American frontier as a story of progress, from Indian trail, to fur trade, to mining camp, to ranching and farming, to city development. His thesis was enormously influential in guiding the thinking of many American historians for decades to come, as well as popular western novelists and story tellers.[6] This thesis suggested, first, that the gold rush was ultimately a story of progress, and second, that the development of cities such as San Francisco were the ultimate accomplishment of the frontier, coming *after* (not with) all the frontier effort.

Historians have long debated the merits and internal inconsistencies of Turner's thesis. But it has resulted in histories of the gold rush that seem celebratory and progressive, despite the realities of the rush, and which begin with the miners then shift to the rise of San Francisco. Such narrative hides many of the brutalities of the gold rush experience. Turner's emphasis on progress, and on the frontier as creating an "American character", also hides the multicultural and multiracial aspects of the rush. The story became one primarily of white Americans, and less about Hispanic and Asian and other outside cultures. His portrayal of Indians in America generally as merely a backdrop to white America's advance also made it easier to sweep the near genocide of California's Indians out of the story tellers' consciousness.[7]

Attitudes about the California gold rush also became entwined with attitudes towards California itself. How could it not? California was a creation of the gold rush, and embraces that heritage on the state seal. Since the gold rush, Americans have approached their memory of this event with a mixture of amnesia and addiction—amnesia as to the rush's ultimate costs, as well as addiction to the idea of a golden dream and easy, fated progress. Perhaps these are two sides of the same coin, after all. The twentieth century rise of the Southern California oil and real estate speculation, and the motion picture industry in Hollywood, not only showed California as a land of eternal sunshine, but also spurred a new migration of "gold seekers," who hoped to make it big in California as movie actors and actresses. The rise of conspicuous consumption in Southern California only further enhanced the notion of California as a golden state.

The mixed message of the gold rush fool gained a new life in the Great Depression, when thousands of dust bowl refugees headed for the golden land of California, seeking a new life. The Great Depression of the 1930s set off a new migration to California, of "dust bowl refugees," who packed

John Steinbeck's "California Dream"

And at last the owner men came to the point. The tenant system won't work any more. One man on a tractor can take the place of twelve or fourteen families. Pay him a wage and take all the crop. We have to do it. We don't like to do it. . . .

But if we go, where'll we go? How'll we go? We got no money.

We're sorry, said the owner men. The bank, the fifty-thousand-acre owner can't be responsible. You're on land that isn't yours. Once over the line maybe you can pick cotton in the fall. Maybe you can go on relief. Why don't you go on west to California? There's work there, and it never gets cold. Why, you can reach out anywhere and pick an orange. Why, there's always some kind of crop to work in. Why don't you go there? And the owner men started their cars and rolled away.

John Steinbeck, *The Grapes of Wrath* (New York: Penguin, 1996), pp. 38–40.

themselves in overloaded automotives and headed to California on the "Mother Road," Route 66, drawn by the image of a golden life in California. The realities of the earlier search for California gold might have been brought back to memory by the Great Depression. Indeed, John Steinbeck's *The Grapes of Wrath* chronicled ironic parallels between the dust bowl refugees and the journey and experiences of the original forty-niners. Steinbeck's Joad family still sees California initially as the golden land, a motif originally set up during the gold rush. But Steinbeck shows that the golden vision of a California paradise hides a hard and brutal life in "paradise." And, like Twain, Steinbeck tried to encompass both the adventurousness as well as the brutal consequences of that move.

World War II had a powerful influence on our public memory of the gold rush. As one historian has noted, it produced the second California gold rush. Hundreds of thousands of soldiers and workers came to California to work in defense plants or to be processed to the Pacific front. With the end of the Depression, the California Dream seemed suddenly recharged. A booming economy and a paradisiacal climate produced many of the same reactions in these young men as the miners had faced in the 1850s.[8] Coming near the hundredth anniversary of the gold rush, California seemed to be fulfilling its old role again.

By the time of the gold rush centennial, in 1949, the image of the California gold rush was largely one of hope, excitement, humorous social arrangements, and ultimate progress. California had already designated the state highway which ran the length of the gold fields "Highway 49," and towns erected markers and renovated old mining camp buildings and artifacts to drum up profits from tourism.[9] Professional historians such as Rodman Paul and John Walton Caughey took a fresh look at the gold rush, noting that gold was the "cornerstone" of the state's development, its foundational event.[10]

Yet, at the same time, attitudes towards the gold rush were undergoing a shift. By the time of the centennial, San Francisco had recently hosted the formation of the United Nations. The United States sought to lead the world in a fight against communism, and a civil rights movement was beginning to stir. The Chinese Exclusion Act had finally been suspended in World War II, as China was an important US ally in that struggle. As a leader of the international community, the California gold rush now could be portrayed popularly as an example of international participation. Thus, when the musical play *Paint Your Wagon* premiered (based in part on a Bret Harte short story, "Tennessee's Partner"), though it joyously proclaimed the humorous and progressive vision of the rush then prevalent, it also included the cosmopolitan nature of the rush—but suggested a peaceful interaction, under American leadership.

Eventually produced both for the stage and on film, *Paint Your Wagon* showed a cosmopolitan mining population, but downplayed any serious ethnic discrimination. Various ethnic groups, such as the Chinese or the Irish, were portrayed in broad stereotypes for light comic effect, never truly disrupting the sense of community that loosely bound the community of fools who create and then destroy the mythical mining camp "No Name City." Yet when the dust settles, the characters move on, singing about being born under a wandering star, and ignore the environmental and social destruction left behind.

The racial reality of the 1950s, however, was far different. The civil rights movement undermined the progressive, cosmopolitan message of the rush as daily headlines proclaimed the continuing problem of deep-seated American racism. The 1950s and 1960s were also the anniversary of the Civil War, and historians understandably sought to find the sources of this problem by turning to the issues of slavery, racism, and states' rights. The gold rush seemed merely a comic sideline, with no direct role in that greater story—and so it was relegated to the side. By not taking the gold rush seriously as a serious event, by treating it merely as a comic interlude, Americans have perpetuated their own amnesia—and their addiction to the idea of easy progress.

Yet if World War II and its Cold War aftermath helped push a benign popular image of the rush, it also produced the GI Bill, which would ultimately send a new generation to college, many of them the first college educated members of their families. At the same time, Federal investments in the military industrial complex would boost the growth of educational institutions, especially the University of California system. Many of these new college students would challenge the traditional image of a white-only history, and of the progressive, benign image of the gold rush. The New Western History of the 1980s especially produced a school of investigators who sought to bring the darker side of the gold rush back into the story. Many of these historians pursued a new array of questions about the gold rush, and uncovered a more gritty and realistic, and less progressive and celebratory, story. While acknowledging the powerful economic and political significance of the rush on the state, these also acknowledged the darker human and environmental costs of the rush.[11]

THE FOOLS' JOURNEY

Ultimately, the California gold rush still remains a critical part of the American culture. It is embodied both in the California State Seal, and also in logos and advertising. The San Francisco Forty-Niners and the

Golden State Warriors keep gold rush symbolism alive. Casinos and lottery games use the imagery and symbolism of the California gold rush to draw in contemporary gamblers by reminding them of the gold fever of 1849. The rise of Silicon Valley and the wealth created in California by software companies making astounding fortunes with IPOs are inevitably referred to as new gold rushes. But the gold rush comparison represents more than simply making a financial fortune. It also suggests the greed and the "after us, the deluge" spirit that had always been a part of the gold rush dream and nightmare.

Figure 7.1 The California State Seal. The state seal portrays a miner at work in the foreground, with gold rush ships in the bay in the background. The state's motto, "Eureka!" meaning *I have found it*, is proclaimed in the sky above. The gold rush experience still casts a powerful influence over the "golden state."

If the two sides of the gold rush fool continue to survive in American history and literature, it is because they touch on a very real human dilemma: What is the proper balance of ambition and morality in American society? Wealth in a capitalistic democracy brings power, and upsets the social and political order. In a society that demands social mobility, wealth is one of the lubricants of the social machine. Like the fool in William Shakespeare's *King Lear*, the gold rush fool clowns and apes the ways of his "betters," but also dares to speak truth to power, to challenge the order of the social hierarchy by ignoring it. When King Lear upsets the social and economic order of his kingdom by giving away his lands and titles, his fool mocks him. "I am better than thou art now; I am a fool, thou art nothing," the Fool tells King Lear.[12] The California gold rush remains a symbolic reminder of one of the most important aspects of the American character: the possibility that America is truly a classless society, or at least, that any American can rise to a higher class in America. Mark Hopkins celebrated this sentiment in the gold rush. In more recent years, the attitude was perhaps best captured in the words of Gordon Gekko in the 1987 film *Wall Street*, "Greed is good."

There is an addictive quality to this belief. No matter how often it does not work out, the dream itself remains. Psychologists note that addicted gamblers have a preoccupation with gambling, that they gamble to escape their problems, that they return to gambling even after losing money, and that they pursue it at the risk of family relationships. Certainly this behavior describes the tragic character of Samuel Nichols. But it seems to also have resonance with all the gold rushers, and with the continuing American fascination with both gambling and the symbolic role of the gold rush in American culture. American culture remains hooked on the get-rich-quick vision of the gold rush. The shine of the vision often makes it hard to tell whether it is a reflection of American progress, or American self-delusion.

★   ★   ★

The gold rush promised to break all the hierarchies of American class in the 1850s, dethroning a rigid social order through access to economic means to social mobility. That aspect of the American gamble, begun in the Declaration of Independence, was reinvigorated and immortalized by the gold rush. It remains as powerful today as then. The California gold rush, after all, was not only a foundation of the California Dream, but was and remains a critical element of the American mind.

NOTES

1   Richard A. Dwyer and Richard E. Lingenfelter, *Songs of the Gold Rush* (Berkeley: University of California Press, 1964), pp. 17–18.

2   Tom Cole, *A Short History of San Francisco* (Berkeley: Heyday Books, 2014), p. 37.

3   Wallace Stegner, "Introduction," in Bret Harte, *The Outcasts of Poker Flat and Other Tales* (New York: Signet, 1961), pp. vii–xvi.

4   Mark Twain, *Roughing It* (Berkeley: University of California Press, 1972), p. 405.

5   Frank Norris, *The Octopus* (New York: Penguin Classics, 1986), pp. 298–299.

6   Frederick Jackson Turner, "The Significance of the Frontier in American History," in *Annual Report of the American Historical Association for the Year 1893* (Washington, DC: GPO and American Historical Association, 1894) pp. 199–227.

7   See Wilbur Jacobs, *On Turner's Trail: 100 Years of Writing Western History* (Lawrence: University of Kansas, 1994).

8   See Gerald D. Nash, *The American West Transformed: The Impact of the Second World War* (Lincoln: University of Nebraska Press, 1985); Marilynn S. Johnson, *The Second Gold Rush: Oakland and the East Bay in World War II* (Berkeley: University of California Press, 1994).

9   For a humorous look at the machinations of one gold rush town trying to come up with a gold rush tourist attraction, see Curt Gentry, *The Last Days of the Late, Great State of California* (Berkeley: Comstock Editions, 1968), pp. 53–77.

10 See, for example, John Walton Caughey, *Gold is the Cornerstone* (Berkeley: University of California Press, 1948).

11 See, for example, Patricia Nelson Limerick, Clyde A. Milner, and Charles E. Rankin, eds., *Trails: Toward a New Western* History (Lawrence: University of Kansas Press, 1991).

12 William Shakespeare, *King Lear*, Act 1, Scene 4.

Documents

DOCUMENT 1

Col. Richard B. Mason's Report, August, 1848

*C*olonel Richard Mason, in charge of the American military forces in California
after the Mexican War (1846–1848), was the first American official to
investigate and report on the early gold discoveries to the US government. His
report was documented with maps and gold samples, and would later be the basis
of President Polk's announcement in December, 1848, usually credited with starting
the gold rush. Mason's report not only accurately reported conditions in the gold
fields, but also warned of the problems that would plague the region for years to
come.

HEADQUARTERS TENTH MILITARY DEPARTMENT, MONTEREY, CALIFORNIA, AUGUST 17, 1848

Sir: I have the honor to inform you that, accompanied by Lieutenant W.
T. Sherman, 3rd artillery, acting assistant adjutant general, I started on the
12th of June last to make a tour through the northern part of California.
My principle purpose, however, was to visit the newly-discovered gold
placer in the valley of the Sacramento. . . .

We reached San Francisco on the 20th, and found that all, or nearly
all, its male population had gone to the mines. The town, which a few
months before was so busy and thriving, was then almost deserted. On
the evening of the 24th, the horses of the escort were crossed to Sausalito
in a launch, and on the following day we resumed the journey, by way
of Bodega and Sonoma, to Sutter's Fort, where we arrived on the morning
of the 2d of July. Along the whole route mills were lying idle, fields of
wheat were open to cattle and horses, houses vacant, and farming going
to waste. At Sutter's there was more life and business. Launches were

discharging their cargoes at the river, and carts were hauling goods to the fort, where already were established several stores, a hotel, &c. Captain Sutter had only two mechanics in his employ—a wagon-maker and blacksmith—whom he was paying ten dollars per day. Merchants pay him a monthly rent of one hundred dollars per room, and whilst I was there a two-story house in the fort was rented as a hotel for five hundred dollars a month.

... on the 5th [of July we] resumed the journey and proceeded twenty-five miles up the American Fork, to a point on it now known as the lower mines, or Mormon diggings. The hill sides were thickly strewn with canvas tents and bush arbors. A store was erected, and several boarding shanties in operation. The day was intensely hot; yet about two hundred men were at work in the full glare of the sun, washing for gold, some with tin pans, some with close-woven Indian baskets, but the greater part had a rude machine known as the cradle. This is on rockers six or eight feet long, open at the foot, and at its head has a coarse grate and sieve; the bottom is rounded, with small cleets nailed across. Four men are required to work this machine; one digs the gravel in the bank close by the stream, another carries it to the cradle and empties it on the grate, a third gives a violent rocking motion to the machine, whilst a fourth dashes water on from the stream itself. The sieve keeps the coarse stones from entering the cradle, the current of water washes off the earthy matter, and the gravel is gradually carried out at the foot of the machine, leaving the gold mixed with a fine heavy black sand above the first cleets. The sand and gold, mixed together, are then drawn off through auger holes into a pan below, are dried in the sun, and afterwards separated by blowing off the sand. A party of four men thus employed at the lower mines averaged a hundred dollars a day. The Indians, and those who have nothing but pans or willow baskets, gradually wash out the earth and separate the gravel by hand, leaving nothing but the gold mixed with sand, which is separated in the manner before described. The gold in the lower mines is in fine bright scales, of which I send several specimens.

As we ascended the south branch of the American Fork, the country became more broken and mountainous, and at the sawmill, twenty-five miles above the lower washings, or fifty miles from Sutter's, the hills rise to about a thousand feet above the level of the Sacramento plain. Here a species of pine occurs, which led to the discovery of the gold. Captain Sutter, feeling the great want of lumber, contracted, in September last, with a Mr. Marshall, to build a saw-mill at that place. It was erected in the course of the past winter and spring—a dam and race constructed; but when the water was let on the wheel, the tail race was found to be too narrow to permit the water to escape with sufficient rapidity. Mr. Marshall, to save labor, let the water directly into the race, with a strong current, so as to wash it wider and deeper. He effected his purpose, and a large bed of mud and gravel was carried to the foot of the race. One day Mr. Marshall, when walking down the race to this deposit of mud, observed some glittering particles at its upper edge: he gathered a few, examined them, and became satisfied of their value. He then went to the fort, told Captain Sutter of his discovery, and they agreed to keep it secret until a certain grist-mill of Sutter's was finished. It however got out, and spread like magic. Remarkable success attended the labors of the first explorers, and in a few weeks hundreds of men were drawn thither. At the time of my visit, but little more than three months after its first discovery, it was estimated that upwards of four thousand people were employed. At the mill there is a fine deposit, or bank of gravel, which the people respect as the property of Captain Sutter, although he pretends to no right to it, and would be perfectly satisfied with the simple promise of a pre-emption, on account of the mill which he has built there, at considerable cost. Mr. Marshall was living near the mill, and informed me that many persons were employed above and below him, that they used the same machines as at the lower washings, and that their success was about the same, ranging from one to three ounces of gold per man daily. This gold too is in scales, a little coarser than those of the lower mines. From the mills Mr. Marshall guided me up the mountain, on the opposite or north bank of the South Fork, where, in the beds of small streams, or ravines, now dry, a great deal of the coarse gold has been found. I there saw several parties at work, all of whom were doing very well. A great many specimens were shown me, some as heavy as four or five ounces in weight; and I send you three pieces, labeled No. 5, presented by a Mr. Spence. You will perceive that some of the specimens accompanying this hold, mechanically, pieces of quartz, that the surface is smooth, and evidently moulded in the crevice of a rock. This gold cannot have been carried far by water, but must have remained near where it was deposited from the rock that once bound it. I inquired of many people if they had encountered the metal in its matrix, but in every instance they said they had not, but that the gold was invariably mixed with washed gravel, or lodged in the crevices of other rocks. All bore testimony that they had found gold in greater or lesser quantities in the numerous small gullies or ravines that occur in that mountainous region. On the 7th of July I left the mill and crossed to a small stream emptying into the American Fork, three or four miles below the sawmill. I struck this stream (now known as Weber's creek) at the washings of Sunal & Co. They had about thirty Indians employed, whom they pay in merchandise. They were getting gold of a character similar to that found in the main fork, and doubtless in sufficient quantities to satisfy them.

I send you a small specimen, presented by this company, of their gold. From this point we proceeded up the stream about eight miles, where we found a great many people and Indians; some engaged in the bed of the stream, and others in the small side valleys that put into it. These later are exceedingly rich, and two ounces were considered an ordinary yield for a day's work. A small gutter, not more than a hundred yards long by four feet wide and two or three feet deep, was pointed out to me as the one where two men, William Daly and Perry McCoon, had, a short time before, obtained in seven days $17,000 worth of gold.

Captain Weber informs me that he knew that these men had employed four white men and about a hundred Indians, and that, at the end of one week's work, they paid off their party and left with $10,000 worth of this gold. Another small ravine was shown me, from which had been taken $12,000 worth of gold. Hundreds of similar ravines, to all appearances, are as yet untouched. I could not have credited these reports had I not seen, in the abundance of the precious metal, evidence of their truth. Mr. Neligh, an agent of Commodore Stockton, had been at work about three weeks in the neighborhood, and showed me, in bags and bottles, over $2,000 worth of gold; and Mr. Lyman, a gentleman of education and worthy of every credit, said he had been engaged, with four others, with a machine, on the American Fork, just below Sutter's saw-mill, that they worked eight days, and that his share was at the rate of fifty dollars a day; but, hearing that others were doing better at Weber's place, they had removed there, and were on the point of resuming operations.

I might tell of hundreds of similar instances; but to illustrate how plentiful the gold was in the pockets of common laborers, I will mention a simple occurrence which took place in my presence when I was at Weber's store. This store was nothing but an arbor of bushes, under which he had exposed for sale goods and groceries suited to his customers. A man came in, picked up a box of seidlitz powders, and asked its price. Captain Weber told him it was not for sale. The man offered an ounce of gold, but Captain Weber told him it only cost fifty cents, and he did not wish to sell it. The man then offered an ounce and a half, when Captain Weber *had* to take it. The prices of all things are high; and yet Indians, who before hardly knew what a breech-cloth was, can now afford to buy the most gaudy dresses.

The country, on either side of Weber's creek, is much broken up by hills, and is intersected in every direction by small streams or ravines, which contain more or less gold. Those that have been worked are barely scratched, and, although thousands of ounces have been carried away, I do not consider that a serious impression has been made upon the whole. Every day was developing new and rich deposits, and the only apprehension seemed to be that the metal would be found in such abundance as seriously to depreciate in value. . . .

Mr. Sinclair, whose rancho is three miles above Sutter's, on the north side of the American, employs about fifty Indians on the North Fork, not far from its junction with the main stream. He had been engaged about five weeks when I saw him, and up to that time his Indians had used simply closely-woven willow baskets. His net proceeds (which I saw) were about $16,000 worth of gold. He showed me the proceeds of his last week's work—fourteen pounds avoirdupois of clean washed gold.

The principal store at Sutter's Fort, that of Brannan & Co., had received in payment for goods $36,000 worth of this gold from the 1st of May to the 10th of July; other merchants had also made extensive sales. Large quantities of goods were daily sent forward to the mines, as the Indians, heretofore so poor and degraded, have suddenly become consumers of the luxuries of life. I before mentioned that the greater part of the farmers and rancheros had abandoned their fields to go to the mines; this is not the case with Captain Sutter, who was carefully gathering his wheat, estimated at 40,000 bushels. Flour is already worth at Sutter's $36 a barrel, and soon will be fifty. Unless large quantities of breadstuffs reach the country, much suffering will occur; but as each man is now able to pay a large price, it is believed the merchants will bring from Chili and Oregon a plentiful supply for the coming winter.

The most moderate estimate I could obtain from men acquainted with the subject was, that upwards of four thousand men were working in the gold district, of whom more than half were Indians, and that $30,000 to $50,000 worth of gold, if not more, was daily obtained. The entire gold district, with very few exceptions of grants made some years ago by the American authorities, is on land belonging to the United States. It was a matter of serious reflection with me how I could secure to the government certain rents or fees for the privilege of procuring this gold; but upon considering the large extent of country, the character of the people engaged, and the small scattered force at my command, I resolved not to interfere, but permit all to work freely, unless broils and crimes should call for interference. I was surprised to learn that crime of any kind was very infrequent, and that no thefts or robberies had been committed in the gold district. All live in tents, in bush houses, or in the open air, and men have frequently about their persons thousands of dollars' worth of this gold; and it was to me a matter of surprise that so peaceful and quiet a state of things should continue to exist. Conflicting claims to particular spots of ground may cause collisions, but they will be rare, as the extent of country is so great, and the gold so abundant, that for the present there is room and enough for all; still the government is entitled to rents for this land, and immediate steps should be devised to collect them, for the longer it is delayed the more difficult it will become. One plan I would suggest is to send out from the United States surveyors, with high salaries, bound to serve specified periods; a superintendent to be appointed at Sutter's Fort, with power to grant licenses to work a spot of ground, say 100 yards square, for one year, at a rent of from $100 to $1,000, at his discretion; the surveyors to measure the grounds and place the renter in possession. A better plan, however, will be to have the district surveyed and sold at public auction to the highest bidder, in small parcels, say from 20 to 40 acres. In either case there will be many intruders, whom for years it will be almost impossible to exclude.

The discovery of these vast deposits of gold has entirely changed the character of Upper California. Its people, before engaged in cultivating their small patches of ground and guarding their herds of cattle and horses, have all gone to the mines, or are on their way thither; laborers of every trade have left their work benches, and tradesmen their shops; sailors desert their ships as fast as they arrive on the coast, and several vessels have gone to sea with hardly enough hands to spread a sail; two or three are now at anchor in San Francisco with no crews on board. Many desertions, too, have taken place from the garrisons within the influence of the mines; 26 soldiers have deserted from the post of Sonoma, 24 from that of San Francisco, and 24 from Monterey. For a few days the evil appeared so threatening that great danger existed that the garrisons would leave in a body; and I refer you to my orders of the 25th of July to show the steps adopted to meet this contingency. I shall spare no exertions to apprehend and punish deserters; but I believe no time in the history of our country has presented such temptations to desert as now exist in California. The danger of apprehension is small, and the prospect of higher wages certain; pay and bounties are trifles, as laboring men at the mines can now earn in *one day* more than double a soldier's pay and allowances for a month, and even the pay of a lieutenant or captain cannot hire a servant. A carpenter or mechanic would not listen to an offer of less than fifteen or twenty dollars a day. Could any combination of affairs try a man's fidelity more than this? And I really think some extraordinary mark of favor should be given those soldiers who remain faithful to their flag throughout this tempting crisis. No officer can now live in California on his pay. Money has so little value, the prices of necessary articles of clothing and subsistence are so exorbitant, and labor so high, that to hire a cook or servant has become an impossibility, save to those who are earning from thirty to fifty dollars a day. This state of things cannot last forever; yet, from the geographical position of California, and the new character it has assumed as a mining country, prices of labor will always be high, and will hold out temptations to desert. I therefore have to report, if the government wish to prevent desertions here on the part of their men, and to secure zeal on the part of the officers, their pay must be increased very materially. Soldiers both of the volunteer and regular service discharged in this country should be permitted at once to locate their land warrants in the gold district. Many private letters have gone to the United States giving accounts of the vast quantity of gold recently discovered, and it may be a matter of surprise why I have made no report of this subject at an earlier date. The reason is, that I could not bring myself to believe the reports that I heard of the wealth of the gold district until I had visited it myself. I have no hesitation now is saying that there is more gold in the country drained by the Sacramento and San Joaquin rivers than will pay the cost of the present war with Mexico, a hundred times over. No capital is required to obtain this gold, as the laboring man wants nothing but his pick, shovel, and tin pan, with which to dig and wash the gravel; and many frequently pick gold out of the crevices of rock with their butcher knives in pieces from one to six ounces. . . .

The placer gold is now substituted as currency of this country: in trade it passes freely at $16 an ounce; as an article of commerce its value is not yet fixed. . . .

I would recommend that a mint be established at some eligible point on the bay of San Francisco, and that machinery, and all the apparatus and workmen, be sent by sea. These workmen must be bound by high wages, and even bonds, to secure their faithful services; else the whole plan may be frustrated by their going to the mines as soon as they arrive in California. If this course be not adopted, gold to the amount of many millions of dollars will pass yearly to other countries, to enrich their merchants and capitalists. . . .

I have the honor to be your obedient servant,

R. B. Mason
Colonel 1st Dragoons, commanding

Source: Colonel Richard B. Mason, *Report*, Monterey, California, August 17, 1848. 31st Congress, 1st session, House Executive Document 17, January 24, 1850, pp. 528–536.

Franklin Buck Argues for Going to the Gold Rush

Franklin Buck struggled to resist the call of the gold rush, but quickly decided to join the adventure. His letters to his sister reveal not only his inner thoughts about going to California, but also suggest his attempt to convince his family to support his decision.

DECEMBER 2, 1848

Have you read the account from there about the Gold? There is no *humbug* about it. I have seen letters from Captains whom I know, who write that their men have all run away and are digging up $20 a day, PURE GOLD, for some of it has been sent home. It has created a real fever here. Two steamships sailed yesterday and there are five vessels advertised for California. Several young men of my acquaintance are going out and you need not be at all surprised to hear of my going. I shall not go unless I can get some chance in trade to fall back on, but if I only had about $1000 to invest in goods, wouldn't I sail! (Oh, Poverty, thou art a crime!) But I shall wait my time.

DECEMBER 17 1848

When I took your letter out of the Post Office this morning I said to myself, "Now here comes a blast from Mary!" for from what Father wrote, I thought I had thrown you all into fits, but I am rejoiced to see from your letter that you think in some measure as I do. When I heard the accounts from the gold region I thought, at first, it was all *humbug*, gotten up to induce people to emigrate. But now I am fully convinced and the most slow to believe are also. I have seen letters from the son of Secretary Macey to a friend in the city. A. G. has received letters from his agent. Uncle Richard has had letters from Captains he sent out and also from two young men who took out goods last Spring. These young men have made $40,000 and one of them is coming home with it. A. G.'s agent, Bob Parker, (you know him) writes that he has sold out his goods at an enormous profit. He kept one man constantly weighing gold dust and he has $100,000 on hand and was going down to Mazatlan to exchange it for coin. Young Macey writes that he did not believe it at San Francisco and went up to the mines to see for himself. He saw them washing out the gold in tin pans and digging it up with sheath knives. One man got $4,000 in one day, but the most of them about $50 to $100 per day. This is hard to believe but all the letters and accounts go to prove that the half has not been told us. Great quantities have been sent here to the banks and Mint. I have *seen* some of it *myself*, in little scales and grains, pure as our gold coin.

But there is another proof, yet. Look out on the docks and you will see from twenty to thirty ships loading with all kinds of merchandise and filling up with passengers, and when I see business firms—rich men— going into it, men who know how to make money too, and young men of my acquaintance leaving good situations and fitting themselves out with arms and ammunition, tents, provisions and mining implements, there is something about it—the excitement, the crossing the Isthmus, seeing new countries and the prospect of making a fortune in a few years—that takes hold of my imagination, that tells me "Now is your chance. Strike while the iron is hot!"

You know that I am in the prime of life—a good constitution, know how to shovel, can live in a log house or a tent, and build one too. You know that I always had a desire to travel, to see something of the world. Now, when shall I ever have a better chance? I can hardly make a living here. We have no capital to carry on business with and it will be a long time before we can get a start. Labor is *capital* out there. I am assured by persons that have lived there that it is a fine country, perfectly healthy and room enough for us all.

I have looked at the subject in all its bearings. I have looked at my chance here and I have made up my mind to go and I am going if I have to go out as a common sailor. It has taken nearly every cent I have made here to pay my expenses as I go along so I have but very little money on hand. Uncle Richard has very kindly given me one hundred dollars and intends to send us a consignment of goods. There are five of us going out together. John Benson goes on Saturday to look after their business. We have paid our passage in the Steam Ship Panama, which sails from Panama on the Pacific, the 15th of February, for San Francisco. We go from here to Chagres in a sailing vessel and cross the land to Panama.

Now, my dear sister, much as I regret leaving you and my parents for so long a time, still I think it is the best thing I can do. I thought you would approve of it and believe me I feel greatly obliged to you for your good intentions. I wish I could see and embrace you once more but there is not time for me to come home. Don't look on the dark side—that's my philosophy—but think of those $4,000 *lumps* that I am going to pick up and remit to you.

Harriett Pond is full of it. Her brother is one of our party and she thinks about going herself.

Captain Cole is in the office now. Says "Tell Mary I am going with my vessel."

It is time for me to go to supper and I must stop. The weather is beautiful and warm. The cholera is still killing them off at Staten Island and there has been one case in the city but, as you suppose, we think nothing of it. The California fever has actually frightened it off.

Source: Katherine A. White, ed. *A Yankee Trader in the Gold Rush, the Letters of Franklin A. Buck.* (Boston: Houghton Mifflin and Company, 1930), pp. 25–29.

Two Early Songs from the California Gold Rush

*M*usic *during the mid-nineteenth century was a participatory activity. The popular songs of the gold rush were usually written by and sung by the miners themselves, who found the lyrics to be both humorous and revealing of their experiences. The following two songs were written during the rush to California. The first, by J. Nichols, was written before the hopeful miners had reached California, and reflects their hopes and dreams. The second song, written by the captain of one of the ships that took miners to California, illustrates the transition from men who had formed associations and mining companies to individualistic miners, out for their own fortunes once the ships actually arrived.*

OH, CALIFORNIA

Air: Oh! Susanna

By J. Nichols, composed November, 1848, while aboard the bark *Eliza* on the way to California

> I came from Salem City, with my washboard on my knee,
> I'm going to California, the gold dust for to see,
> It rained all night the day I left, the weather it was dry
> The sun so hot I froze to death, oh, brothers don't you cry.
> Oh, California, that's the land for me!
> I'm bound for San Francisco with my washbowl on my knee.
>
> I jumped aboard the 'Liza ship and traveled on the sea
> And every time I thought of home I wished it wasn't me!
> The vessel reared like any horse that had of oats a wealth:
> I found it wouldn't throw me, so I thought I'd throw myself!

I thought of all the pleasant times we've had together here
I thought I ought to cry a bit, but couldn't find a tear.
The pilot's bread was in my mouth, the gold dust in my eye,
And though I'm going far away, dear brothers don't you cry!

I soon shall be in Frisco, And there I'll look around,
And when I see the Gold lumps there I'll pick them off the ground.
I'll scrape the mountains clean, my boys, I'll drain the rivers dry,
A pocketful of rocks bring home—so brothers don't you cry!

ARRIVAL OF THE SAN FRANCISCO

Air: The Washing Day

By Captain Isaac W. Baker, member of the Beverly Joint Stock San Francisco Company, which set sail aboard the bark *San Francisco* for California, composed in August, 1849.

The San Francisco Company, of which I've often told,
At Sacramento has arrived in search of glittering gold.
The bark hauled in, the cargo out and that is not the worst,
The Company like all the rest, has had a talk and burst.
    For 'twas talk, talk, talk, growl, growl, talk, talk away,
    The devil a bit of comfort's here in Californi-a.

While on the passage all was well and everything was nice,
And if there was a civil growl, 'twas settled in a trice.
But here example has been set by Companies before,
Who'd all dissolved and nothing less, so we did nothing more.
    But talk, talk, etc.

We'd forty men of forty minds, instead of one alone,
And each wished to convert the rest but still preferred his own.
Now in some places this might do, but here it won't, you see,
For independence is the word in Californi-e.
    And you may talk, talk, etc.

At first the price of lumber fell, which made it bad for us,
Some wished to sell and some did not, which made the matter
    worse,
Some longed to start to the mines and let the barkey stay,
While others said it wouldn't do for all to go away.
    For 'twas talk, talk, etc.

Some longed to get their ounce a day, while others knew they
   couldn't,
And wished to share and keep all square, but then the workers
   wouldn't.
A meeting of the whole was called, the question put and tried,
Our constitution voted down, our by-laws null and void.
   For 'twas talk, talk, etc.

Now carpenters can take a job and work for what they please,
And those who do not like to work can loaf and take their ease,
And squads can form for traveling or any thing they chose,
And if they don't a fortune make, they'll not have it to lose,
   And can chat, chat, sing, sing, chat, chat away,
   And take all comfort that they can in Californi-a.

Now whether it's good or bad, since time alone can show,
The deed is done with our consent and that at least we know,
So let us all contented be and do the best we can,
And may a fortune be in store for every honest man.
   Chat, chat, sing, sing, chat, chat away.
   And leave for home whene'er he likes from Californi-a.

Source: J. Nichols, "Oh, California," and Captain Isaac Baker, "Arrival of the San Francisco," in Richard A. Dwyer, and Richard E. Lingenfelter, eds. *The Songs of the Gold Rush* (Berkeley: University of California Press, 1964), pp. 17, 20.

Mark Hopkins Assesses California

Mark Hopkins set out for California in 1849 with his brother and cousin, and promised to keep his remaining brother Moses informed of his progress, and advise him on whether he should join them in California. Hopkins wrote regular letters while at sea and mailed them at ports of call. Once he arrived in California he assessed the situation and set out for the gold fields. It took him a full year before he wrote home again. By that time, his plans had changed considerably. Hopkins would quickly realize that he could make more money mining the miners than in digging for his gold. He would later turn his business sense into an astounding fortune, as one of the founding partners of the Central Pacific Railroad.

CAMP IN PLEASANT VALLEY NEAR SAN FRANCISCO CALIFORNIA, AUGUST 30, 1849

Brother Moses,

I arrived here at this far-famed San Francisco on the 6th August inst & was much pleased to find your letters (three sheets) from the 11th March to 25th May inclusive. Their contents and detailed items of news were very interesting. I hope you will find time to continue them. . . .

We have not been idle since we arrived, now nearly four weeks. We anchored Sunday & Monday pitched our tents in a valley, looking out upon the bay just above the town. We then commenced receiving our goods which is no small labor on the beach where there are no docks. Our board roofed house which cost us, freight & all, delivered here $300. We sold and agreed to put it up for $2250. We were six days putting it up. On the arrival of the last steamer our boat with a party of four got

51$in the afternoon landing passengers and their luggage. Augustus last week took a horse and cash to keep & work until he had broke the horse to the harness and to draw. He earned in hard coin over and above all expenses in six days $101. I mention these items to show you that we have not been idle. I as one of the business committee have been too much engaged to make much money except in landing and disposing of our company property. I did however make $34.50 on a little lot of flour. Living however is very high here board and lodging is worth from $3 to $5 a day, washing $5 to $7 per doz, Eggs $6 a dozen, Potatoes 3 dc per pound. Still where we live in camp it is comparatively cheap. I have seen good flour sold at $8 pr Bbl, good salt miss beef for $9 & prime pork for $8 and many kinds are thus forced off at auction at serious prices. Labor is high. Common laborers $6 to $8 a day, and sort of Carpenter $10 to $12 & to the mechanics in proportion. Rents are enormous. A building 15 by 25 will rent from $400 to $600 a month, payable always in advance & not half houses enough at that. Lumber's worth $400 pr thousand feet. It costs $26 a ton to lighter goods from the ship to the beach. These captains who like the Pacific were not sharp enough to have their bills of lading read "deliverable at the ships side" will have to pay a good part of their freight money to get their cargo discharged & landed. This is the case with the ship Pacific. How I pity him.

I can't tell yet much better than you how much gold is to be found, but I believe if a man will submit to this hard life and the privations of this country and will work hard he can find gold here. He certainly can't live long in idleness here without a plenty of gold. I expect to go to the mines next week & when next I write perhaps I can tell you more about the diggings. I think many men will get plenty of gold & many will be disappointed & go back without it. I can't tell yet which party I belong to.

SACRAMENTO CITY, AUGUST 29, 1850

Thousands of emigrants are now arriving by sea and land. On their arrival many are confused and know not how to make their time and energies available. Hundreds seek employ at moderate wages rather than rely on themselves and strike out on their own account. The feverish excitement which sustained them until they reached here has left them and they seem irresolute and desponding. They often wish they had staid at home. I have no doubt very many will return as empty handed as they came. But even they cannot fail to gain a rich experience, of more value than gold without it. It seems to me that in no part of the world and under no circumstances so much of the philosophy of men and things is presented to view & visible to all the senses & so mixed in the functional concerns of every day life. There is a freedom of thought and action that seems to characterize the people of this country which is unusual. If a man has nefarious propensities and passions he is certain to exhibit them and if good qualities, they too will be visible. Men seem to act themselves and exhibit their true character. Deception, the worst of the vices, because it cloaks the ugly deformity of all others, seems least practiced here. The gambler is a gambler openly. The libertine and frequenter of licentious brothels, is ditto. Their current value is known and established. There is no counterfeit.

When I say hundreds seek employ at moderate wages, I mean at prices far below what was expected by most persons who start for California, say $3 to $4 per day. Success in the mines is as various this year as it was last. A few make their fortunes & these the public always hears of while the success of the thousands who make but a small per diem allowance is not so certain to be heralded. After deducting the sacrifice that every man makes who suddenly closes his affairs at home to come here—deducting six or eight months time in getting here, and three or four for returning—deducting time spent in looking up a good location, or prospecting as it is called—deducting four months of the winter season when the ground is too full of water to dig to much advantage—and deducting expenses and incidental casualties and a man must be very successful what time he actually spends in the mines, if he gets home at the end of two years with a large heap of gold, the produce of his own digging. All this every man knows, or might have known, before starting as well as after. Still very many came here with extravagant expectations founded on an indistinct something (a kin to nothing) in the distance, which vanishes like a vapor when they approach the realities of the pick and shovel under a midday sun. Notwithstanding this sad disappointment, there are some who soon recover from it and set themselves about something & do well, much better than they could do at home. Industry of any kind is well rewarded. Common laborers, mechanics, and good businessmen I think can gain a thousand dollars surplus money as easy here as they can a hundred in the States. Many fail to gain the hundred there, & all such will be likely to fail to get the thousand here, and they are not a few.

SACRAMENTO CITY OCTOBER 13TH, 1850

Brother Moses,

Mr Mossman (who you will remember as a Drayman in Lockport driving Jonathan Ingall's big gray horses) happened yesterday in our store, and although I had not seen him or heard from him for eleven years, I recognized him at first sight as an old acquaintance. He leaves here tomorrow for his home in Wisconsin via New York, and has offered to take this letter to you. He has been at work in the mines all the time he has been in this country, now about fourteen months, and says he thinks with good luck in his voyage home he will have made $100 average per month from the time he left his home to come to this country across the plains which will be about twenty one months by the time he gets back to his wife and four children, twenty miles from Milwaukee. There he owns a hundred and twenty acres of good land and good improvements and this twenty one hundred dollars, the produce of two years labor and privation, will render him comparatively independent and his family quite happy. It really does me good to know of the success of such men, men of moral character and industry, who were never intoxicated with the golden visions of California in the distance, to become dispirited and discouraged by the realities of gold digging. Mr Mossman has met with no "big lumps" or particularly "rich diggings," but has been content with $8 to $12 a day because it was ten times as well as he could do at home and because he thought of the comforts and happiness it would purchase for those he loves at home. No doubt these considerations have nerved his arm to strike deeper the pick, and daily to undergo what he would otherwise have shunned.

I cannot but share with such men the pleasure they feel in the possession of the means of educating their children & augmenting the happiness of their domestic firesides. The case of Mr Mossman is not a solitary instance. I have known many such here, very many. They leave here quite happily. Visions of home as they left it make them forget their toils here. Bouyant in spirit they bid us good bye and speed their way, leaving us to finish our pilgrimage and follow after them. My time I hope will come next January. . . .

A kind remembrance to friends

Affectionately

Mark Hopkins

Source: Mark Hopkins, *Letters to Brother, Moses,* August 30, 1849; August 29, 1850; and October 13, 1850; Huntington Library manuscripts, HM 26039, 26042, 26044.

DOCUMENT 5

The Death of Samuel Nichols

If Hopkins suggests the possible riches to be had in California, the letter Sarah Nichols received in the fall of 1850 suggests the depth of misery that the gold rush also created. Samuel had set off for California in 1849, with his oldest son George, who died on the way to California, Samuel returned with his son's body before the end of the year. Several months later, Samuel set off for California again. He sent several letters to Sarah, who was distraught over her oldest son's death, and who, in the absence of her husband, struggled to raise and support their remaining two sons and keep his faltering business from collapsing. In the fall of 1850, Samuel wrote to his wife that he was finally beginning to succeed, and he sent her a few nuggets, which she had to sell for back taxes and food. Then she received the following letter from her husband's mining partner.

SACRAMENTO CITY, OCT 25, 1850

Mrs. S Nichols,

By the request of your lamented and respected husband, I write to you to inform you several of the particulars of his death. He was taken with a slight diarrhea, but complained of no pain whatever, but appeared to be very weak, yet refused to have a physician or to take medicine till the next week when by his consent I called in a physician which attended him till he died. When his physician informed him that he thought his case a very critical one, he said he thought he should not live but a few days. I was with him every day and night during his sickness. The day he died he requested me to write you the following note.

In the first place, abandon the Virginia land suit at once, pay nothing whatever on it. Return all property under your own control, and jurisdiction. Keep all in your own hands, keep the boys under you control till they are old enough to go into business for themselves. Give Sister Mariah one specimen (he said to me &) have everything sold and sent to my wife. And may God be all your protector during life. Before the last words was pronounced he closed his eyes, and when he finished the sentence, draft away without a struggle. The Dr. and myself was with him when he died. I never saw any one who appeared to suffer so little during his illness and at the hour of his death as your deceased husband. The Dr. wish me to say that he had everything done that was necessary after he was called to him. But still thinks that if he had been called sooner he might have checked his disease. But still there was no certainty of it. Your husband said he put his trust in the great creator of the universe, and I have no doubt but that his wish accomplished in removing your late husband to a better world above. His effects will be sent home the first convenient opportunity. Permit me now as one who knows something of his kindness, and highly appreciated his friendship, to sympathize with you in part the loss of your late lamented husband.

Yours truly,

Luther Cleaves

He was buried in the Sutter burring ground and a slab put to his head with his inscription.

He sent some gold to you by Hawley and Adams Express not long since.

L.C.

Source: Luther Cleaves, Letter to Sarah Nichols, October 25, 1850; Huntington Library manuscript, HM 48250.

Miners' Songs

Songs written and sung by the miners and performed in gold rush saloons reflected the experiences of the miners in California. The following excerpts suggest the variety of mining experiences, as well as their sense of homesickness and the pressure they felt to succeed.

The Happy Miner

I am a happy miner, I love to sing and dance;
    I wonder what my love would say, if she could see my pants,
With canvas patches on the knees, and one upon the stern;
    I'll wear them while I'm digging here, and home when I return.
CHORUS:
So I get in a jovial way, I spend my money free,
And I've got plenty, will you drink lager beer with me?

             *   *   *

The Sensible Miner

I'm mining in a dry ravine, That may not pay at all;
    I've dug a long and fancy drain, to sluice through in the Fall;
But should the rains hold off till late, And keep me in suspense,
    I'll write a line and tell dear Kate, My hide is on the fence!

             *   *   *

The Lousy Miner

It's four long years since I reached this land,
In search of gold among the rocks and sand;
And yet I'm poor when the truth is told,
I'm a lousy miner, I'm a lousy miner in search of shining gold

* * *

An "Honest" Miner

When first I went to mining, I was uncommon green,
    With a "gallus" rig I went to dig, and claimed a whole ravine;
But when I could not make my grub, with implements to gag,
    An honest miner might have been seen at night with a pig in a
    bag!
As he lugged it away from the pen, was thinking how lucky he'd
    been,
    Went into a hole, dug deep after gold, With pig in a bag
    tumbled in.

* * *

I Often Think of Writing Home

I often think of writing home, but very seldom write;
    A letter now and then I get, which fills me with delight,
But while I'm here with Romans I'll do as Romans do, —
    And let it rip, till I return, and tell them all I know.
CHORUS:
    For it keeps a man a humping round, to keep up with the
    times,
        And "pen and ink" is very scarce with people in the
    mines,
    And writing don't amount to much, unless you have the dimes.

Source: Excerpts from Richard A. Dwyer, and Richard E. Lingenfelter, eds. *The Songs of the Gold Rush* (Berkeley: University of California Press, 1964), pp. 87, 85, 155, 83, 166.

William Carpenter's California Adventure

The following excerpts from the letters of William Carpenter to his fiancée suggest the problem that faced many miners. Many who set out on the adventure were condemned for being foolish and irresponsible by neighbors and family members who stayed at home. William Carpenter, like many of these young men, promised to stay moral and righteous among the temptations of a life in California. In his early letters, he described the region as immoral, barbarous, and no place for a woman. Yet, when he switched from mining to shop keeping, he now had to convince his fiancée that California was not so bad, and that she should move west herself. But having painted such a dismal picture of California, how could he now change his tune without appearing to have slipped morally?

SEPT. 1, 1850

. . . I will give you a brief history of my adventures since I left San Francisco. Started from there July 19; arrived at Sacramento on the morning of the 20th. The valley of the Sacramento is beautiful to look upon, as far as I had a view of it in coming up, which was only for about thirty miles in the morning before arriving at Sacramento. At this place I found the news most discouraging, but kept up good courage and am doing well now. This place demands more courage and determined perseverance than any other, I believe, in the world. I am making this time from ten to twelve dollars per day and believe I shall do well with the blessings of Providence attending me. My place of labor at this time is on the middle fork of the American River at a bar called Oregon opposite to a bar by the name of Spanish Bar.

My health is first rate. All the rest of the company good, save Q. Adams. Calvin Gates is dead. He died after an illness of only five and 1/2 days. His disease was inflammation of the brain. . . . We were strangers in a strange land and knew not what to do in regard to burying him, the cost of a coffin being about 35 or 40 dollars, and knew not where to get one, and when got only made of rough boards planed a trifle. We bethought us of our brother Odd Fellows and called on some four or five, and they prompt in their assistance, sending themselves for a coffin and bearing a part of the expense, giving us all the sympathy and aid in their power. . . . We buried him in the evening with no light save the glimmering of the stars. For a shroud we wrapt his blanket around him, reminding me of the lines describing the burial of Sir John Moore.

The mines as I find them are filled to overflowing—plenty of gold, but not to be got by all the thousands come to the mines, and are not courageous enough to strike among all those difficulties that beset them on the first onset, and so they go back discouraged and disheartened to their homes, if they have money enough to get them home. I find the longer I stay here the more I find I can do well. The prospects are better than I first supposed. There will be more gold taken out this year than last by two to one. You may understand how it affects most men here by one fact I will give you. In the vessel we came in from Panama to San Francisco were about 250 passengers. They came in to the mines, and 130 of them returned on her when she sailed back, which was in about four weeks. Climate here first rate. Cloudless days and nights. Air pure. But what a place for a woman to be in! I pity those women here. . . . Farming can be done here in spots only, save on the banks of the River Sacramento and San Joaquin. I mean to be home one year from this fall, but perhaps not till one year from next spring, and may be successful enough to come before, but mean to come as soon as I can and get a small sum to bring back. I expect to become a barbarian before I come back, for society is indeed a blank here. . . . I have received a letter from back home only yesterday, giving me the only information of you I have had since I left you in Middlebury. . . . Direct your letters to Sacramento. I have no time for more, for got a distance of eight miles to travel, which is equal to about twelve in the States, and it is between two and three o'c. More in the future. I am about 60 miles from Sacramento.

FROM ROSES BAR, YUBA RIVER, NO DATE

I have nerved my heart and steeled my hand to write to you from this barbarous land. I have laid down shovel and pick to take up paper, pen and ink and write you a few lines from this State where the golden placers be; and sure it is a barbarous land for vice of every kind, dissipation, sloth and crime, men of every nation, rank and station, name, shape, color and hue abound. All ages from children to the gray-haired man just tottering into the grave are here. No place in all God's creation like this self same California. Men at home of respectable habits and standing come here and soon become reckless and dissolute from want of the success they dreamed of, expecting to make their fortune without any effort; too indolent to work or make the necessary efforts in this country that are required in any country. The consequence is vice, immorality, gambling of ever kind abound. Liquors of every kind, not used as a drink but poured down these worse than brutes, making society a perfect sink of pollution. One cause of this is the want of woman's restraining influence, the want of . . . some one at home to call the wanderer from evil influence after a day of toil or to cheer one after disappointment and misfortune. . . . Many of these evils are incidental to a new country. Gold, where will not man go to obtain it, on the top of the loftiest mountains, or in the lowest valleys, or into the bowels of the earth; through rain, snow, ice, or heat of the severest kind, through hardships of every kind—all for gold. And it is so with man here. He dreams of golden treasures, and how often his bright anticipations of the future end in disappointment or in the grave. This is the fate of very many that come to this clime.

California will never be used to any extent for farming purposes, in spite of what Butler King says of the farming qualities in his celebrated report last winter. The country will be a mining country and that will be its chief characteristic. Who ever heard of a mining country being a desirable country to live in? I never did. Neither is this. Nor will I stay after I get a decent sum of its glittering dust.

Now for a short description of my mining in this country. I began in Georgetown. There helped dig three holes in the earth about twelve feet deep, about the same square. We took out of those holes about three dollars per day a piece. We were about two weeks digging there. We moved down on to the Spanish Bar, and there dug about five weeks, or six, making about two hundred dollars for my share. Then moved on to the place I am at now; and have made in all about eleven hundred dollars. Am going to send my brother about eight or nine hundred dollars in a few days. The best day's work I have made $96, next $64, next best $50. The last day I worked a half day before high water I made sixty dollars and should have made without doubt one hundred and twenty or thirty, if the water had not risen so fast that we had to pull our tools out in double quick time. You see the rainy season is upon us by this. We thought things poked dubious in our first debut in the mines, and so they did; but kept good courage and have done well, and the prospect before us first rate. Thus you see the chance for me to come home in a short time comparatively speaking is good. Four others and myself have three claims that will realize us two thousand dollars a piece next summer if they turn out as well as those above them or below have done. . . . The house we live in is made of cloth about twelve feet in diameter and round. Over this we have another cloth drawn within about four inches of it, and these two together keep us dry and warm with a fireplace.

I have not received any letter from you yet, but expect to; nor any from my brother or sister save one written in July by them. The resin, I expect, is this: there are three persons of the same name as myself in this country and I expect they have got them and have not sent them back to the office as they should. . . . In order to avoid this I am going to have my middle name used after this. So please direct to me as signed by myself, and to Sacramento City. William Oscar Carpenter.

LETTER OF NOV. 15, 1851, FROM "SAC. CITY, CAL."

I am in trade here and doing well. Have made (since I sent home some $800.00 dollars to Brother Augustus) in the neighborhood of four thousand dollars. . . . I have had two partners, one a man by the name of Clark, and Wells of our place. Mr. Clark has done the selling and I the buying. Having claims to tend to we had Wells get a third partner, whom we have bought out, and before this gets to you he will be in Pike. I can tell you our amount of business by saying that I have paid out for the last three months from eight to fifteen hundred dollars every week for goods in gold dust. . . .

Do not fail to put on the outside of every letter my middle name in full, as there is a person by the name of W. O. Carpenter in this city besides myself. (Signed) William Oscar Carpenter

SAC. CITY, DEC. 21ST, 1851

. . . It seems to me now, from being accustomed to this beautiful clime and genial skies, as though it were impossible to feel as well in that cold bleak country as we do in this sunny clime. Oh! It is a beautiful climate to live in; scenery which none can surpass. Would you see nature in all its grandeur, it is here. Would you see fields covered with green verdure, it is to be seen, but not in all parts of the country. Nature seems to parcel out to each its precise location, from plains covered with naught but withered vegetation to valleys green, and parts of the plains also covered with green fields along the river sides. Then we come to the mountains, and then to the snow-capped peaks far in the distance, all lending enchantment to the view. . . . California is bound to be a great state.

If you were only here I could live contented for three or four years at least; but it is a poor society to bring a woman to as yet, although the prospect is that next year will bring an influx of ladies into this country that will change society in a great measure. . . .

I am in business in Sacramento and shall be for the next year. I am in the iron foundry business and hope to do well.

Source: William Carpenter, *A California Pioneer of the Fifties*, no date. Edited by Frederic Ives Carpenter; Huntington Library typewritten manuscript, HM16777.

Albert Benard de Russailh's Toothpick Fortune

*T*here were two ways to make a fortune in California: digging for gold, or selling goods to the miners. California was an incredible sellers' market, as nearly everyone who arrived in San Francisco quickly discovered. Frenchman Albert Bernard de Russailh was astounded to find ordinary items selling for outrageous prices, and decided to open a "store" of his own in the city by the bay. An unusual encounter with a potential customer suggested that even he had under-estimated the potential for making money in California. As he summed up, in a sentence that could become the motto of the gold rush, "in California nothing is given away; everything is sold."

The following day I spent unpacking my cases in preparation for my new career as shopkeeper. Early next morning, I conquered my vanity, put on a red flannel shirt, and went down to the Long Wharf, where I chose a good place, and with a few old boards rigged up my open-air shop. My goods were soon spread out to attract customers. I had many things of no particular value: brushes, gloves, perfumes, cutlery, colored shirts, and other articles; but it was enough to begin with; and my little stock transformed me into an important San Francisco merchant. After all, my shop was not much smaller than the best in town, and my different lines were fairly complete.

My business began superbly; my sales were steady, and I made good profits. I sold a pair of suspenders for more than six times what I had paid for them, and a toothbrush for ten times its cost. Jars of cold cream, bottles of eau de Cologne and perfume went for high prices, $1 or $1.50 apiece. It seemed quite magnificent. A hundred old magazine illustrations, which I had by chance stowed away in the bottom of my trunk, paid my hotel expenses for more than a week. Among them some caricatures by Gavarni, clipped five or six years before from Charivari, brought me $2 each. But

I made my biggest profit from a wholly worthless article. In Paris no restaurant charges for these articles, they are carelessly thrown away and trodden under foot, and a man will break twenty-five a day at lunch or dinner. I am speaking of toothpicks. I had brought with me two packages of them (about 248 small packs) for my own use, or to give away to my friends and acquaintances. One day I decided to lay several packs on my counter. They had scarcely left the box when a grave gentleman paused before my shop and began to examine my merchandise. He picked up the illustrations and a few other things, but laid them down again, and he seemed about to walk away, when his eye happened to light on the toothpicks. He reached for a pack, held it up, and said:

"How much?"

I was quite taken aback, for I had no idea what to charge. It had never occurred to me that anyone would buy them, and I had rather planned to give them away. But I remembered suddenly that in California nothing is given away; everything is sold. With as serious an expression as I could command, I replied:

"Half a dollar, sir."

He gave me a long look.

"It is not possible," he said finally. "That is very little."

At first, I thought he was joking. Then I feared that he would fly into a rage. I smiled and was about to say politely: "That is nothing for you, sir." But he quietly gathered up four packs, handed me $2, nodded pleasantly, and moved away.

My happiness was even greater than my amazement, and I congratulated myself on being such a good business man. Next day I laid out twice as many toothpicks for sale, and in a few minutes they were all snapped up at the same price. "If this is a country where toothpicks are valuable," I said to myself, "and if I have the only supply on the market, I must certainly take advantage of the situation and do something on a grand scale."

Elated by my success, I hurried home and sat up far into the night splitting the packs of toothpicks in two. After this process of division, packs originally containing twenty-four toothpicks had only twelve. The plan was excellent and I was not disappointed: in less than a week they had all gone for 50c a pack. I could hardly restrain my laughter whenever a man paid me half a dollar for only twelve. If I had a 1500-ton ship loaded to the gunwale with toothpicks, my fortune would have been made, and I could have gone home to France in a steamer. But, unluckily, I had only 496 packs.

For a while my shop was well patronized and my business flourished, for I was beginning to learn the tricks of the trade. I discovered the value of a friendly word here and there, a smile for a woman, a jest or a timely remark for a man, all of which helped to attract customers. Destiny seemed propitious. But my goods were nearly exhausted, and I knew that I should have to lay in a fresh supply, if I wished to continue operations.

Source: Albert Benard de Russailh, *Last Adventure: San Francisco in 1851. Translated from the original journal of Albert Benard de Russailh by Clarkson Crane* (San Francisco: The Westgate Press, 1931), pp. 43–47.

Bayard Taylor on the Rise of San Francisco

The development of the cities of California, especially San Francisco, astounded the miners. It was a visual representation of the rush itself, a magical sense of the accomplishment of the rush, something that even those who had been unlucky in the mines could feel they shared in. Bayard Taylor was a prominent travel writer, already well known when he set out to report on the gold rush for the New York Tribune. *His account is a classic of gold rush reporting.*

Of all the marvellous phases of the history of the Present, the growth of San Francisco is the one which will most tax the belief of the Future. Its parallel was never known, and shall never be beheld again. I speak only of what I saw, with my own eyes. When I landed there, a little more than four months before, I found a scattering town of tents and canvas houses, with a show of frame buildings on one or two streets, and a population of about six thousand. Now, on my last visit, I saw around me an actual metropolis, displaying street after street of well-built edifices, filled with an active and enterprising people and exhibiting every mark of permanent commercial prosperity. Then, the town was limited to the curve of the Bay fronting the anchorage and bottoms of the hills. Now it stretched to the topmost heights, followed the shore around point after point, and sending, back a long arm through a gap in the hills, took hold of the Golden Gate and was building its warehouses on the open strait and almost fronting the blue horizon of the Pacific. Then, the gold-seeking sojourner lodged in muslin rooms and canvas garrets, with a philosophic lack of furniture, and ate his simple though substantial fare from pine boards. Now, lofty hotels, gaudy with verandas and balconies, were met with in all quarters, furnished with home luxury, and aristocratic restaurants presented daily their long bills of fare, rich with the choicest technicalities of the Parisian cuisine. Then, vessels were coming in day after day, to lie deserted and useless at their anchorage. Now scarce a day passed, but some cluster of sails, bound outward through the Golden Gate, took their way to all the corners of the Pacific hike the magic seed of the Indian juggler, which grew, blossomed and bore fruit before the eyes of his spectators, San Francisco seemed to have accomplished in a day the growth of half a century.

When I first landed in California, bewildered and amazed by what seemed an unnatural standard of prices, I formed the opinion that there would be before long a great crash in speculation. Things, it appeared then, had reached the crisis, and it was pronounced impossible that they could remain stationary. This might have been a very natural idea at the time, but the subsequent course of affairs proved it to be incorrect. Lands, rents, goods and subsistence continued steadily to advance in cost, and as the credit system had been meanwhile prudently contracted, the character of the business done was the more real and substantial. Two or three years will pass, in all probability, before there is a positive abatement of the standard of prices there will be fluctuations in the meantime, occasioning great gains and losses, but the fall in rents and real estate, when it comes, as it inevitably must in the course of two or three years, will not be so crushing as I at first imagined. I doubt whether it will seriously injure the commercial activity of the place. Prices will never fall to the same standard as in the Atlantic States. For rules will always be made by the sober, intelligent, industrious, and energetic; but no one who is either too careless, too spiritless or too ignorant to succeed at home, need trouble himself about emigrating. The same general rule holds good, as well here as elsewhere, and it is all the better for human nature that it is so.

Not only was the heaviest part of the business conducted on cash principles, but all rents, even to lodgings in hotels, were required to be paid in advance. A single bowling-alley, in the basement story of the Ward House—a new hotel on Portsmouth-Square—prepaid $5,000 monthly. The firm of Findley, Johnson & Co sold their real estate, purchased a year previous, for $20,000, at $300,000; $25,000 down, and the rest in monthly instalments of $12,500. This was a fair specimen of the speculations daily made. Those on a lesser scale were frequently of a very amusing character, but the claims on one's astonishment were so constant, that the faculty soon wore out, and the most unheard-of operations were looked upon as matters of course Among others that came under my observation, was one of a gentleman who purchased a barrel of alum for $6, the price in New York being $9. It happened to be the only alum in the place, and as there was a demand for it shortly afterwards, he sold the barrel for $150. Another purchased all the candle-wick to be found, at an average price of 40 cts per lb., and sold it in a short time at $2.25 per lb. A friend of mine expended

$10,000 in purchasing barley, which in a week brought $20,000 The greatest gains were still made by the gambling tables and the eating-houses. Every device that art could suggest was used to swell the custom of the former. The latter found abundant support in the necessities of a large floating population, in addition to the swarm of permanent residents.

For a month or two previous to this time, money had, been very scarce in the market, and from ten to fifteen per cent monthly, was paid, with the addition of good security. Notwithstanding the quantity of coin brought into the country by emigrants, and the millions of gold dust used as currency, the actual specie basis was very small compared with the immense amount of business transacted. Nevertheless, I heard of nothing like a failure; the principal firms were prompt in all their dealings, and the chivalry of Commerce—to use a new phrase—was as faithfully observed as it could have been in the old marts of Europe and America. The merchants had a Change and News-room, and were beginning to cooperate in their movements and consolidate their credit. A stock company which had built a long wharf at the foot of Sacramento Street declared a dividend of ten per cent within six weeks after the wharf was finished. During the muddy season, it was the only convenient place for landing goods, and as the cost of constructing it was enormous, so were likewise the charges for wharfage and storage.

There had been a vast improvement in the means of living since my previous visit to San Francisco. Several large hotels had been opened, which were equal in almost every respect to houses of the second class in the Atlantic cities. The Ward House, the Graham House, imported bodily from Baltimore- and the St. Francis Hotel, completely threw into the shade all former establishments. The rooms were furnished with comfort and even luxury, and the tables lacked few of the essentials of good living, according to home' taste. The sleeping apartments of the St. Francis were the best in California. The cost of board and lodging was $150 per month—which was considered unusually cheap. A room at the Ward House cost $250 monthly, without board. The principal restaurants charged $35 a week for board, and there were lodging houses where a berth or "bunk"—one out of fifty in the same room—might be had for $6 a week

The model of these establishments—which were far from being "model lodging-houses"—was that of a ship. A number of staterooms, containing six berths each, ran around the sides of a large room, or cabin, where the lodgers resorted to read, write, smoke and drink at their leisure. The state-rooms were consequently filled with foul and unwholesome air, and the noises in the cabin prevented the passengers from sleeping, except between midnight and four o'clock.

The great wart of San Francisco was society. Think of a city of thirty thousand inhabitants, peopled by men alone! The like of this was never seen before. Every man was his own housekeeper, doing, in many instances, his own sweeping, cooking, washing and mending. Many home-arts, learned rather by observation than experience, came conveniently into play. He who cannot make a bed, cook a beefsteak, or sew up his own rips and rents, is unfit to be a citizen of California. Nevertheless, since the town began to assume a permanent shape, very many of the comforts of life in the East were attainable. A family may now live there without suffering any material privations; and if every married man, who intends spending some time in California, would take his family with him, a social influence would soon be created to which we might look for the happiest results.

Source: Bayard Taylor, *Eldorado, or Adventures in the Path of Empire*, 18th edition (New York: G.P. Putnam, 1861), pp. 301–305.

DOCUMENT 10

Dust vs Coin

*T*he gold rush evolved quickly. Placer mining by individuals soon gave way to partnerships, and in a few years to corporate mining. The adventurous days of the rush seemed to fade quickly, as even the miners themselves realized. In the spring of 1851, the Sacramento Transcript editor described the changes that had come over California. The sense that the "good old times" had passed is astounding, considering that this was only two years after the international rush had begun.

SACRAMENTO *TRANSCRIPT*, MARCH 8, 1851

One year ago there seemed to be only one kind of circulating medium. It was "dust," and nothing else. The miner, when he came to the city, hauled out his huge buckskin purse and paid for his "section of gingerbread," or meal at a restaurant, in "dust." . . . Gold dust seemed to have lost its conventional value in his estimation, and the free spirited miner parted with it without a sigh, a why, or a wherefore. How things have changed in one year.

Those were good old times, when the miners paid for everything in dust—when the red-shirted gentry were the nabobs of the land—when the dirty shirt and coatless party were worth their thousands. It may seem strange, yet it is not less true, that thousands of persons in this State last fall a year did not own a coat, and yet they may have had several thousand dollars in the pocket. The fact of it was, coats were a sort of useless appendage, and but few seemed willing to trouble themselves with packing them about. Last September a year, a floating population of at least six thousand persons were in and around Sacramento, yet out of this entire number there were not over one dozen coated persons. As for "tiles," we doubt if there were a dozen respectable looking hats in the city—they were a perfect mongrel breed—of all shapes, sizes, and conditions—some crownless, some rimless, and so patched and worn that the looker on could not have told whether they had originally been "plush" or "wool." . . .

Those days have passed, and with the change has come idleness, vagrancy, and coin as the circulating medium. Instead of that free and don't care spirit of spending money, men now regard dollars as much as they once esteemed ounces. They grip a dollar with more tenacity than they formerly did their pounds of dust. Instead of old time apparel, nothing will do now but clothes of the fanciest hue and finest fabric, and "tiles" of the latest and most fashionable style. We doubt indeed whether there is a more rigid adherence to fashion anywhere, than is now visible in the resident population of Sacramento.

Source: F.C. Ewers, editor, Sacramento *Transcript*, March 8, 1851.

The "Ragged Coat" Returns Home

Many returning miners feared that they would be seen as failures, especially if they did not return with a vast fortune. The following song speaks both to these fears and to the sense of inner worth which many miners developed during the rush.

The Ragged Coat

Oh, what a world of flummery—there's nothing but deceit in it—
    So you'll find, if you'll mind, as through this life you travel on;
Old and young, rich and poor, every one you meet in it,
    All judge you by appearances, and I'll prove it in my song.
Eight years ago I left New York—I hadn't nary red, sirs;
    My folks were rich, but wouldn't lend a single dollar note;
So I started off across the plains, and really almost dead, sirs—
    I had no hat, no shirt, no boots, and this very ragged coat.

But being in the land of gold, my spirits soon got lighter—
    I got a pick and shovel, and I started off to work;
I made a very lucky strike—my prospects soon got brighter—
    I made a handsome fortune, though I worked like any Turk.
And then I thought that I'd return, and see my friends at home,
    sirs;
    So I bought a first class passage on board of a steamboat.
I had a heap more cash then than when I 'gan to roam sirs,
    But to fathom out deception I kept my ragged coat.

The boat was very crowded, but I got a first rate berth, sirs,
    And tried to make myself at home with the passengers on
    board;
But their behavior oftentimes it caused me lots of mirth, sirs—

I'd commence a conversation, but they wouldn't say a word.
When I heard a silly puppy say, though lowly he did breathe it,
  "It's a shame to let a ragged man in this part of the boat";
Said I, "You foppish rascal, there's a good heart beats beneath
  it—
  So don't despise a man because he wears a ragged coat."

My journey being ended, I put my foot on shore, sirs,
  Glad enough, indeed, I was of them to get relief.
I walked up to my cousin's and straight knocked at the door, sirs,
  But he banged it in my face again, as though I was a thief.
I told him plainly who I was—my *face* he didn't know, sirs.
  I told him I had made a pile—he quickly chang'd his note;
He wanted to borrow, but, I said, "Oh, dear me, no, sirs,
  For you despised the *man* because he wore a ragged coat."

Source: J. Woodward and J. E. Johnson, "The Ragged Coat" in Richard A. Dwyer, and Richard E. Lingenfelter, eds. *The Songs of the Gold Rush* (Berkeley: University of California Press, 1964), p. 179.

Revisiting California by Rail in 1890

Transportation advances within the later nineteenth century, especially the railroad, soon joined California much more closely to the nation. After only about forty years, miners who had made the harsh journey to California in 1849 could return to tour the gold fields quickly from the comfort of a railroad car. The shock of returning to the former mining camps, some now developed cities, brought disturbing memories to some miner-tourists.

SACRAMENTO, CAL., APRIL 27, 1890.

MY DEAR SON:

When I entered the [railroad] cars for Auburn, my first mining-camp in 1849, I thought of how I went there forty-one years ago, walking beside a four-yoke ox-team in the rain; for, on that very day, November 1, the rainy season commenced. The first day we only made twelve miles, and nine the next, on account of rain and mud. On the second night, in a tent which had at one end, to keep the rain off, a piece of cotton cloth held down by a stone, we found a negro cooking biscuits hard as a rock, boiling black coffee—to be served without sugar—and baking beans; but we were delighted to share his dinner at seventy-five cents apiece. We were eight days traveling the forty miles to Auburn.

When we left the cars, I looked for the spot where I had pitched my tent, built a stone chimney at one end, made a mattress of fir boughs, and thought myself well fixed for the winter. On the identical spot stood a nice, two-story house, with a fine garden, neatly fenced. I then looked around where not a building stood then, and saw churches, schoolhouses, fine brick buildings, and children in the wide streets. It was hard to realize that this was the place where I had dug for gold, and that the hills of red clay we thought good for nothing, were really the charming slopes now covered with grape vines, peach, apple, and pear trees, and other evidences of fertility.

I stood and reflected upon the past, and thought of all the hardy men who had helped to build the place; but, by diligent inquiry, I could not find one of all who wintered here in '49 and '50. I suppose most of them have gone to their long home, and that the others are widely scattered. It makes me feel sad as I think of the old days.

Your affectionate father,

CHARLES T. STUMCKE

Source: Nicholas Ball, *The Pioneers of '49: A History of the Excursion of the Society of California Pioneers of New England, from Boston to the Leading Cities of the Golden State, April 10–May 17, 1890, with Reminiscences and Descriptions* (Boston: Lee and Shepard, 1891), p. 97.

Suggested Readings

Both scholarly and popular studies of the California gold rush are extensive. Malcolm Rohrbough's *Days of Gold* (1997), a masterful overview of the gold rush experience, provides a strong starting point. Other excellent overviews are H. W. Brand's *Age of Gold* (2003); Mary Hill's *Gold: The California Story* (2002); J. S. Holliday's *Rush for Riches* (1999); and Edward Dolnick's *The Rush* (2014). Rodman Paul's early pioneering works, *California Gold* (1965) and *Mining Frontiers of the Far West* (1963), as well as John Walton Caughey's *The California Gold Rush* (1975) remain foundational works.

A number of excellent articles have been published coinciding with the 150th anniversary of the rush, and compiled in anthologies. Of these Kenneth Owens's *Riches for All* (2002) is perhaps the best short, single volume. The *California History Sesquicentennial Series*, a four volume series published between 1998–2003, collects recent articles relating to the period before and during the American conquest and California. These volumes include Ramón A. Gutiérrez and Richard J. Orsi, *Contested Eden: California Before the Gold Rush* (1998); James J. Rawls and Richard J. Orsi, *A Golden State: Mining and Economic Development in Gold Rush California* (1999); Kevin Starr and Richard J. Orsi, *Rooted in Barbarous Soil: People, Culture, and Community in Gold Rush California* (2000); and John F. Burns and Richard J. Orsi, *Taming the Elephant: Politics, Government, and Law in Pioneer California* (2003). The many articles in these anthologies delve into a variety of aspects of the rush and suggest many possibilities for further gold rush studies.

More detailed and specialized studies of the gold rush have recently been published, including Gunther Barth's *Instant Cities* (1975); Brian Robert's *American Alchemy* (2000); Susan Lee Johnson's *Roaring Camp* (2001); Leonard Richards's *The California Gold Rush and the Coming of the*

Civil War (2008); Mark A. Eifler's *Gold Rush Capitalists* (2003); Alexander Saxton, *The Indispensable Enemy: Labor and the Anti-Chinese Movement in California* (1975); Stacey L. Smith *Freedom's Frontier: California and the Struggle over Unfree Labor, Emancipation, and Reconstruction* (2013); and Andrew C. Isenberg, *Mining California: An Ecological History* (2005).

Studies of California Native peoples in the gold rush deserve particular attention, and have been getting more play recently, including Albert L. Hurtado, *Indian Survival on the California Frontier* (1990); James J. Rawls, *Indians of California: The Changing Image* (1986); Brendan C. Lindsay, *Murder State: California's Native American Genocide, 1846–1873*; Robert F. Heizer, *The Destruction of California Indians* (1993); Clifford E. Trafzer and Joel R. Hyer, eds, *Exterminate Them: Written Accounts of the Murder, Rape, and Enslavement of Native Americans during the California Gold Rush* (1999).

Studies of the international aspects of the rush have lagged behind, but new work is being done here. Recent publications include Malcolm J. Rohrbough, *Rush to Gold: The French and the California Gold Rush, 1848–1854* (2013); Aims McGuinness, *Path of Empire: Panama and the California Gold Rush* (2008); Elizabeth Sinn, *Pacific Crossing: California Gold, Chinese Migration, and the Making of Hong Kong* (2013); David Goodman, *Gold Seeking: Victoria and California in the 1850's* (1994); Douglas Fethering, *The Gold Crusades: A Social History of Gold Rushes, 1849–1929* (2015) have made great strides in this direction. Earlier works, however, are worth perusing, such as two books by Jay Monaghan: *Australians and the Gold Rush* (1966) and *Chile, Peru, and the California Gold Rush of 1849* (1973).

The best way to really get into the California gold rush experience, however, it to read through some of the many accounts of the rush written by the participants themselves. J. S. Holliday's account of William Swain's experience, *The World Rushed In* (1983) is an excellent miner's account, fleshed out with additions from other miners who travelled along with Swain. Rodman Paul's collection of accounts of the original gold discovery, *The California Gold Discovery* (1967) have gathered a rich collection of sources on this moment. Bayard Taylor's reports for Horace Greeley's *New York Tribune* have been published as *El Dorado: Adventures in the Path of Empire*, and provide an excellent reporter's view of the rush.

Women's accounts of the rush have been especially rich—see, for example, May Jane Macquier's letters, recently re-edited and published by Polly Welts Kauffman as *An Apron Full of Gold* (1994), Louise A. K. S. Clappe's *The Shirley Letters* as a collection of letters describing the Gold Rush, and Sarah Royce's *Frontier Lady*. JoAnn Levy's *They Saw the Elephant: Women in the California Gold Rush* (1990) nicely surveys women's experiences in the rush.

Richard A. Dwyer and Richard E. Lingenfelter, eds, *The Songs of the Gold Rush* (1964) offers an interesting musical and social insight into the experience of the rush. Likewise, Janice T. Driesbach, et al., *Art of the Gold Rush* (1998), provides an artistic view of the rush. Peter Blodgett's *Land of Golden Dreams* (1999) provides not only a good gold rush overview, but also a fine introduction to the Huntington Library's gold rush holdings.

Websites and e-books on the gold rush are becoming more plentiful and a rich source of miner's accounts, as well as images of gold rush artifacts and artwork. Good starting places are:

California State Library site: www.library.ca.gov/goldrush/

Oakland Museum of California: http://explore.museumca.org/goldrush/

University of California site: www.calisphere.universityofcalifornia.edu/
calcultures/eras/era4.html

Bancroft Library site: http://vm136.lib.berkeley.edu/BANC/Exhibits/
Goldrush/introduction.html

Huntington Library "Land of Golden Dreams" site: www.huntington.org/
education/goldrush/index.html

The Virtual Museum of the City of San Francisco site: www.sfmuseum.
org/hist/chron1.html

SF Maritime Heritage site: www.maritimeheritage.org/captains/hillBen
jamin.html

PBS: American Experience, The Gold Rush site: www.pbs.org/wgbh/
amex/goldrush/

The Sacramento Bee Gold Rush site: www.calgoldrush.com

Coloma Gold Discovery site: www.coloma.com/california-gold-dis
covery/

Bibliography

Manuscript Collections and Newspapers

Daily Alta California, March 6, 1853.

Carpenter, William. *A California Pioneer of the Fifties*, no date. Manuscript, H. E. Huntington Library, HM16777.

Hopkins, Mark. *Letters*. Manuscripts, H. E. Huntington Library, HM 26034–26046.

Nichols, Samuel. *Letters*. Manuscripts, H. E. Huntington Library, HM 48250–48298.

Sacramento *Transcript*, March 8, 1851.

Published First Person Accounts

Ball, Nicholas. *The Pioneers of '49: A History of the Excursion of the Society of California Pioneers of New England, from Boston to the Leading Cities of the Golden State, April 10–May 17, 1890, with Reminiscences and Descriptions*. Boston: Lee and Shepard, 1891.

Barker, Malcolm E. ed. *San Francisco Memoirs, 1835–1851: Eyewitness Accounts of the Birth of a City*. San Francisco: Londonborn Publications, 1994.

Christman, Enos. *One Man's Gold*. New York: Whittlesey House, 1930.

Delano, Alonzo. *Life on the Plains and Among the Diggings: An Overland Journey to California, 1849*. Auburn and Buffalo: Miller, Orton & Mulligan, 1854.

Dwyer, Richard A. and Richard E. Lingenfelter, eds. *The Songs of the Gold Rush*. Berkeley: University of California Press, 1964.

Haskins, Charles Warren. *The Argonauts of California: Being the Reminiscences of Scenes and Incidents That Occurred in California in Early Mining Days*. New York: Fords, Howard & Hulbert, 1890.

Helper, Hinton. *The Land of Gold, Reality versus Fiction*. Baltimore, Published for the Author, By Henry Taylor, Sun Iron Building, 1855.

Holliday, J. S. *The World Rushed In: The California Gold Rush Experience*. New York: Touchstone, 1983.

James, Edwin. *An Account of an Expedition from Pittsburgh to the Rocky Mountains, Performed in the Years 1819, 1820.* London: Longman, Hurst, Rees, Orme, and Brown, 1823.

Kaufman, Polly Welts ed. *Apron Full of Gold: The Letters of Mary Jane Megquier from San Francisco, 1849–1856,* 2nd edition. Albuquerque: University of New Mexico Press, 1994.

Paul, Rodman. *The California Gold Discovery: Sources, Documents, Accounts, and Memoirs Relating to the Discovery of Gold at Sutter's Mill.* Georgetown, CA: Talisman Press, 1966.

Sherman, William T. *Memoirs of General William T. Sherman, by Himself,* 2 vols. New York, 1875.

Taylor, Bayard. *Eldorado: Adventures in the Path of Empire.* Berkeley: Heyday Books, 2000.

Thompson, Willard. *Going For The Gold: By Sea to the California Gold Rush* (Chronicles of Western Pioneers). Rincon Publishing. Kindle Edition.

Tucker, J. C. *Diary of a Voyage Around Cape Horn in 1849 to California.* Kindle Edition.

Twain, Mark. *Roughing It.* Berkeley: University of California Press, 1972.

White, Katherine A. ed. *A Yankee Trader in the Gold Rush, the Letters of Franklin A. Buck.* Boston: Houghton Mifflin and Company, 1930.

General Bibliography

Abbott, Carl. *How Cities Won the West.* Albuquerque: University of New Mexico Press, 2008.

Andrist, Ralph K. *The Long Death: The Last Days of the Plains Indian.* New York: Collier Books, 1964.

Avella, Steven M. *Sacramento: Indomitable City.* Charleston, SC: Arcadia Publishing, 2003.

Bain, David Haward. *Empire Express: Building the First Transcontinental Railroad.* London: Penguin Books, 1999.

Barth, Gunther. *Bitter Strength: A History of the Chinese in the United States, 1850–1870.* Cambridge, Ma.: Harvard University Press, 1964.

Barth, Gunther. *Instant Cities: Urbanization and the Rise of San Francisco and Denver.* Albuquerque: University of New Mexico Press, 1975.

Brands, H. W. *The Age of Gold: The California Gold Rush and the New American Dream.* New York: Anchor, 2003.

Burns, John F. and Richard J. Orsi, eds. *Taming the Elephant: Politics, Government, and Law in Pioneer California.* Berkeley: University of California Press, 2003.

Castaneda, Christopher J. and Lee M. A. Simpson, eds. *River City and Valley Life: An Environmental History of the Sacramento Regions.* Pittsburgh, PA: University of Pittsburgh Press, 2013.

Caughey, John Walton. *Gold is the Cornerstone.* Berkeley: University of California Press, 1948.

Cole, Tom. *A Short History of San Francisco.* Berkeley: Heyday Books, 2014.

Dasmann, Raymond F. *The Destruction of California.* New York: Collier Books, 1975.

Dolnick, Edward. *The Rush: America's Fevered Quest for Fortune, 1848–1853*. Boston: Little, Brown and Company, 2014.

Eifler, Mark A. *Gold Rush Capitalists: Greed and Growth in Sacramento*. Albuquerque: University of New Mexico Press, 2002.

Fetherling, Douglas. *The Gold Crusades: A Social History of Gold Rushes, 1849–1929*. Toronto: University of Toronto Press, 1997.

Fradkin, Philip. *Stagecoach: Wells Fargo and the American West*. New York: Simon and Schuster, 2002.

Frederick, J. V. *Ben Holladay: The Stagecoach King*. Lincoln: University of Nebraska Press, 1968.

Gentry, Curt. *The Last Days of the Late, Great State of California*. Berkeley: Comstock Editions, 1968.

Gonzales, Manuel G. *Mexicanos: A History of Mexicans in the United States*. Bloomington: Indiana University Press, 2000.

Gray, Jack. *Rebellions and Revolutions: China from the 1800s to 2000*, 2nd edition. New York: Oxford University Press, 2003.

Harlow, Neal. *California Conquered: The Annexation of a Mexican Province, 1846–1850*. Berkeley: University of California Press, 1982.

Hill, Mary. *Gold: The California Story*. Berkeley: University of California Press, 1999.

Hurtado, Albert L. *Indian Survival on the California Frontier*. New Haven: Yale University Press, 1988.

Isenberg, Andrew C. *Mining California: An Ecological History*. New York: Hill and Wang, 2006.

Jacobs, Wilbur. *On Turner's Trail: 100 Years of Writing Western History*. Lawrence: University of Kansas, 1994.

Johnson, Marilynn S. *The Second Gold Rush: Oakland and the East Bay in World War II*. Berkeley: University of California Press, 1994.

Johnson, Steven. *The Ghost Map: The Story of London's Most Terrifying Epidemic—And How it Changed Science, Cities, and the Modern World*. New York: Riverhead Books, 2006.

Johnson, Susan Lee. *Roaring Camp: The Social World of the California Gold Rush*. New York: W.W. Norton, 2000.

Lawson, Melinda. *Patriot Fires: Forging a New American Nationalism in the Civil War North*. Lawrence: University Press of Kansas, 2002.

Limerick, Patricia Nelson. *The Legacy of Conquest: The Unbroken Past of the American West*. New York: W.W. Norton, 1987.

Limerick, Patricia Nelson, Clyde A. Milner and Charles E. Rankin, eds. *Trails: Toward a New Western History*. Lawrence: University of Kansas Press, 1991.

Lotchin, Roger W. *San Francisco, 1846–1856*. Urbana: University of Illinois Press, 1997.

Matthews, Glenna. *The Golden State in the Civil War*. New York: Cambridge University Press, 2012.

McDougall, Walter A. *Let the Sea Make a Noise: Four Hundred Years of Cataclysm, Conquest, War and Folly in the North Pacific*. New York: Avon Books, 1993.

McDougall, Walter A. *The Throes of Democracy: The American Civil War Era, 1829–1877*. New York: Harper Collins Publisher, 2008.

McGuinness, Aims. *Path of Empire: Panama and the California Gold Rush*. Ithaca: Cornell University Press, 2008.

McPherson, James M. and James K. Hogue. *Ordeal by Fire: The Civil War and Reconstruction*, 4th edition. New York: McGraw-Hill, 2010.

Nash, Gerald D. *The American West Transformed: The Impact of the Second World War*. Lincoln: University of Nebraska Press, 1985.

Norris, Frank. *The Octopus*. New York: Penguin Classics, 1986.

Owens, Kenneth N. ed. *Riches for All: The California Gold Rush and the World*. Lincoln: University of Nebraska Press, 2002.

Paine, Lincoln. *The Sea and Civilization: A Maritime History of the World*. New York: Knopf, 2013.

Paul, Rodman W. *California Gold: The Beginning of Mining in the Far West*. Lincoln: University of Nebraska Press, 1947.

Potter, David M. *The Impending Crisis, 1848–1861*. New York: Harper & Row, 1976.

Rapport, Mike. *1848: Year of Revolution*. New York: Basic Books, 2010.

Rawls, James J. *Indians of California: The Changing Image*. Norman: University of Oklahoma Press, 1984.

Rawls, James J. and Richard J. Orsi, eds. *A Golden State: Mining and Economic Development on Gold Rush California*. Berkeley: University of California Press, 1999.

Remini, Robert V. *At the Edge of the Precipice: Henry Clay and the Compromise that Saved the Union*. New York: Basic Books, 2010.

Roberts, Brian. *American Alchemy: The California Gold Rush and Middle-Class Culture*. Chapel Hill: The University of North Carolina Press, 2000.

Robinson, W. W. *Land in California*. Berkeley: University of California Press, 1979.

Rohrbough, Malcolm J. *Days of Gold: The California Gold Rush and the American Nation*. Berkeley: University of California Press, 1997.

Roland, Alex. *The Way of the Ship: America's Maritime History Re-envisioned, 1600–2000*. New York: Wiley, 2007.

Rosenberg, Charles E. *The Cholera Years: The United States in 1832, 1849, and 1866*, 2nd edition. Chicago: University of Chicago Press, 1987.

Saxton, Alexander. *The Indispensable Enemy: Labor and the Anti-Chinese Movement in California*. Berkeley: University of California, 1975.

Scott, Mel. *The San Francisco Bay Area: A Metropolis in Perspective*, 2nd edition. Berkeley: University of California Press, 1985.

Starr, Kevin and Richard Orsi, eds. *Rooted in Barbarous Soil: People, Culture, and Community in Gold Rush California*. Berkeley: University of California Press, 2000.

Stegner, Wallace. "Introduction," in Bret Harte, *The Outcasts of Poker Flat and Other Tales*. New York: Signet, 1961.

Steinbeck, John. *The Grapes of Wrath*. New York: Penguin, 1996.

Stillson, Richard T. *Spreading the News: A History of Information in the California Gold Rush*. Lincoln: University of Nebraska Press, 2006.

Turner, Frederick Jackson. "The Significance of the Frontier in American History," in *Annual Report of the American Historical Association for the Year 1893*. Washington, DC: GPO and American Historical Association, 1894: 199–227.

Twain, Mark. "The Late Benjamin Franklin," *The Galaxy*, July 1870.

Unruh, John D. *The Plains Across: The Overland Immigrants and the Trans-Mississippi West, 1840–1860*. Urbana: University of Illinois Press, 1993.

Utley, Robert M. *The Indian Frontier of the American West, 1846–1890*. Albuquerque: University of New Mexico Press, 1984.

West, Elliott. *The Way to the West: Essays on the Central Plains*. Albuquerque: University of New Mexico Press, 1995.

Index